A PENGUIN BOOK

THE REAL STATE OF
AMERICA ATLAS

Cynthia Enloe is Research Professor at Clark University, Worcester, MA. She has lectured throughout the world on feminism, militarization, and globalization, written for Ms. Magazine and Village Voice and appeared on National Public Radio and the BBC. She serves on the editorial boards of scholarly journals, including *Signs* and the *International Feminist Journal of Politics*, and is the author of 11 other books, including *Bananas, Beaches and Bases: Making Feminist Sense of International Politics, The Curious Feminist* and, most recently, *Nimo's War, Emma's War: Making Feminist Sense of the Iraq War.* She is the recipient of two major awards from the International Studies Association as well as being named Clark's 'Outstanding Teacher of the Year' three times and the University Senior Faculty Fellow for Excellence in Teaching and Scholarship. In 2010 she was awarded the Howard Zinn Lifetime Achievement in Peace Studies Award.

Joni Seager, Professor and Chair of Global Studies at Bentley University in Boston, is a geographer and global policy expert. She has achieved international acclaim for her work in feminist environmental policy analysis, the international status of women, and global political economy. She is the author of many books, including four editions of the award-winning *Atlas of Women in the World*, two editions of *The State of the Environment Atlas*, and *Earth Follies: Coming to Feminist Terms With the Global Environmental Crisis.* Joni has been an active consultant with the United Nations on several gender and environmental policy projects, including consulting with the United Nations Environmental Programme on integrating gender perspectives into their work on disasters and early warning systems, and with UNESCO on gender in water policy.

"Invaluable...I would not be without
the complete set on my own shelves."
Times Educational Supplement

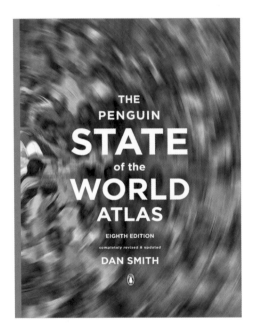
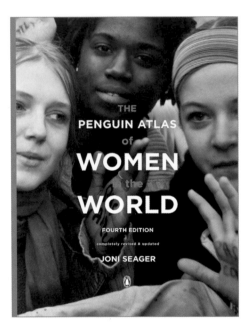

"No-one wishing to keep a grip on the reality of the world should be without
these books." *International Herald Tribune*

"Fascinating and invaluable." *The Independent*

"A new kind of visual journalism." *New Scientist*

—Iconic Places—

LOCATIONS IN THE US that have become cultural legends or that resonate with Americans because of historic or traumatic events.

6. *Seneca Falls, New York*
Town where the first American women's suffrage rights convention was held, 1848.

7. *Woodstock, New York*
Site of large outdoor music festival, August 1969.

8. *Love Canal, New York*
Neighborhood near Niagara Falls polluted by Hooker Chemical Company, forcing residents to abandon their homes.

9. *Stonewall, New York*
Bar where gay men and lesbians first resisted a police raid in June 1967, launching the gay liberation movement.

10. *Broadway, New York*
Center of American theater and neon lights.

11. *The Dakota, New York*
Apartment building where Beatles singer John Lennon lived and was murdered on December 8, 1980.

12. *Ground Zero, New York*
Site of World Trade Center towers, destroyed in terrorist plane attacks, September 9, 2011.

13. *Statue of Liberty, New York*
Gift of France, dedicated 1884, celebrating liberty and welcoming immigrants.

14. *Ellis Island, New York*
Over 12 million immigrants entered the US through this station,1892–1954.

15. *Three-Mile Island, Pennsylvania*
Site of nuclear reactor partial meltdown in March 1979.

16. *Gettysburg, Pennsylvania*
Site of July 1863 Civil War battle, leaving 50,000 killed or wounded, and where Abraham Lincoln delivered his "Gettysburg Address" in November 1863,

17. *Watergate, DC*
Apartment complex where burglars broke into Democratic Party offices in 1972. The ensuing scandal led to 1974 resignation of President Nixon.

18. *The Lincoln Memorial, DC*
Celebrating President Lincoln, site of Martin Luther King's "I Have a Dream" speech in 1963.

19. *The Pentagon, Virginia*
US Department of Defense headquarters.

20. *Arlington Cemetery, Virginia*
Military cemetery established during the Civil War. Burial place of John F. Kennedy and Robert Kennedy.

21. *Kennedy Space Center, Florida*
On Cape Canaveral, site of launches for every US human NASA space flight since 1968.

22. *Guantánamo, Cuba*
US Naval Base, forcibly leased from Cuba, 1903. In 2001, it became a detention center for men captured in the Afghanistan war.

23. *The Lorraine Motel, Tennessee*
Martin Luther King assassinated here on April 4, 1968. Now a civil rights museum.

24. *Graceland, Tennessee*
Home of singer Elvis Presley.

25. *Little Rock, Arkansas*
Site of school desegregation confrontation, 1957, when federal troops protected Black students entering the all-White Central High School.

26. *Selma, Alabama*
Town where Martin Luther King led a voting rights march in the face of brutal police resistance in 1965.

THE REAL STATE OF
AMERICA ATLAS

Mapping the Myths and Truths of the United States

Cynthia Enloe and Joni Seager

PENGUIN BOOKS

PENGUIN BOOKS

Published by the Penguin Group

Penguin Group (USA) Inc., 375 Hudson Street, New York, New York 10014, U.S.A.

Penguin Group (Canada), 90 Eglinton Avenue East, Suite 700, Toronto,
Ontario, Canada M4P 2Y3 (a division of Pearson Penguin Canada Inc.)

Penguin Books Ltd, 80 Strand, London WC2R 0RL, England

Penguin Ireland, 25 St Stephen's Green, Dublin 2, Ireland
(a division of Penguin Books Ltd)

Penguin Group (Australia), 250 Camberwell Road, Camberwell, Victoria 3124,
Australia (a division of Pearson Australia Group Pty Ltd)

Penguin Books India Pvt Ltd, 11 Community Centre, Panchsheel Park,
New Delhi – 110 017, India

Penguin Group (NZ), 67 Apollo Drive, Rosedale, Auckland 0632,
New Zealand (a division of Pearson New Zealand Ltd)

Penguin Books (South Africa) (Pty) Ltd, 24 Sturdee Avenue, Rosebank,
Johannesburg 2196, South Africa

Penguin Books Ltd, Registered Offices: 80 Strand, London WC2R ORL, England

This first edition published in Penguin Books 2011

1 3 5 7 9 10 8 6 4 2

Penguin paperback ISBN is 978-0-14-311935-7

Produced for the Penguin Group by
Myriad Editions
59 Lansdowne Place
Brighton, BN3 1FL, UK
www.myriadeditions.com

Edited and coordinated by Corinne Pearlman, Candida Lacey and Jannet King
Designed by Isabelle Lewis and Corinne Pearlman
Maps and graphics by Isabelle Lewis

Printed on paper produced from sustainable sources.
Printed and bound in Hong Kong through Lion Production
under the supervision of Bob Cassels, The Hanway Press, London.

Contents

Introduction

AMERICANS HAVE BEEN BUOYED AND BURDENED by myths since the continent's settlement. "The City on the Hill" is what early English settlers imagined they were creating on these shores; they almost starved during those harsh early winters. "The Golden Mountain" is what Chinese arrivals imagined they were sailing to; thousands instead worked as indentured laborers laying rails through rugged mountain passes. Still more immigrants came, seeking "the Land of Opportunity," its "streets paved with gold"; once here, many of them toiled in sweatshops and steel mills, or ploughed hardscrabble farms. More recently, people arriving from Somalia, India, Senegal, Guatemala, Vietnam, Afghanistan and Iraq have been attracted by neon-lit promises of "freedom," though they have found, in post-9/11 America, that it helps to tape an American flag on their home, shop or taxi cab window to ward off fellow-Americans' hostility.

Of course, many arrived here harboring no illusions. Early African newcomers to these shores struggled to survive The Middle Passage and were "welcomed" with chains and the auction block. And for the First Peoples of North America, the arrival of waves of immigrants brought disease and displacement.

At the same time, the United States has been – and remains – a land of social mobility, economic energy, and individual freedom to an extent found in few other countries. If there is a single conclusion about the US, it is that it represents a perplexing mix of contradictions and contrasts. This book explores the push and pull between the myths and the realities as they are being lived by Americans in the 21st century. One of the reasons that the recent Great Recession came as such a blow, not only to individuals but to the national self-image, is because it knocked the pins out from under the "American Dream." Cherished assumptions that to live in America is to live in a land of equal opportunity, homeownership, and social mobility have been hollowed out by the economic earthquake that still rumbles through the landscape, and by the corruption, greed, malfeasance, raw incompetence, and timid public policy that the recession exposed. But if the American Dream is listing, is hasn't yet gone under.

What does it really mean to live in America? Who lives what kinds of lives here? In this book, we try to follow the tangible threads of the interplay of the material, the cultural and the ideological. We trace these relationships in things such as homeownership, religiosity, militarism, healthcare and health politics, jobs and job losses, battles over same-sex marriage, the export of Starbucks, movies and guns, and the economic flows of wealth and debt from global to local. Meaning is refracted through experiences that vary with race, gender, and class, and we map the consequences of these too: the racial and gender skews in wages, jobs, schooling, political representation, health, wellbeing, and unemployment, among many others.

Mapping is a powerful tool of display and analysis. It simultaneously exposes sameness and difference. Mapping shows *what* is happening *where*. Maps reveal simultaneous patterns that would not be apparent in statistical tables or even in narratives. Mapping allows all kinds of readers to enter the conversation: at its simplest, looking at a map allows a reader to ask "why": why are California and Montana so different in their military enlistment rates? Why are Minnesota and Colorado the same in their low state minimum wages? In the US, as elsewhere, it matters where you live. Healthcare is not the same in Massachusetts and Texas. The prevalence of guns in everyday life may seem a nationwide phenomenon to an outside observer, but in fact Americans' relationship to guns differs markedly if they live in Arizona rather than New York.

The US is not an island. It is simultaneously a player, a participant, and a user of global products, global ideas, global alliances. We have tried to raise the visibility of some of these. Who in the world drinks the most Coca Cola? Where do American defense manufacturers sell most of their weapons? The people of which countries are most admiring of the US? Which international treaties have the US refused to ratify? Together, the answers to these questions define Americans' relationships to the rest of this complex contemporary world.

We address 40 topics here. These become 40 windows opened onto this sprawling, dynamic, diverse American society. The views through all the windows reveal the US in its warts and its glory. This is a book, we hope, that will spark conversations among readers: What is surprising? What existing beliefs about this country are up-ended? What American realities inspire further exploration or new social commitments? Maps and graphics can provide the kindling for those conversational sparks. Our hope is to enliven conversations among family members, among friends, among students and teachers, as they pore over these essays, graphics and maps together.

On an even larger scale, we hope that revealing these often-surprising patterns in contemporary American life will promote a public conversation grounded in gritty realities, and will enhance the inspection and introspection of what it means to be an American today. Is this the society we want to create? Do the lives of most Americans match our self-images, our dreams and aspirations, the principles we say we embrace?

We could not possibly have produced such an information-rich, graphically vibrant book without the skills, dedication and stunningly creative imaginations of the team at Myriad Editions. Corinne Pearlman, the Creative Director of Myriad, took on a staggering load with this atlas. She was a wonder to work with, calm, collected, and great fun. Candida Lacey, Myriad's Managing Director, has been with us from the start and stuck with us through each of the literally hundreds of steps it has taken to produce this atlas. Isabelle Lewis is the amazing graphics designer who, along with Corinne, turned our data into the engaging graphics you see here. Thank you, too, to Richard Corr for design help at the start, creating our "outline" map and suggesting a visual approach for this atlas. Behind the scenes, Jannet King contributed vital editorial attentiveness to this demanding project, and Dawn Sackett her proofreading skills. Liz Hudson tracked down much of the early information for the State Profiles. Bob Benewick is at the heart of Myriad and lent his good advice and comradeship to the atlas at crucial junctures.

Julie Clayton, an editorial consultant and researcher, and Amy Lang, a prominent American Studies scholar, provided subtle, in-depth research leads and assistance for several of these complex spreads. We are grateful to them each. Gilda Bruckman, one of our closest friends as well as a literary and political sounding board, provided advice and guidance throughout, and, at the final stages, excruciatingly careful proofreading. We want to express our sincere thanks also to Jeff Ballinger, Kareen Bar-Akiva, Donald Bruckman, Ann Fleck-Henderson, Matt Hannah, Beth Herr, Susan Jackson, Mary Katzenstein, Lory Manning, Marc Mauer, and Rod Palmquist: each is a specialist in one of the areas we explore here and each generously provided us with guidance through the often dense thickets of data.

Cynthia Enloe and Joni Seager
Cambridge, Massachusetts, 2011

11

Part One

This Land is Whose Land?

Who We Are

ACCORDING TO THE NUMBERS, the "typical American" is a White woman born in the United States of German ancestry. She is in her late thirties, living in a household with one or more family members (most likely she's married). Her household has at least one car, quite likely two. She thinks of herself as middle class. She lives in an urban area, quite possibly in the Southern region (one that stretches roughly from Maryland to Texas). She doesn't own a passport, she most likely voted in the last presidential election, and holds a waged job but earns less than her male counterparts. She knows someone who is gay or lesbian. She lives in a neighborhood that is racially segregated, where almost all her neighbors are also White.

This portrait of "averageness," derived from the US Census, gives us the snapshot of who we are, or think we are, from which we build outwards to capture the diversity that is the *real* America.

VITAL STATISTICS
2009

Sex

49% *Men*   51% *Women*

Median age

Women	38.2 years
Men	35.4 years

Who we live with

Unmarried partner 1%   6% *Other*

Alone 11%

82% *Family*

Racial/ethnic segregation

Percentage living in neighborhood dominated by people of their own racial/ethnic group *2009*

White	79%
Black	44%
Hispanic	45%

Black–White residential segregation

In 100 largest metropolitan areas

Most segregated
Milwaukee
Detroit
New York
Chicago
Cleveland

Least segregated
El Paso
Las Vegas
Modesto
Raleigh
Colorado Springs

A country of citizens
2009

Born in territories 1%

By naturalization 5%

7% *Not a US citizen*

86% *Born in USA*

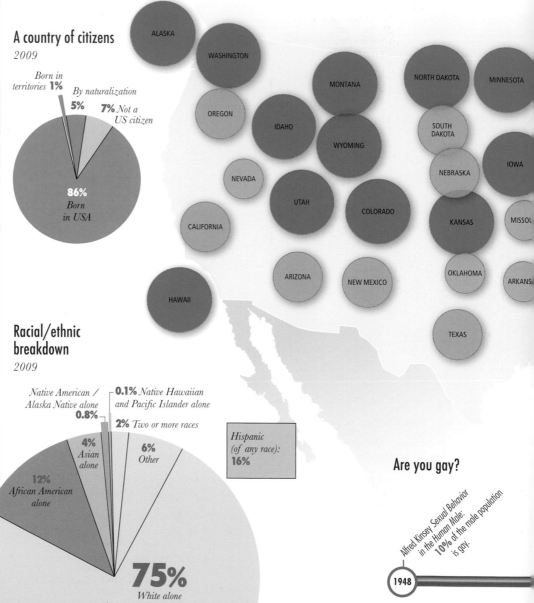

Racial/ethnic breakdown
2009

Native American / Alaska Native alone 0.8%

0.1% *Native Hawaiian and Pacific Islander alone*

2% *Two or more races*

4% *Asian alone*

6% *Other*

12% *African American alone*

Hispanic (of any race): 16%

75% *White alone*

Are you gay?

Alfred Kinsey Sexual Behavior in the Human Male: **10%** of the male population is gay.

1948

14

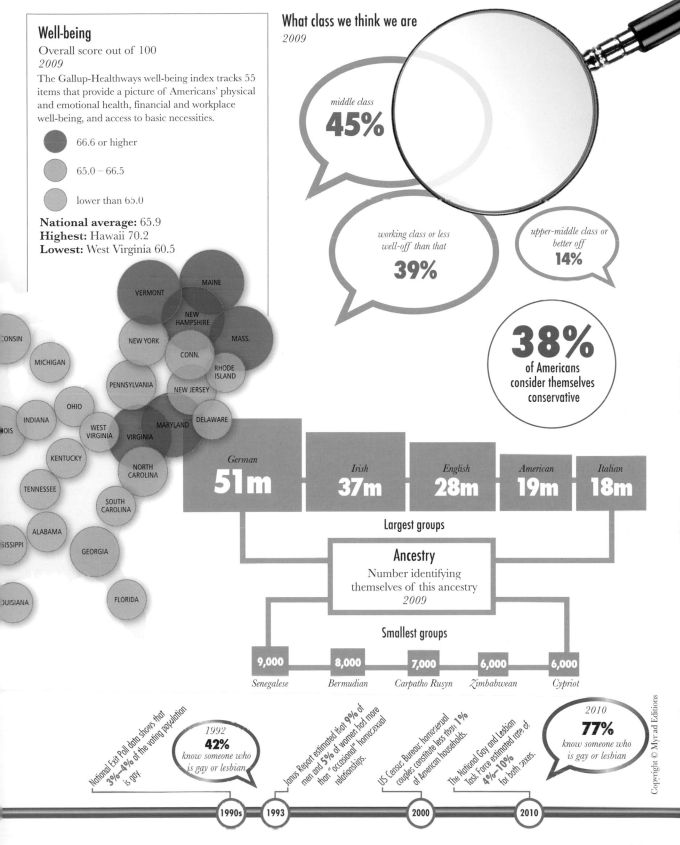

Well-being

Overall score out of 100
2009

The Gallup-Healthways well-being index tracks 55 items that provide a picture of Americans' physical and emotional health, financial and workplace well-being, and access to basic necessities.

- 66.6 or higher
- 65.0 – 66.5
- lower than 65.0

National average: 65.9
Highest: Hawaii 70.2
Lowest: West Virginia 60.5

VERMONT · MAINE · NEW HAMPSHIRE · NEW YORK · MASS. · CONN. · RHODE ISLAND · PENNSYLVANIA · NEW JERSEY · DELAWARE · WEST VIRGINIA · MARYLAND · VIRGINIA · OHIO · INDIANA · KENTUCKY · NORTH CAROLINA · TENNESSEE · SOUTH CAROLINA · ALABAMA · GEORGIA · FLORIDA · MICHIGAN · CONSIN · OIS · ILLINOIS · SISSIPPI · OUISIANA

What class we think we are
2009

middle class
45%

working class or less well-off than that
39%

upper-middle class or better off
14%

38%
of Americans consider themselves conservative

Ancestry
Number identifying themselves of this ancestry
2009

Largest groups

German	*Irish*	*English*	*American*	*Italian*
51m	**37m**	**28m**	**19m**	**18m**

Smallest groups

Senegalese	*Bermudian*	*Carpatho Rusyn*	*Zimbabwean*	*Cypriot*
9,000	**8,000**	**7,000**	**6,000**	**6,000**

National Exit Poll data shows that **3%–4%** of the voting population is gay.

1992
42%
know someone who is gay or lesbian.

Janus Report estimated that **9%** of men and **5%** of women had more than "occasional" homosexual relationships.

US Census Bureau: homosexual couples constitute less than **1%** of American households.

The National Gay and Lesbian Task Force estimated rate of **4%–10%** for both sexes.

2010
77%
know someone who is gay or lesbian

| 1990s | 1993 | 2000 | 2010 |

15

Indian Country

Number of Americans of fully or mixed Native American or Alaska Native descent:
4.3 million

Percentage of all Native Americans and Alaska Natives who live on Indian reservations, trust lands or in Native Alaskan villages:
36%

NATIVE AMERICANS AND ALASKA NATIVES – counting everyone of sole and mixed ancestry – together comprise only 1.5% percent of the US population today. However, their cultural, environmental, and political significance looms large. Their history, their activism, and their impoverished material conditions remind other Americans that this country was founded not only on high ideals, but on theft. Most European Americans don't think they stole indigenous peoples' lands: they imagine that those lands were "empty," were fairly "bought," or that the indigenous peoples were "uncivilized" and didn't deserve or make good use of these rich natural resources.

Yet, new accounts of the slaughter and displacement of indigenous peoples make it harder to hold on to those old narratives. And, since the 1960s, the political activism of some Native Americans, Alaska Natives, Native Hawaiians, and Pacific Islanders has upset myths of the Disappearing Indian, the happy First Thanksgiving, and images of cartoon Indians favored as sports teams' logos. At the same time, Native Americans' spiritual beliefs, artistic creativity, and stewardship of the land offer other Americans an appealing alternative set of values.

Indigenous peoples

In non-contiguous US lands *2008*

indigenous peoples as percentage of total population

GUAM

37%

The indigenous people, the Chomorros, whose forebears arrived 4,000 years ago, currently comprise 37% of Guam's population. The US government controls 31% of Guam's land, which it uses chiefly for military purposes. The government of Guam controls another 25% of the land. The remaining 45% of the territory's land is owned privately, with no residency or nationality limits on local landownership.

HAWAII

9%

Following the 1893 US overthrow of the Hawaiian monarchy, 1.2m acres of land were taken from the indigenous people and placed under federal control. Today, much of that land is used by the US military. Native Hawaiians lost a major land claim suit before the Supreme Court in 2009, but continue to press Congress for land restoration.

ALASKA

15%

89% of land is controlled by federal and state agencies. Discovery of Alaska's valuable natural resources, including oil and natural gas, mobilized indigenous communities to assert their right to share equitably in their profits. The result: the 1971 Alaska's Native Claims Settlement Act giving control of 12% of Alaskan land to Native Indian, Aleut and Eskimo (Inuit) Regional and Village Corporations.

PUERTO RICO

The indigenous people were the Taino. They were virtually wiped out by the Spanish, who enslaved them and brought smallpox to the island. Today, there is some DNA evidence that a few Taino descendants may survive, but they have made no land claims.

Alaska

Commonwealth of Northern Mariana Islands

Hawaii

Guam

Puerto Rico

US Virgin Islands

AMERICAN SAMOA

93%

90% of the land is held communally, following the indigenous land system, though private land ownership is growing. Thousands of native Samoans have emigrated to Hawaii and mainland US.

American Samoa

NORTHERN MARIANA ISLANDS

36%

The largest group of indigenous peoples are the Chamorros. Asians (most prominently Filipinos) comprise 56%. The US Defense Department occupies 13% of the land. Land ownership for the remainder is restricted to Northern Marianans of Pacific Island descent. The restriction is controversial and up for local government review in 2011.

US VIRGIN ISLANDS

The first indigenous people were the Ciboney, thereafter displaced by the seafaring Arawaks, and then the Caribs. Spanish conquest decimated the Arawaks and Caribs. Today, there are no indigenous people left to make land claims.

Between 1620 and 1900, Native American tribes lost virtually all of their land to Europeans. Today, Indian reservations are scattered across the US, and the federal government's Bureau of Indian Affairs determines who qualifies as an American Indian and what tribes are officially recognized (there are 564). Treaties between individual tribes and the federal government recognize tribes as sovereign nations, though that sovereignty is partial, and constantly vulnerable to dilution.

World War II marked a turning point, with 25,000 American Indians serving in the US military, and many more leaving rural areas for jobs in defense industries. Political organizing has been spurred by a new sense of shared American Indian and indigenous identity. Activists have challenged claims on Native lands made by the US military, state governments, mining companies and private developers.

TURNING NATIVE AMERICANS INTO SOMEONE ELSE'S LOGOS

All across America high schools, colleges and professional sports teams have adopted Native Americans as logos – "Indians", "Braves", "Redskins" are the most common. The teams have not consulted with Native Americans and include very few Native American players and coaches. Many Americans consider these names – and the images, dances and chants that accompany them – merely innocent, but being turned into somebody else's cartoon is deeply offensive to Native Americans, who have organized against such practices. Some teams have changed their names in response, and newly created teams have avoided such insulting references, but many remain.

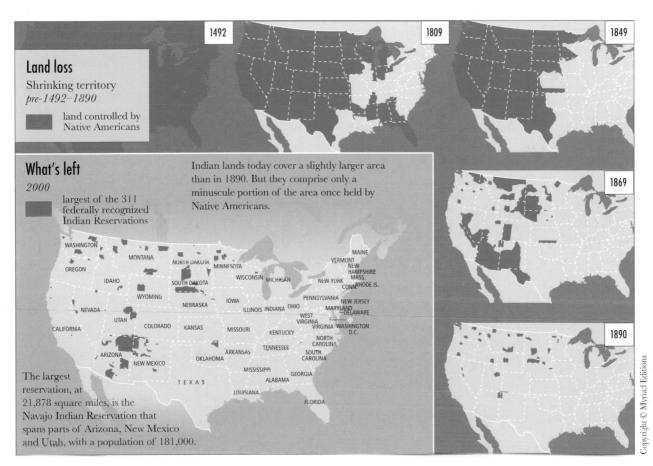

Land loss

Shrinking territory
pre-1492–1890

☐ land controlled by Native Americans

What's left

2000

☐ largest of the 311 federally recognized Indian Reservations

Indian lands today cover a slightly larger area than in 1890. But they comprise only a minuscule portion of the area once held by Native Americans.

The largest reservation, at 21,878 square miles, is the Navajo Indian Reservation that spans parts of Arizona, New Mexico and Utah, with a population of 181,000.

American Empire

Population

Largest inhabited territories
2009

48,317

*Commonwealth of
Northern Mariana
Islands*

66,432

American Samoa

109,775

US Virgin Islands

181,865

Guam

3,971,663

Puerto Rico

In the late 19th century, when colonial empires were at their height, the United States was not considered one of the great imperial powers, but at the beginning of the 21st century more than 4 million people are colonized subjects of an American empire that stretches from the Caribbean to the Pacific. In addition to five territories with sizable populations, the US claims another 12 uninhabited small atolls or islands, and several small countries are in an ambiguous legal and sovereign relationship to it. Many are places most Americans know little about. Several have proved of significant value as military bases and, in the 1950s and 1960s, as nuclear test sites. Some are now designated National Wildlife Refuges (NWR).

The US gained some of its territories in the treaty settlements of 1898 after the Spanish-American War, and some were placed in its trust by the UN in 1947. Others were "acquired" following the Guano Act of 1856. Guano deposits (bird droppings) are an effective fertilizer, and huge amounts, built up over millennia on uninhabited islands, were "mined" and traded around the world. The Act stated that if a US citizen discovered deposits of guano on an island, rock, or key not already within the lawful jurisdiction of any other government and took "peaceable possession thereof," the land subsequently "appertained" to the United States.

DIEGO GARCIA

The US leases this strategic military island base from the UK (1966–2016, with an option for extension), and has used it to launch operations in wars in the Gulf and Afghanistan. It is one of the Chagos Islands, controlled by the UK. A group of Chagossians has sued the UK for the right to return to Diego Garcia. Mauritius also lays claim to the islands.

INDIAN OCEAN

*Chagos
Islands*

Diego Garcia

MAURITIUS

Commonwealth
of Northern
Mariana
Islands

Saipan

Guam

*Federated States
of Micronesia*

Republic
of Palau

The US overseas

2010

- inhabited territories
- uninhabited territories
- *de facto* territories
- compacts of free association

COMPACT OF FREE ASSOCIATION

Under a compact, the US provides financial assistance, defends a country's territory, and allows its citizens access to the US. In exchange, the country grants the US unlimited and exclusive access to its land and waterways for strategic and military purposes.

REPUBLIC OF PALAU

Compact signed 1994. Population: 21,000. In 1981, Palau voted for the world's first nuclear-free constitution. Years of struggle with the US ensued as the US would not agree to a Compact until the anti-nuclear clause was repealed, which it was after fierce political pressure and controversy. In 2009, Palau agreed to accept Uighur prisoners released from US prison in Guantánamo.

FEDERATED STATES OF MICRONESIA

*Compact signed 1986, renewed 2003.
Population: 107,000*

GUAM

1898 Treaty with Spain.
An important military strategic base fully controlled by US, which plans to spend over $13 billion on expanding military facilities – a process started in the 1990s, after the Philippines refused to extend the lease for the US Navy base at Subic Bay. The US also plans to relocate more than 8,000 Marines and an estimated 9,000 dependants from Okinawa, Japan to Guam.

NORTHERN MARIANA ISLANDS

Made a US Trust Territory under a UN Mandate after WWII. In the 1970s the islanders voted not to seek independence but to become a US territory, which came into force in 1976. Saipan is a haven for the garment industry, with no requirement to pay the US minimum wage, yet the right to import products into the US without tariff restrictions. The large number of female migrant workers from China and Vietnam has distorted the sex ratio: there are 133 females for every 100 males.

SMALL PACIFIC TERRITORIES

Wake Island
Annexed 1899. Since 1974 has served as launch platform for testing of anti-missile systems. Access restricted.

Midway Island
Annexed 1867. Naval base played pivotal role in Korean, Vietnam, and Cold wars. Environmental contamination supposedly cleaned up. NWR (1998) and ecotourism industry being developed.

GUANTANAMO

The US Navy has authority over the base, built on land leased from Cuba under agreements in 1903 and 1934. The claim that it was not part of the US, and that the post-2001 detention center need not adhere to laws regarding prisoners' rights was rebuffed by the Supreme Court in 2008. The US is closing the detention center, but not the base. Cuba considers the US to be an occupying force.

PUERTO RICO

The US has long seen PR as its security bulwark in the Caribbean; the Cuban Missile Crisis of 1962 reinforced this view. In the 20th century, Puerto Rico also became an offshore industrial site for garment sweatshops, textiles, and pharmaceuticals. Puerto Rico's Commonwealth status is much debated; in 2008, a survey indicated for the first time that a majority of islanders would prefer statehood within the US.

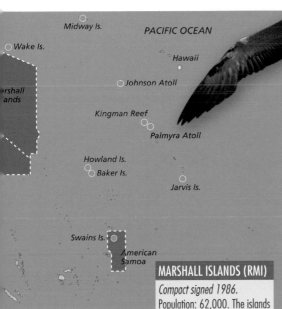

Midway Is.   PACIFIC OCEAN
Wake Is.
                    Hawaii
                Johnson Atoll
rshall
ands   Kingman Reef
                Palmyra Atoll
        Howland Is.
        Baker Is.
                        Jarvis Is.

Guantánamo
                                    Puerto Rico
                            Navassa Is
                                    US Virgin Islands
            Serranilla   Petrel Is.
            Bank

Swains Is.
        American
        Samoa

SMALL PACIFIC TERRITORIES

Johnson Atoll
Acquired 1859 under Guano Act. Contaminated by 12 thermonuclear tests in 1950s and 1960s. Used as storage site for Agent Orange containers from Vietnam War, and highly toxic chemicals from ex-USSR and East Germany. Access restricted.

Kingman Reef
Acquired 1860 under Guano Act. Administered by US Navy 1934–2001. Now a NWR. Closed to public.

Palmyra Atoll
Acquired 1898. Privately owned through much of 20th century. Made a NWR (2001).

Howland Island
Acquired 1857 under Guano Act. Mined until about 1890. A short-lived attempt at colonization was disrupted by WWII and abandoned. Made a NWR (1974).

MARSHALL ISLANDS (RMI)

Compact signed 1986.
Population: 62,000. The islands were made a US Trust Territory under a UN mandate after WWII and were used for US nuclear testing. The Marshallese suffer medical problems, environmental contamination, displacement, and social upheaval as a result. Became an independent state in 1986, but the US exerted excessive pressure to retain its use of 750,000 square miles of Kwajalein Atoll as a missile test range.

AMERICAN SAMOA

1899 Treaty with Germany.
Major naval station for US. During World War II, US Marines in Samoa outnumbered the local population, and American militarization has altered the cultural fabric of Samoa.

SMALL PACIFIC TERRITORIES

Baker Island
Acquired 1856 under Guano Act. Guano mining peaked in the 1860s and 1870s. 1942–44: occupied by 2,000–3,000 US forces. Made NWR in 1974 but there are environmental concerns about debris from military occupation.

Jarvis Island
Claimed 1856 under Guano Act. Guano mined until 1879. US colony established in 1936. Evacuated in 1942 after attacks by Japan. Established as NWR (1974).

Swains Island
Population approximately 40 people. Claimed also by Tokelau.

US VIRGIN ISLANDS

During WWI, the US feared Germany might seize the islands for a submarine base, and so bought them from Denmark. The economy is largely driven by tourism, but Saint Croix hosts Hovensa, a large petroleum refinery that processes Venezuelan crude oil for US markets.

Uninhabited Caribbean Territories
All claimed under Guano Act

Petrel Island
Claimed 1869. Under US military. No public access. Claimed also by Jamaica and Colombia.

Navassa Island
Claimed 1857. Guano mining until 1898. NWR 1999. Access by permit only. Claimed also by Haiti.

Serranilla Bank
Acquired 1879–80. Largely under water.

This Land is Our Land

Land use in USA
2002

Forest	**29%**
Grassland and pasture	**26%**
Cropland	**20%**
Special uses e.g. military, national parks	**13%**
Urban	**3%**
Other	**9%**

At just over 2.3 billion acres, the United States is big. It boasts the eighth-longest coastline in the world, the longest undefended border (with Canada), and the third-largest land area. It is a country of geographic superlatives. The early history of the US, from one perspective, is all about land: land stolen or coerced from Native Americans, land wrested from colonizers, battles with Mexico for territory, land purchases from France and Russia.

In the American imagination, land looms even larger. The most cherished elements of the stereotyped (masculine) American character – independence, resilience, don't-fence-me-in attitude – are said to be forged on the anvil of the frontier, that mythical borderless space. Although almost all Americans are now urban dwellers, impingements on the presumed right to unimpeded use of land are amongst the most divisive, and represent the rawest edges in the culture wars. Does the government have the right to ban development to protect endangered species? What about snowmobiling in National Parks, all-terrain vehicles or off-road beach buggies in the National Seashore? Does a private developer have the right to drain a wetland, build on a floodplain, or clear-cut a forest? Can private landowners prevent others from hunting on their property or block access to the beach?

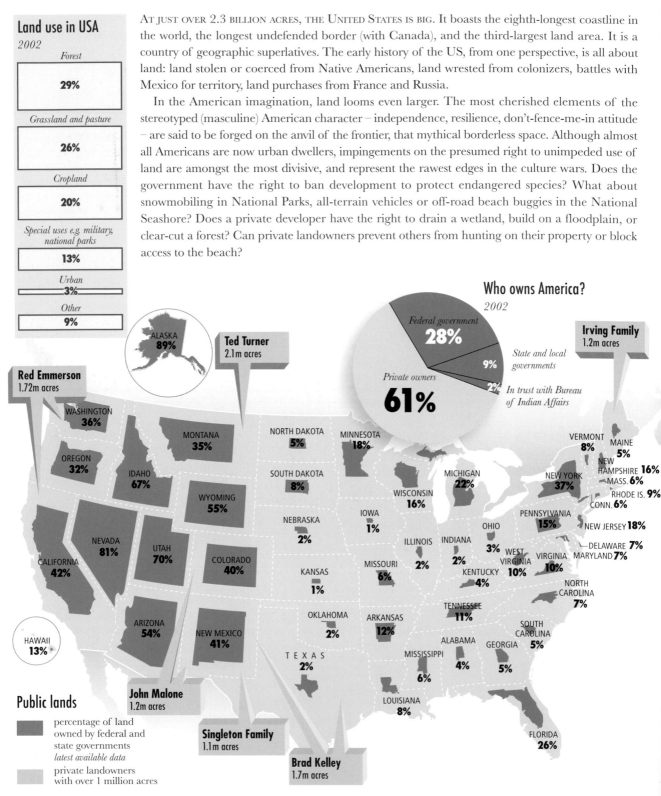

Who owns America?
2002

Federal government **28%**

State and local governments **9%**

In trust with Bureau of Indian Affairs **2%**

Private owners **61%**

Irving Family
1.2m acres

ALASKA **89%**

Ted Turner
2.1m acres

Red Emmerson
1.72m acres

WASHINGTON **36%**

OREGON **32%**

MONTANA **35%**

NORTH DAKOTA **5%**

MINNESOTA **18%**

VERMONT **8%**

MAINE **5%**

NEW HAMPSHIRE **16%**

MASS. **6%**

IDAHO **67%**

SOUTH DAKOTA **8%**

MICHIGAN **22%**

NEW YORK **37%**

RHODE IS. **9%**

CONN. **6%**

WYOMING **55%**

WISCONSIN **16%**

PENNSYLVANIA **15%**

NEW JERSEY **18%**

NEBRASKA **2%**

IOWA **1%**

OHIO **3%**

NEVADA **81%**

UTAH **70%**

COLORADO **40%**

ILLINOIS **2%**

INDIANA **2%**

WEST VIRGINIA **10%**

VIRGINIA **10%**

DELAWARE **7%**

MARYLAND **7%**

CALIFORNIA **42%**

MISSOURI **6%**

KENTUCKY **4%**

NORTH CAROLINA **7%**

KANSAS **1%**

ARIZONA **54%**

NEW MEXICO **41%**

OKLAHOMA **2%**

ARKANSAS **12%**

TENNESSEE **11%**

SOUTH CAROLINA **5%**

HAWAII **13%**

ALABAMA **4%**

GEORGIA **5%**

TEXAS **2%**

MISSISSIPPI **6%**

John Malone
1.2m acres

LOUISIANA **8%**

FLORIDA **26%**

Public lands

Singleton Family
1.1m acres

Brad Kelley
1.7m acres

- percentage of land owned by federal and state governments
  latest available data
- private landowners with over 1 million acres

Hunting is a particularly privileged activity. Although only one adult American in 20 hunts, the "right to hunt" is a cherished part of the "freedom to roam" American ideology. Hunters' rights trump landowners' rights in most parts of the US: in more than half the states, for example, hunters have the presumptive legal right to hunt on private lands unless the owners specifically post prohibitions against it. Hunting is allowed on most public lands, including wildlife refuges, national forests, and all Bureau of Land Management property.

For many Americans, leery about what they see as the long reach of government, the amount of public land – and the extent to which governments may regulate behavior on that land – is worrying. On the other hand, grazing and logging interests have managed to secure leases and permits that allow the holders to exploit resources on public lands at staggeringly low costs. And while land is a source of subsistence for fewer and fewer Americans, it is a source of wealth for many more.

Hunters: 91% male 96% White

Making a killing

Regional average percentage of adults who hunt
2006

- 12%
- 6% – 8%
- 2% – 5%

National average: 5%

PACIFIC
MOUNTAIN
WEST NORTH CENTRAL
EAST NORTH CENTRAL
NEW ENGLAND
MIDDLE ATLANTIC
WEST SOUTH CENTRAL
EAST SOUTH CENTRAL
SOUTH ATLANTIC

Where hunters hunt
2006

On private lands only
58%

On public lands only
15%

On both
24%

Unknown
3%

Top 5 hunting states

Texas
Pennsylvania
Wisconsin
Michigan
Missouri

PUBLIC LAND, PRIVATE PROFIT

Mining

The General Mining Law of 1872 allows companies to mine gold, silver, platinum, and other hardrock minerals on public land without paying royalties to the federal government, and with limited responsibility for environmental cleanup. The law further permits companies to buy the land for $2.50 to $5 per acre. Efforts in 2007 and 2009 to reform this law were vigorously opposed by mining interests and were not enacted.

The Congressional Budget Office estimates that roughly $1 billion worth of hardrock minerals are extracted each year from public lands, and that federal agencies spent at least $2.6 billion cleaning up abandoned hardrock mines between 1998 and 2007.

Grazing

Most public lands in the western states are open for livestock grazing. Ranchers pay a fee for this use. The Government Accounting Office estimated that in 2004 the federal government spent at least $144 million managing the livestock grazing program, including controlling wildlife and remediating environmental damage, but took in only $21 million in grazing fees.

13%
of American adults go fishing

Part Two

American Dreams

A Land of Homeowners

HOMEOWNERSHIP has become a central pillar of American public policy and national identity. In reality, it is beyond the reach of many Americans.

There is not a level playing field in buying a home, and homeownership varies with race, region, gender, and marital status. It has taken social movements, targeted legislation, and law suits to level out some of the worst inequalities in buying a home, including rampant racial discrimination that was, until recently, the norm. Yet, inequalities remain. Today, homeownership is more common in many other countries than it is in the United States. Women who are single-parent heads of households are the least likely to be homeowners.

Nevertheless, over the past century, the percentage of Americans owning their own homes has been rising, and the quality of their residences has been improving. But even here there are striking inequalities: while some Americans are living in McMansions, others still don't have central heat. Americans are building ever-bigger houses, even though fewer people are living in them.

American attitudes to home ownership
2010

Owning is preferable to renting
66%

Homeownership is important to the economy
80%

Buying a house is a safe investment
2003: **83%**
2010: **70%**

Top reasons to own:
"safety of neighborhood" and "positive environment for children"

State of housing

Percentage of houses with complete plumbing amenities
1950–90

99%
93%
64%
1950   1970   1990

12% of Native American houses on reservations in 2000 lacked complete plumbing.

How we compare

Homeownership in selected countries
Most recent rates since 2002

Country	%
Hungary	92%
Mexico	84%
UK	72%
Australia	71%
USA	68%
Japan	61%
Germany	44%

Keyholders

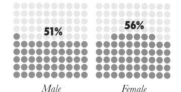

The ability to buy and own a home depends on:

- jobs that pay well enough
- banks and lending institutions that play fair
- mortgage rates that are low enough
- the absence of racial and other social discriminations in real-estate transactions that affect what houses are shown and sold
- the absence of racial and other social discrimination in the mortgage lending process
- the perceived desirability of owning over renting, which in part depends on whether renters have protection

Most likely to own
Homeownership among different types of household *2009*

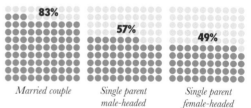

Family households

83%
Married couple

57%
Single parent male-headed

49%
Single parent female-headed

Single-person households

51%
Male

56%
Female

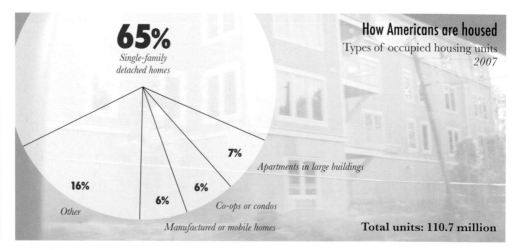

65%
Single-family detached homes

16%
Other

6%
Manufactured or mobile homes

6%
Co-ops or condos

7%
Apartments in large buildings

How Americans are housed
Types of occupied housing units
2007

Total units: 110.7 million

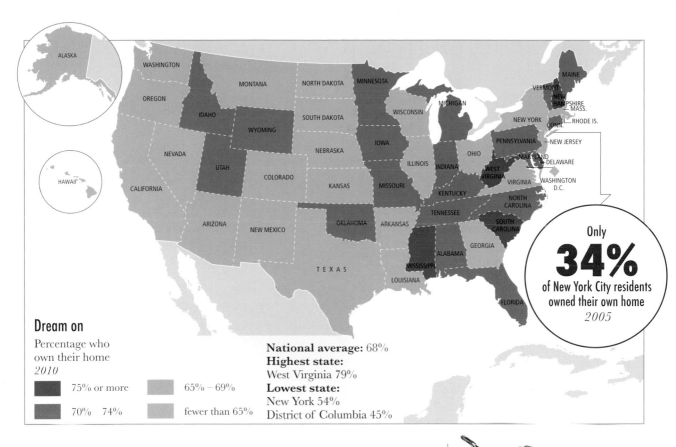

Dream on

Percentage who
own their home
2010

- 75% or more
- 70% – 74%
- 65% – 69%
- fewer than 65%

National average: 68%
Highest state:
West Virginia 79%
Lowest state:
New York 54%
District of Columbia 45%

Only
34%
of New York City residents
owned their own home
2005

Race and homeownership

The gap in homeownership between White and African American households has fluctuated over the last 100 years. Two factors widened the gap in the mid-20th century: the increase in homeownership by Whites as they benefited from post-war economic growth, and the migration of African Americans to northern cities, where renting was prevalent and racist discrimination by bankers and real estate agents common and legal.

The urban race riots in the mid-1960s sparked a greater political concern over housing inequality, and the passage of federal and local laws made such discriminatory practices illegal. It persisted in more informal ways, though, and combined with continuing income differences between Whites and non-Whites to preserve the homeownership gap.

**Black homebuyers reporting discrimination
when asking about homes advertised for sale:**

1989:
29%

2000:
17%

Dreams come true

Percentage of Americans
who own their own home
2008
average by racial/ethnic group

- 1994
- 2008

**Homeownership
gap between
Non-Hispanic Whites
and Blacks**

1970:
24%

2009:
29%

US average	Non-Hispanic White	Asian/ Hawaiian/ Pacific Islander	Native American/ Alaska Native	Hispanic	Black
64% / 68%	70% / 75%	51% / 60%	52% / 57%	41% / 49%	42% / 47%

Dreams Foreclosed

1 in 78 housing units received a foreclosure notice in the first half of 2010

MILLIONS OF AMERICANS HAVE LOST THEIR HOMES, and with it their equity, their dignity, and their main means of survival. By 2010, one out of every 78 houses in the United States was in foreclosure; for almost a quarter of homeowners, their houses are worth less than their mortgages. The "collateral damage" is extraordinary: pets are being abandoned in record numbers as people are forced from their homes; abandoned boats are piling up in coastal waterways; vacant houses – foreclosed and then forgotten by the big banks that own them – mar communities and produce a spiral of neighborhood decline.

Regulatory responses to this crisis have been anemic. Huge bank bailouts and modest assistance to homeowners in crisis have staunched the flow, but for most Americans there is little relief.

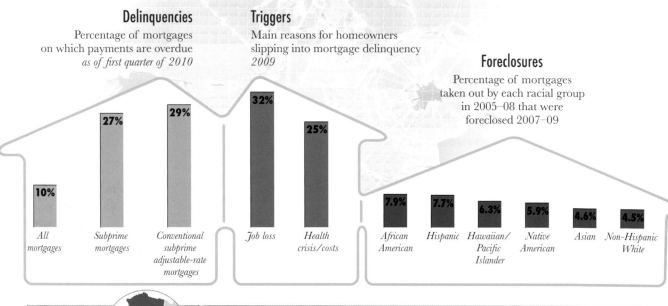

Delinquencies
Percentage of mortgages on which payments are overdue *as of first quarter of 2010*

- All mortgages: 10%
- Subprime mortgages: 27%
- Conventional subprime adjustable-rate mortgages: 29%

Triggers
Main reasons for homeowners slipping into mortgage delinquency *2009*

- Job loss: 32%
- Health crisis/costs: 25%

Foreclosures
Percentage of mortgages taken out by each racial group in 2005–08 that were foreclosed 2007–09

- African American: 7.9%
- Hispanic: 7.7%
- Hawaiian/Pacific Islander: 6.3%
- Native American: 5.9%
- Asian: 4.6%
- Non-Hispanic White: 4.5%

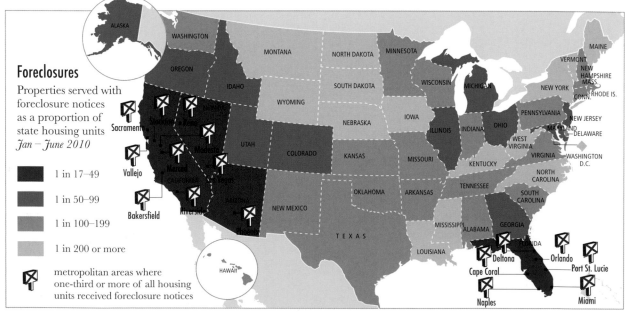

Foreclosures
Properties served with foreclosure notices as a proportion of state housing units *Jan – June 2010*

- 1 in 17–49
- 1 in 50–99
- 1 in 100–199
- 1 in 200 or more
- metropolitan areas where one-third or more of all housing units received foreclosure notices

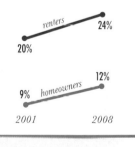

The American homeownership dream is mired in debt. For most Americans, their home is their biggest asset but also their biggest liability. About two-thirds of owner-occupied houses have mortgages on them, with rates higher for African American (69 percent) and Hispanic (74 percent) home owners.

Homeownership used to be a sure path to financial stability and social mobility. Home values increased, a mortgage was considered to be a responsible debt, and a home was a reliable investment. Between 2005 and 2006, this all changed. The run-up in house prices – described with hindsight as a housing bubble – ended, and values in most of the country plunged dramatically; sales of homes in some markets all but stopped. The value of stocks and other securities linked to the housing market plummeted. Credit tightened, trade declined, and the economy went into a tailspin. Job losses piled on top of housing value losses. Millions of Americans were suddenly in financial trouble and without equity in their homes to bail them out. Many couldn't even sell their homes for break-even money.

The housing and economic crisis was linked to a mortgage crisis. Mortgage regulations were relaxed in the 1990s, and new lenders and new types of mortgages flooded the market, often chasing ever more marginal borrowers. "Subprime" mortgage lenders emerged in the late 1990s as serious players, and by 2005 represented more than 20 percent of all mortgages issued.

Subprimes were typically pitched at people with thin credit and were issued at higher rates than ordinary (or "prime") mortgages. Many subprime lenders sought out people excluded from the traditional mortgage markets, including women, minorities, the elderly, and new immigrants. Some used fraud and deception to lure people into high-cost loans that were beyond their capacity to pay. Borrowers, entranced by easy credit, colluded in the deception. As long as house prices kept going up, this gamble appeared to work for everyone. But by 2007, the subprime industry had collapsed, and with it the dreams of millions of homeowners.

Who were sold the subprimes?

Percentage of all mortgage borrowers who took out subprime mortgages for home purchase
2005

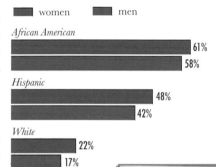

	women	men
African American		61% / 58%
Hispanic		48% / 42%
White		22% / 17%

46%
of those renting spent more than 30% of their income on housing
2006

Increase in severely cost-burdened households

Percentage of households spending more than half their income on housing

renters 20% → 24%

homeowners 9% → 12%

2001   *2008*

Copyright © Myriad Editions

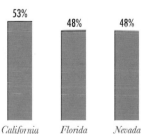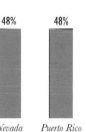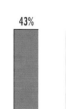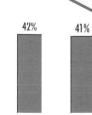

Top 10 in trouble

Proportion of mortgaged owners paying more than 30% of their income on housing
2006–08

California	Florida	Nevada	Puerto Rico	Hawaii	New Jersey	Rhode Island	Massachusetts	New York
53%	48%	48%	48%	47%	46%	43%	42%	41%

Homelessness

Who are the homeless?

When compared to the national population, homeless people are disproportionately adult males, African-Americans, alone, and disabled:

Of the total homeless population who used a shelter Oct 2008– Sept 2009

78% were adults
of whom
64% were male

14% were military veterans

36% were African American
12% were Hispanic
3% were American Indian/ Alaska Native
<1% were Asian

38% had a mental or physical disability

12% were victims of domestic violence

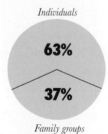

Individuals
63%
37%
Family groups

30%
The increase in the number of families using homeless shelters between 2007 and 2009

HOMELESSNESS IS OFTEN TEMPORARY; many people cycle through homeless periods over the course of a year. Because of this, and because homeless people have no stable address, it is almost impossible to get an accurate count of their numbers. Two main methods are used to count the homeless: point-in-time snapshots are usually taken one night a year, when hundreds of volunteers fan out across cities to count how many people are on the streets and in shelters on that night; and shelter-use statistics, which track how many people use shelter services over a year. The numbers are fluid and approximate. Nonetheless, there is general agreement that between 2 million and 3 million Americans experience periods of homelessness each year, and that this number is increasing. Near-homelessness is a way of life for many millions more: families doubling-up on accommodations, people sleeping on the couch of family or friends, informal arrangements that are temporary and that lead to a constant round of moving and resettling.

Homelessness is the end point of job cuts, economic crisis, and poverty. For many people, the slide into homelessness starts with foreclosures – not necessarily because the now-homeless were previous homeowners, but the foreclosure crisis has put pressure on the housing rental market as well; as more former homeowners enter the rental market, rental price hikes push out precarious renters. Public assistance cuts over the past 15 years, especially in welfare, and state funding cuts during the current economic crisis, have reduced "safety net" services, making people increasingly vulnerable to homelessness. People who are precariously housed are one crisis away from homelessness; in the USA, this is often a health crisis and its associated costs. Substance abuse, previous incarceration, and domestic violence are all catalysts for homelessness.

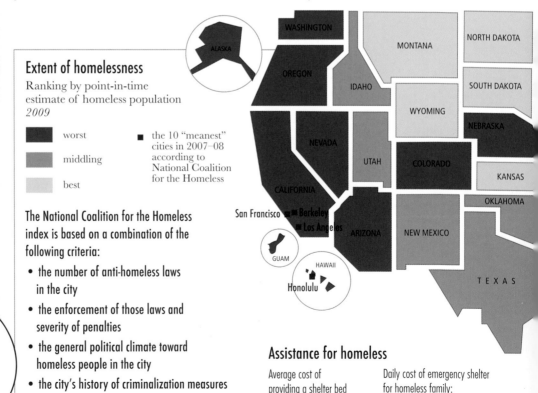

Extent of homelessness

Ranking by point-in-time estimate of homeless population *2009*

- worst
- middling
- best

■ the 10 "meanest" cities in 2007–08 according to National Coalition for the Homeless

The National Coalition for the Homeless index is based on a combination of the following criteria:

- the number of anti-homeless laws in the city
- the enforcement of those laws and severity of penalties
- the general political climate toward homeless people in the city
- the city's history of criminalization measures
- the existence of pending or recently enacted criminalization legislation in the city.

Assistance for homeless

Average cost of providing a shelter bed for one year in California:
$47,000

Daily cost of emergency shelter for homeless family:
DC: **$123**
Houston: **$46**

Without adequate shelter space or affordable housing in most cities, many people are forced to live on the streets, where they are vulnerable to violence, and for homeless women the threat of sexual violence is always present. Billions of dollars is spent by city, state and federal agencies, private charities, and nonprofits, providing healthcare, employment assistance, clothing, housing, nutrition, and emergency shelter services for the homeless. But many cities are responding to the homelessness crisis by making the activities of homeless people illegal. Among other prohibitions, some cities have outlawed food sharing programs, often run by churches or private nonprofit groups, which offer food to the homeless in public spaces.

ODDS OF BECOMING HOMELESS
2009

all persons	1 in 195
persons in families	1 in 296
children	1 in 214
adult men	1 in 145
adult women	1 in 269
all minorities	1 in 105

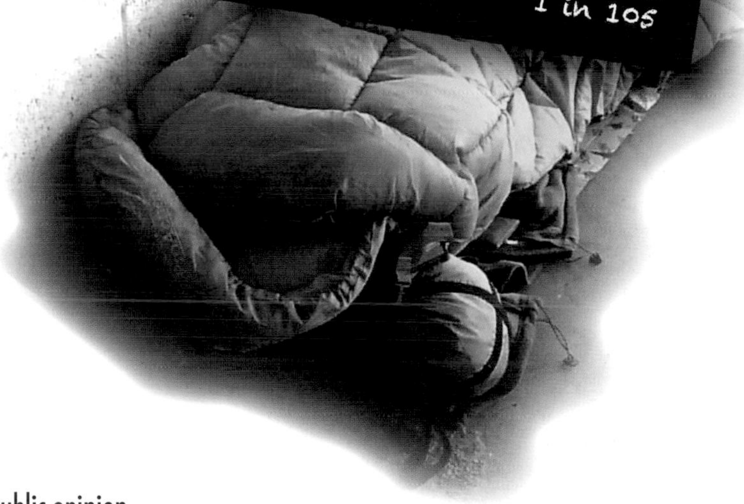

39% of homeless are found in Florida, California and New York states

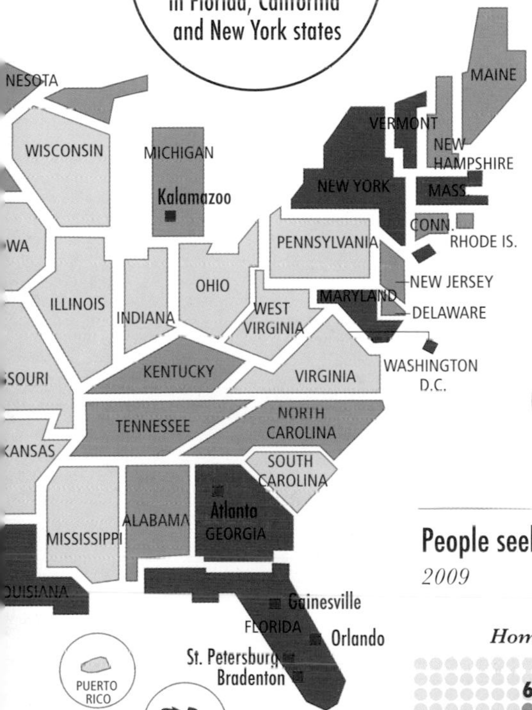

MAINE
NESOTA
VERMONT
WISCONSIN
MICHIGAN
NEW HAMPSHIRE
Kalamazoo
NEW YORK
MASS.
CONN.
RHODE IS.
WA
PENNSYLVANIA
NEW JERSEY
ILLINOIS
OHIO
DELAWARE
INDIANA
WEST VIRGINIA
MARYLAND
SOURI
KENTUCKY
VIRGINIA
WASHINGTON D.C.
KANSAS
TENNESSEE
NORTH CAROLINA
SOUTH CAROLINA
ALABAMA
Atlanta
GEORGIA
MISSISSIPPI
OUISIANA
Gainesville
FLORIDA
Orlando
St. Petersburg
Bradenton
PUERTO RICO
US VIRGIN ISLANDS

Public opinion

Percentage of people who worry a "great deal" about homelessness as a social problem in the US
2005

52% *Of Non-whites*

33% *Of Whites*

45% *Of women*

28% *Of men*

People seeking shelter services
2009

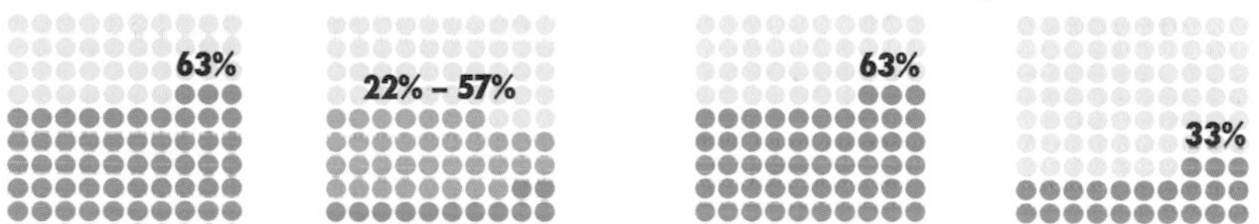

Homeless individuals

63%
Came from another homeless situation

22% – 57%
Of women reported domestic violence as the immediate cause of their homelessness

Homeless families

63%
Came from a housed situation

33%
Had a chronic substance abuse problem

Copyright © Myriad Editions

Religious Identities

Most people in the United States identify with an organized religion. Most Americans believe in a god. Most are Christian. And almost two-thirds belong to a church or synagogue. But the American religious landscape has been shifting: the religions Americans identify with are more diverse, and more people are nonbelievers. In 1990, 86 percent of American adults identified themselves as Christian; by 2008, this had dropped to 76 percent. By contrast, the proportion of those with no religious preference, and those who are atheist or agnostic – commonly known as "the nones" – grew from 8 percent in 1980 to 16 percent in 2010.

Religious affiliations and activities vary considerably by ethnicity and gender. Religious affiliations and political leanings are strongly linked: Christians, and amongst them the Mormons, are the most conservative, while Jews are the most liberal.

Despite the overwhelmingly "Christian" identity of Americans, this masks a dizzying diversity of Protestant branches, Baptist churches, and Pentecostal identities. Religious relations are often fractious. It was only in 1961 that the first (and, to date, only) Catholic President, John F. Kennedy, was elected, and he had to explicitly counter strong suspicions that he would be a puppet of the Vatican. The 6 percent of Americans who acknowledge prejudice against Buddhists reflect the general distrust of non-Christian "others" that is a foundation of the American religious landscape.

Native American religious traditions were suppressed and in many cases outlawed in the course of European colonization. This was not fully remedied until the 1978 American Indian Religious Freedom Act, and successor legislation in 1994 and 1996 that offered a degree of protection for Indian sacred sites, and that reinstated the legality of certain Indian sacred items, including peyote and eagle feathers and bones used in ceremonies.

Religious identification among racial/ethnic groups

The single-largest categories *2008*

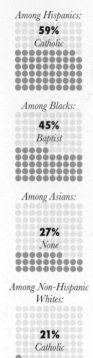

Among Hispanics:
59%
Catholic

Among Blacks:
45%
Baptist

Among Asians:
27%
None

Among Non-Hispanic Whites:
21%
Catholic

Importance of religion within racial/ethnic groups

Percentage who say religion is an important part of their daily life *2009*

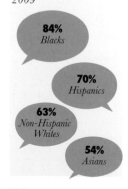

84% *Blacks*

70% *Hispanics*

63% *Non-Hispanic Whites*

54% *Asians*

Religious identification

of US adult population
2008

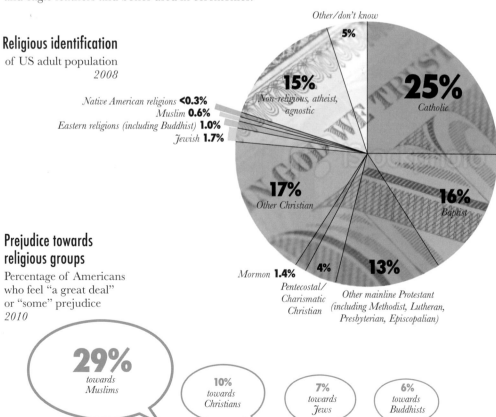

Native American religions **<0.3%**
Muslim **0.6%**
Eastern religions (including Buddhist) **1.0%**
Jewish **1.7%**

Other/don't know **5%**

15%
Non-religious, atheist, agnostic

25%
Catholic

17%
Other Christian

16%
Baptist

Mormon **1.4%**

4%
Pentecostal/ Charismatic Christian

13%
Other mainline Protestant (including Methodist, Lutheran, Presbyterian, Episcopalian)

Prejudice towards religious groups

Percentage of Americans who feel "a great deal" or "some" prejudice *2010*

29%
towards Muslims

10%
towards Christians

7%
towards Jews

6%
towards Buddhists

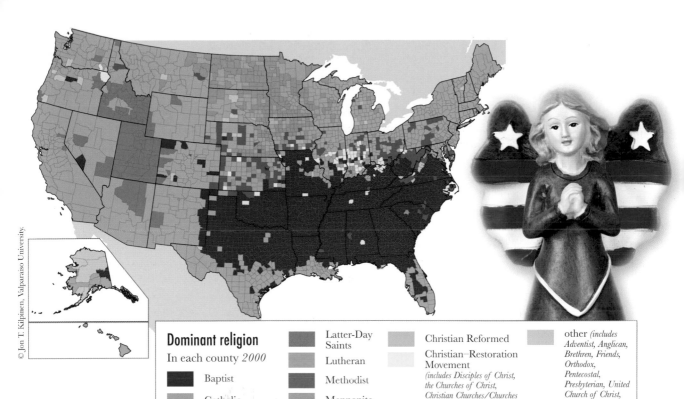

Dominant religion

In each county *2000*

- Baptist
- Catholic
- Latter-Day Saints
- Lutheran
- Methodist
- Mennonite
- Christian Reformed
- Christian–Restoration Movement *(includes Disciples of Christ, the Churches of Christ, Christian Churches/Churches of Christ)*
- other *(includes Adventist, Anglican, Brethren, Friends, Orthodox, Pentecostal, Presbyterian, United Church of Christ, None)*

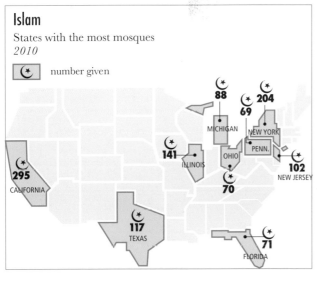

Islam

States with the most mosques *2010*

(C* number given

- 88 MICHIGAN
- 204 NEW YORK
- 69 OHIO
- 102 NEW JERSEY
- 141 ILLINOIS
- PENN.
- 70
- 295 CALIFORNIA
- 117 TEXAS
- 71 FLORIDA

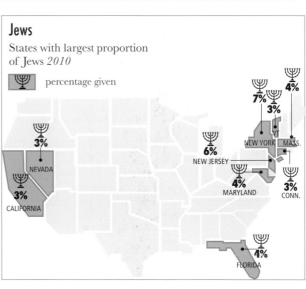

Jews

States with largest proportion of Jews *2010*

percentage given

- 7%
- 3%
- 4%
- NEW YORK
- VT
- MASS.
- 6% NEW JERSEY
- 3% NEVADA
- 4% MARYLAND
- 3% CONN.
- 3% CALIFORNIA
- 4% FLORIDA

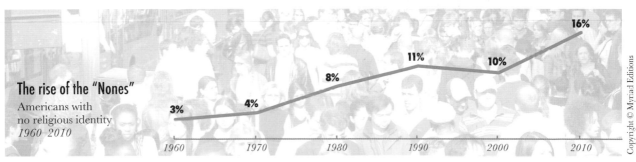

The rise of the "Nones"

Americans with no religious identity *1960–2010*

- 3% — 1960
- 4% — 1970
- 8% — 1980
- 11% — 1990
- 10% — 2000
- 16% — 2010

God and Politics

By its constitution, the United States government is secular, founded on the principle of the separation of church and state. However, the nature of that principle, and the location of that boundary line, have been sources of constant and increasing debate in American life. Prayers in school, reproductive rights for women, sex education for children, and the Pledge of Allegiance have long been hot-button legal and public policy issues that test the boundaries between state and religion. The rise of activist Evangelicals in the past few years has influenced new public policy debates and outcomes on issues that include stem cell research, science education (especially evolution), and same-sex marriage.

While overall religiosity in the US has diminished in recent decades, the insertion of religion into public policy has been accelerated by the rise of Protestant evangelicalism and the organizing base provided by "megachurches." Religious intensity is strongly associated with political inclination: the more religious Americans are also the more conservative.

The emergence of the organized Religious Right is usually dated to the founding of "Focus on the Family" in 1977 and the "Moral Majority" in 1979. The Christian Right is now a highly effective political force, with Washington-based lobbying offices, sharply refined electoral strategies, and deep financial resources. The political Christian Right is a distinctively American phenomenon, although this model is now being exported globally.

The secular state?

- Every President since the early 1800s, except Franklin Pierce, has sworn the oath of office on a Bible.
- The US Congress opens its daily sessions with a prayer.

Religious beliefs

Among Americans
2008

Believe in God with absolute certainty: 71%

Pray at least once a day: 58%

Believe God created humans, as is, within the past 10,000 years: 44%

Attend religious services at least once a week: 39%

Believe in evolution: 39%

The great solution

Percentage of Americans who believe religion can answer all or most problems

- 80%
- 63%
- 58%

1960 1980 2010

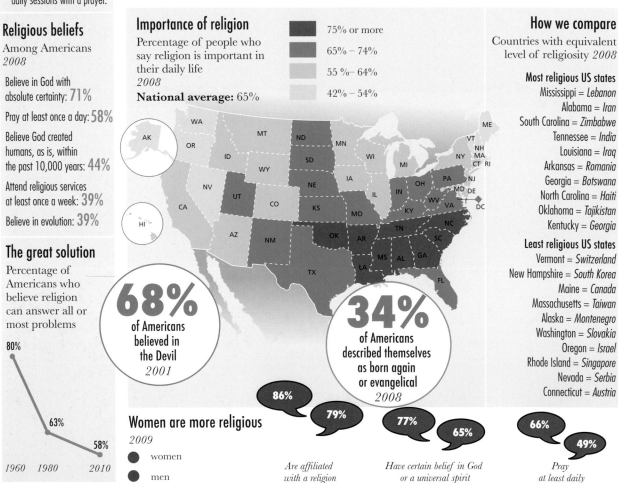

Importance of religion

Percentage of people who say religion is important in their daily life
2008
National average: 65%

- 75% or more
- 65% – 74%
- 55 % – 64%
- 42% – 54%

68% of Americans believed in the Devil 2001

34% of Americans described themselves as born again or evangelical 2008

Women are more religious
2009

● women
● men

86% 79%
Are affiliated with a religion

77% 65%
Have certain belief in God or a universal spirit

66% 49%
Pray at least daily

How we compare

Countries with equivalent level of religiosity 2008

Most religious US states
Mississippi = *Lebanon*
Alabama = *Iran*
South Carolina = *Zimbabwe*
Tennessee = *India*
Louisiana = *Iraq*
Arkansas = *Romania*
Georgia = *Botswana*
North Carolina = *Haiti*
Oklahoma = *Tajikistan*
Kentucky = *Georgia*

Least religious US states
Vermont = *Switzerland*
New Hampshire = *South Korea*
Maine = *Canada*
Massachusetts = *Taiwan*
Alaska = *Montenegro*
Washington = *Slovakia*
Oregon = *Israel*
Rhode Island = *Singapore*
Nevada = *Serbia*
Connecticut = *Austria*

Megachurches

Protestant churches with sustained weekly attendance of 2,000 or more, megachurches are usually associated with a charismatic pastor, and often offer a mix of politics and theology. Many have large media empires; most mass-produce books by their pastors. They often provide social welfare for congregants in need. Church services take place in vast arenas and typically emphasize joyfulness, music, and congregant participation. In 2009, the average annual income of a megachurch was $6.5 million.

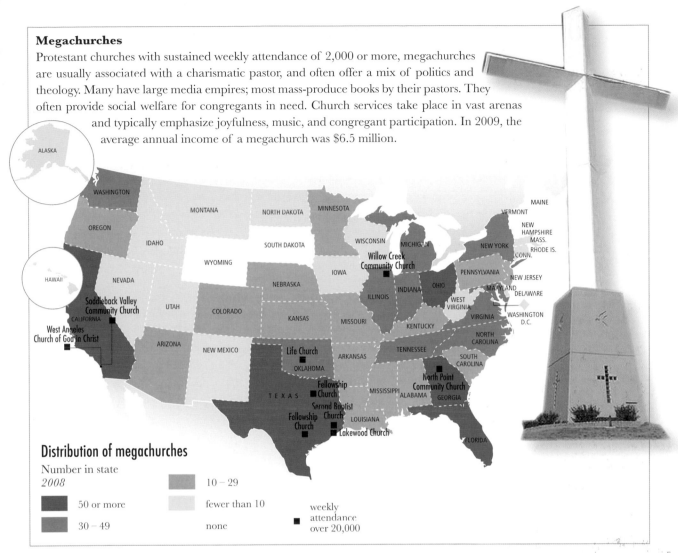

Distribution of megachurches
Number in state
2008

- 50 or more
- 30 – 49
- 10 – 29
- fewer than 10
- none
- ■ weekly attendance over 20,000

Map labels: ALASKA, WASHINGTON, OREGON, HAWAII, MONTANA, NORTH DAKOTA, MINNESOTA, IDAHO, WYOMING, SOUTH DAKOTA, WISCONSIN, MICHIGAN, MAINE, VERMONT, NEW HAMPSHIRE, MASS., RHODE IS., NEVADA, UTAH, COLORADO, NEBRASKA, IOWA, ILLINOIS, INDIANA, OHIO, NEW YORK, PENNSYLVANIA, NEW JERSEY, CONN., CALIFORNIA, ARIZONA, NEW MEXICO, KANSAS, MISSOURI, KENTUCKY, WEST VIRGINIA, VIRGINIA, MARYLAND, DELAWARE, WASHINGTON D.C., OKLAHOMA, ARKANSAS, TENNESSEE, NORTH CAROLINA, SOUTH CAROLINA, TEXAS, MISSISSIPPI, ALABAMA, GEORGIA, LOUISIANA, FLORIDA

Church labels: Willow Creek Community Church, Saddleback Valley Community Church, West Angeles Church of God in Christ, Life Church, Fellowship Church, Second Baptist Church, Fellowship Church, Lakewood Church, North Point Community Church

Big players in the religious right

Current annual revenue, founder and date of foundation
latest available

Christian Broadcasting Network *Pat Robertson, 1961*	**$295m**
Focus on the Family *James Dobson, 1977*	**$130m**
Alliance Defense Fund *Coalition of 30 religious leaders, 1993*	**$30m**
Concerned Women for America *Tim & Beverly LaHaye, 1979*	**$13m**
Family Research Council *James Dobson, 1983*	**$12m**
Christian Coalition *Jerry Falwell, 1989*	**$1.3m**

Political ideology

Percentage of members of religious groups who identify themselves as politically conservative
2010

Mormon	**59%**
Protestant and other Christian	**46%**
Catholic	**39%**
Muslim	**23%**
Jewish	**20%**
Other non-Christian religions	**20%**

The sex of faith

Majority sex among affiliated members
2008

- women
- men

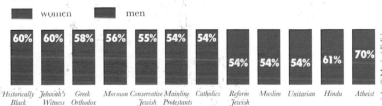

Historically Black Protestant Churches	Jehovah's Witness	Greek Orthodox	Mormon	Conservative Jewish	Mainline Protestants	Catholics	Reform Jewish	Muslim	Unitarian	Hindu	Atheist
60%	60%	58%	56%	55%	54%	54%	54%	54%	54%	61%	70%

The Road to Suffrage

VOTE HERE ▶

WHEN AMERICANS LAUNCHED THEIR "GREAT EXPERIMENT" in democracy in the late 1700s, only a small handful of people were imagined capable of casting a vote to determine who should make public policy: white adult men owning property. Everyone else – the great majority of people residing in the former colonies – was deemed too "uncivilized," too "dependent," too "untrustworthy," too "alien," or too "irrational" to be capable of calculating their own and their country's best interest. Each effort to make voting more inclusive has had not just to change laws but to challenge these cultural assumptions.

The writers of the Constitution – themselves white men of property – gave most of the powers to determine who could and could not vote to the states. Only sporadically has the federal government intervened to alter the rules. Even when it has – for instance, in passing the post-Civil War 14th and 15th Amendments, the later 19th Amendment, and the 1965 Voting Rights Act – it has left implementation mainly to state officials, some of whom have been notably unenthusiastic about expanding the pool of voters.

Members of each disenfranchised group have debated among themselves whether voting matters and, if so, how best to achieve it. Some white women, for instance, contemptuous of "unrespectable" suffragists, joined anti-suffrage clubs. Moreover, disenfranchised groups have not always seen each other as allies.

Charting the twisting, rocky road to fuller suffrage reveals the energies and commitments it has taken to create today's broad electorate. Yet many eligible voters who have voting rights do not exercise those rights. And other Americans still remain on the margins of suffrage or excluded altogether: people who become homeless; people who have had to move repeatedly; people who live in the District of Columbia, Puerto Rico, American Samoa, Guam, and the US Virgin Islands; people who have served prison sentences for felonies. The American road to suffrage requires constant maintenance, and stretches of it are still under construction.

The road to suffrage
A chronology of voting
1776–2010

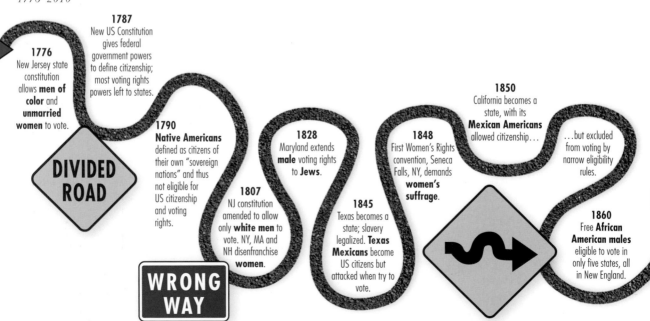

1776
New Jersey state constitution allows **men of color** and **unmarried women** to vote.

1787
New US Constitution gives federal government powers to define citizenship; most voting rights powers left to states.

DIVIDED ROAD

1790
Native Americans defined as citizens of their own "sovereign nations" and thus not eligible for US citizenship and voting rights.

1807
NJ constitution amended to allow only **white men** to vote. NY, MA and NH disenfranchise **women**.

WRONG WAY

1828
Maryland extends **male** voting rights to **Jews**.

1845
Texas becomes a state; slavery legalized. **Texas Mexicans** become US citizens but attacked when try to vote.

1848
First Women's Rights convention, Seneca Falls, NY, demands **women's suffrage**.

1850
California becomes a state, with its **Mexican Americans** allowed citizenship...

...but excluded from voting by narrow eligibility rules.

1860
Free **African American males** eligible to vote in only five states, all in New England.

34

Suffrage

Under construction

2007
Maryland repeals its voting ban for **ex-felons** who have served their sentences.

1992
NY Appeals Court declares unconstitutional state rule that requires voters to live in a **traditional dwelling**.

1984
Federal act requires states to ensure voting place access for **elderly** and **handicapped**.

1981
American Samoans win voting rights in political parties' presidential primaries.

1971
26th Amendment lowers voting age from **21 to 18**.

1967
Martin Luther King leads first **Black** civil rights voter registration drive in a northern city, Cleveland, OH.

1965
Voting Rights Act authorizes Attorney General to enforce voting rights for **African Americans** in those states (all in the South) where less than 50% of Black adults have been registered and voted.

PASS WITH CARE

1960
23rd Amendment grants **residents of DC** the right to vote in presidential elections.

1952
Walter McCarren Act restricts **Asian** immigration, but grants **Americans of Asian descent** the right to become citizens and thus to vote.

1948
Federal Court overturns last state laws in ME, AZ and NM, limiting **Native Americans'** voting rights.

1943
Congress repeals **Chinese** Exclusion Act.

1936
Puerto Rican women win voting rights.

GO

SHARE THE ROAD

YIELD

1924
Congress passes Indian Citizenship Act granting **Native Americans**, including those on reservations, full US citizenship rights.

1924
CA, MN, ND, OK, WI still require that voters must be **"civilized."**

1922
Supreme Court rules it is legal to deny **Japanese Americans** naturalized citizenship and thus right to vote.

1920
19th Amendment grants full voting rights to **women** citizens on same terms as men.

1917
Women win full voting rights in: ND, OH, IN, RI, NE, MI, NY, AR.

1917
Puerto Rican men win right to vote for their own legislature.

GO

1906
Burke Act grants US citizenship to **Native Americans** with land outside reservations.

1890
Wyoming becomes first state in which **women** win right to vote. UT, ID, CO, WA, CA soon follow.

NARROW BRIDGE

1867
14th Amendment extends citizenship to all **African Americans**…

1866
Post-Civil War Civil Rights Acts grant citizenship to **everyone** born in US.

…but for the first time **women of all races** explicitly excluded from voting by the Constitution.

1870
15th Amendment declares **citizens** cannot be denied the right to vote based on "race, color, or previous condition of servitude"

…**African American** men in the South start voting and running for office…

…but **women** still excluded.

DEAD END

1877–1965
Southern **white men** regain control of state governments, pass "Jim Crow" laws enforcing racial segregation and exclusion of **Black men** from voting. Western states enact laws limiting **Asians'** and **Hispanics'** voting rights. Federal officials stop enforcing voting rights acts.

1882
Chinese Exclusion Act bars **Chinese** laborers from entering the US, becoming naturalized citizens and voting.

DIVIDED ROAD

36–37 Representatives;
38–39 Yes We Can!

Representatives

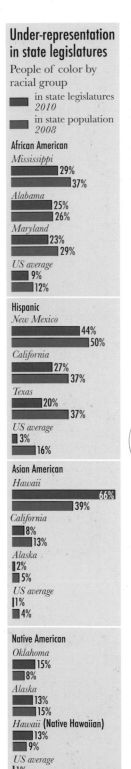

Under-representation in state legislatures

People of color by racial group

▮ in state legislatures 2010
▮ in state population 2008

African American

Mississippi
29%
37%

Alabama
25%
26%

Maryland
23%
29%

US average
9%
12%

Hispanic

New Mexico
44%
50%

California
27%
37%

Texas
20%
37%

US average
3%
16%

Asian American

Hawaii
66%
39%

California
8%
13%

Alaska
2%
5%

US average
1%
4%

Native American

Oklahoma
15%
8%

Alaska
13%
15%

Hawaii (Native Hawaiian)
13%
9%

US average
1%
1.5%

UNTIL RECENTLY, MOST AMERICAN representative institutions operated as if White Christian men could represent the interests of everyone. The first 43 out of 44 American presidents and all vice presidents were White men; until 1981, all of the justices sitting on the Supreme Court were men; until recently, all but a handful of senators were White men. It took multi-stranded civil rights movements, a gay rights movement, and two waves of the women's movement to repaint this bland portrait. Still, a mere 17 percent of members of the 112th Congress are women. Hispanics in Congress also lag behind their proportion of the population. Since World War II, only one African American at a time has sat in the 100-member Senate; the 112th Congress (2011–12) has none. It was deemed a breakthrough in 2010 when three women Justices were serving simultaneously on the Supreme Court. Presidents have been appointing more diverse cabinets, yet only White men have ever headed the powerful departments of Defense and Treasury. And it remains politically risky for a candidate or member of Congress to come out as gay or lesbian.

Race, ethnicity, sexuality, and gender do not, however, translate automatically into ideology. In the aftermath of the Civil War, before the segregationist backlash, those few African American men who won Congressional seats in the South ran as Republicans, "the party of Lincoln." Several pioneering women winning Congressional seats in the 1920s and 30s were Republicans. Yet in the 21st century, majorities of both people of color and women sitting in state legislatures and Congress are Democrats.

Congressional districts are drawn by state legislatures. Often these are drawn with the goal of creating "safe seats" for a particular party, and the districts that result from these manipulations are called "gerrymanders." This power to draw the Congressional districts after each census escalates partisan rivalry to control state legislatures.

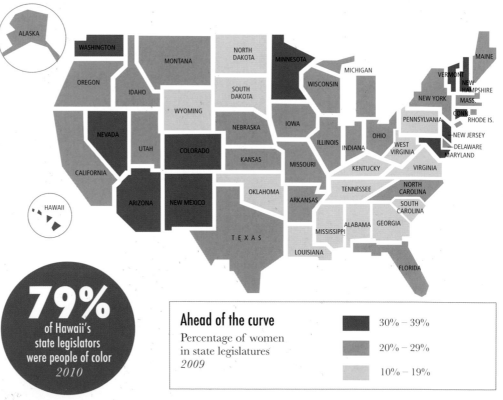

79% of Hawaii's state legislators were people of color 2010

Ahead of the curve

Percentage of women in state legislatures 2009

▮ 30% – 39%
▮ 20% – 29%
▮ 10% – 19%

People of color in the Senate and House of Representatives

Members of the 112th Congress *2011–12*

- ■ African Americ**n**
- ■ Asian American
- ■ Hispanic
- ■ Native American
- ● Democrat
- ● Republican
- ● Independent

51 *Democrat*

47 *Republican*

Senate
Total : 100 members

African American: **0**
Asian American: **2**
Hispanic: **2**
Native American: **0**

192 *Democrat*

242 *Republican*

65 of the 90 women in the 112th Congress are **Democrats**

House of Representatives
435 voting members

African American: **44**
Asian American: **9**
Hispanic: **23**
Native American: **1**

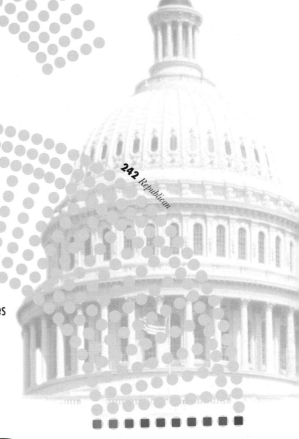

Let the redistricting begin

States that will lose or gain Congressional seats as a result of the 2010 Census population count

Due to the 2010 Census, some states will gain seats (votes) in the House of Representatives; others (especially industrial northern states) will lose. For the states losing seats/votes, this is politically traumatic: some voters will lose their familiar representative; the state as a whole will lose clout in Washington. State legislatures will redraw the voting district lines. Republicans have increased their control of state legislatures, so it is their party that will wield particular influence in these crucial redistricting decisions, which will go into effect in the 2012 Congressional elections.

Gains

Texas	**+4**
Florida	**+2**
Arizona	**+1**
Georgia	**+1**
Nevada	**+1**
South Carolina	**+1**
Utah	**+1**
West Virginia	**+1**

−1	*Illinois*
−1	*Kansas*
−1	*Louisiana*
−1	*Massachusetts*
−1	*Michigan*
−1	*Missouri*
−1	*New Jersey*
−1	*Pennsylvania*
−2	*Ohio*

Losses

Patsy Mink, Democrat from Hawaii, was the first woman of color elected to the US Congress, serving 1965–77 and 1990–2002. A Japanese American, Mink was an opponent of the Vietnam War and an outspoken supporter of women's rights, civil rights and the welfare state.

Illinois' 4th District

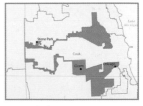

Gerrymanders, named after an early governor of Massachusetts, are Congressional districts drawn in odd shapes by state legislators intent upon crafting boundaries that will ensure that candidates from their own party will win. Only occasionally has the Supreme Court struck down a gerrymandered district as unconstitutional. Both Democrat and Republican state legislators have gerrymandered, leaving voters in these odd districts struggling to find common issues.

37

Yes We Can!

NOVEMBER 2008 WAS AN HISTORIC MOMENT in American history. While race still plays a powerful role in American society – shaping jobs, sports, education, housing, policing, marriage, health – the election of Barack Obama to the office of President lifted many Americans' hopes that a new era of race relations had begun.

The election occurred as the US waged two costly wars, the housing "bubble" burst, and the economy sank. Both major parties conducted prolonged primary contests to select their final nominees, John McCain for the Republicans, Barack Obama for the Democrats. Voting in the United States is complicated. Each voter had to decide whether to: 1) register to vote, and, if so, whether as an "independent" or as affiliated with a political party; 2) vote in a primary; 3) vote in November; 4) vote for McCain, Obama or a minor candidate; 5) vote for the same party's Congressional candidates as its presidential candidate.

Only 63 percent of eligible voters voted in the 2008 election. Yet this was the highest turnout since 1960. The Obama campaign mobilized young people, although only 46 percent of those aged 18 to 24 actually voted, and it wasn't clear whether they would stay engaged for future elections. The "gender gap" that had emerged in the 1980s persisted: women were more likely than men to vote for Democrats than Republicans. Hispanic voters wielded new electoral clout in the Southwest. African Americans voted in record numbers, both in the final election and in Democratic primaries, playing a decisive role in Barack Obama's win over his closest Democratic rival, Hillary Clinton.

In the 2008 election, voters also chose Democrats for a majority of seats in both the Senate and the House. For two years – until the November 2010 "mid-term" Congressional elections – Barack Obama would have substantial majorities of his own party as allies in Congress. It would prove an uneasy alliance.

Gender gap

The gender gap in voting refers to the difference in the percentage of women and the percentage of men voting for a given candidate. A gender gap in voting for presidential candidates has been apparent in every election since 1980.

In the Obama-McCain election, **56%** of women and **49%** of men voted for Obama, a gap of **7%**.

Turnout

Percentage of all eligible voters who voted in presidential elections

2008	63%
2004	61%
2000	54%
1996	51%
1992	58%
1988	53%
1984	56%
1980	55%

Turnout according to gender and race/ethnicity

Turnout as percentage of each group's eligible voters
November 2008

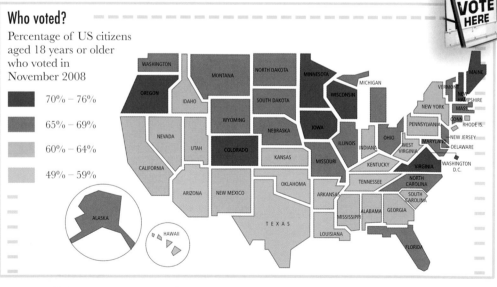

Who voted?

Percentage of US citizens aged 18 years or older who voted in November 2008

- 70% – 76%
- 65% – 69%
- 60% – 64%
- 49% – 59%

Black	White	Hispanic	Asian/Pacific Islander
64% / 56%	62% / 57%	34% / 29%	33% / 32%
Women / Men	Women / Men	Women / Men	Women / Men

2008 Presidential Election

Candidate who received the majority of the popular vote by county

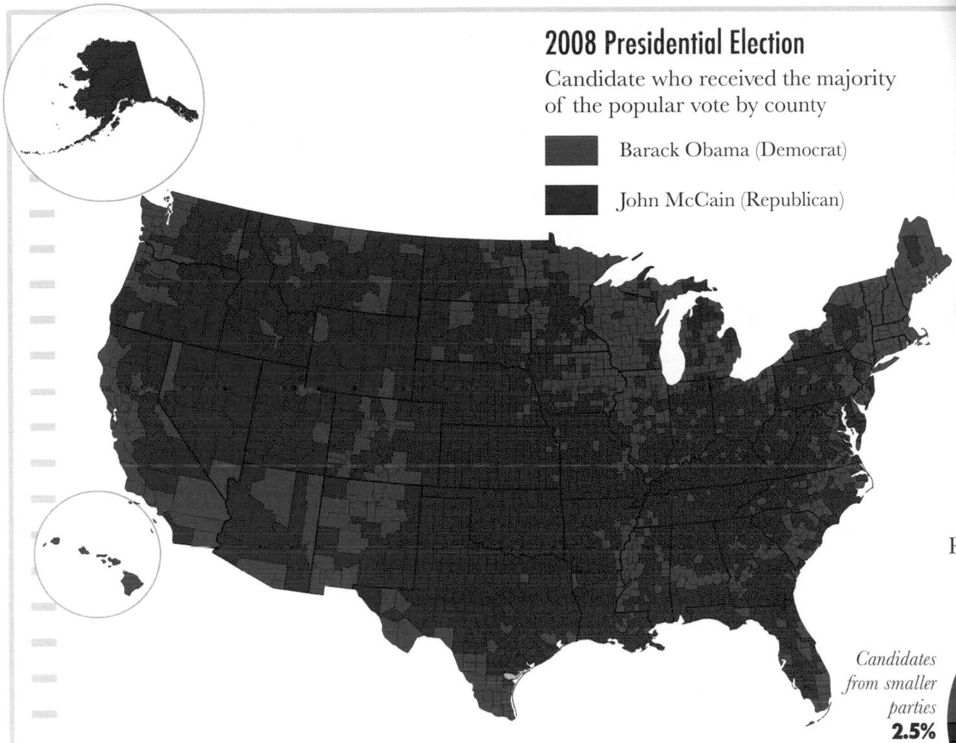

■ Barack Obama (Democrat)

■ John McCain (Republican)

Votes cast

Percentage of total votes
2008

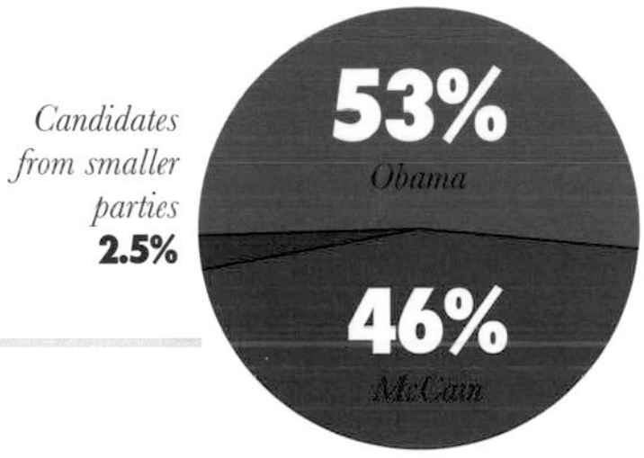

Candidates from smaller parties
2.5%

53%
Obama

46%
McCain

Who voted for whom?

Percentage of each group that said they voted for the candidates
Exit poll data, Election Day 2008

■ Obama   ■ McCain

Voting patterns by family income

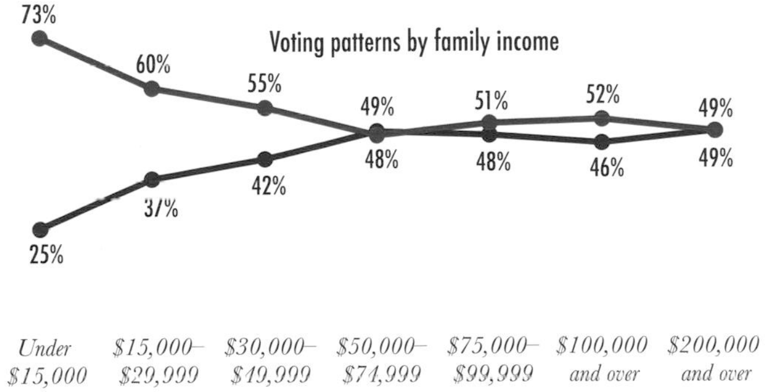

73%
60%
55%
49% 51% 52% 49%
48% 48% 46% 49%
42%
37%
25%

| Under $15,000 | $15,000– $29,999 | $30,000– $49,999 | $50,000– $74,999 | $75,000– $99,999 | $100,000 and over | $200,000 and over |

Voting patterns according to age

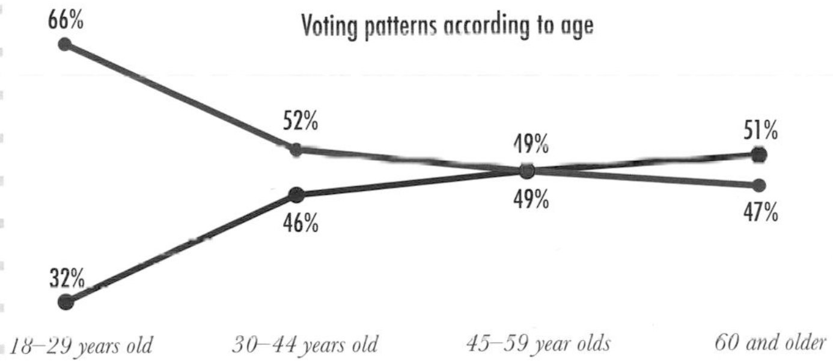

66%
52%
49% 51%
49%
46% 47%
32%

18–29 years old   30–44 years old   45–59 year olds   60 and older

Voting patterns by gender and race/ethnicity

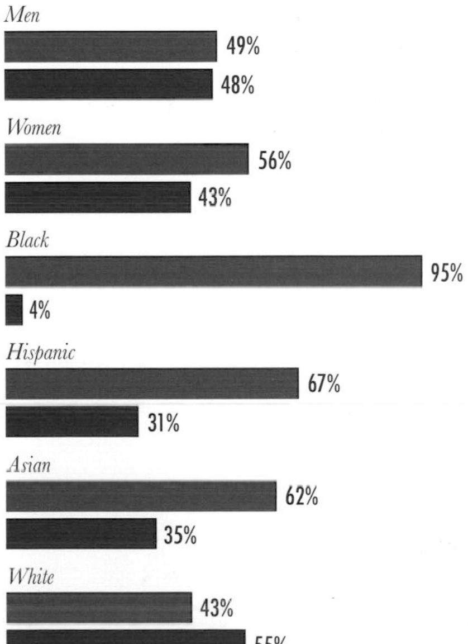

Men
49%
48%

Women
56%
43%

Black
95%
4%

Hispanic
67%
31%

Asian
62%
35%

White
43%
55%

39

Media

A FREE PRESS is a pillar of any democracy. "Congress shall make no law…abridging the freedom of speech, or of the press" reads the Constitution's First Amendment. The Federal Communications Commission is mandated to ensure fairness in the use of the public's air waves, but Congress passed the 1996 Telecommunications Act radically deregulating the media business sector. The resultant proliferation of television channels, radio stations, and internet sites seems to offer Americans a dizzying array of information and entertainment. Today, one can watch golf 24/7, listen only to golden oldies, or surf among channels in multiple languages. Media democracy appears to be in full flower.

In practice, large media corporations control the country's press, radio, publishing, film production and television. Fewer cities have competing local newspapers. Clear Channel Communications, the country's largest radio company, owns 700 radio stations across the United States. Most local TV channels are affiliates of national companies. City councils in California, Oregon, and Tennessee are contracting out their public libraries to private companies. Prominent American book publishers – Random House, Knopf, Simon and Schuster – are now subsidiaries of

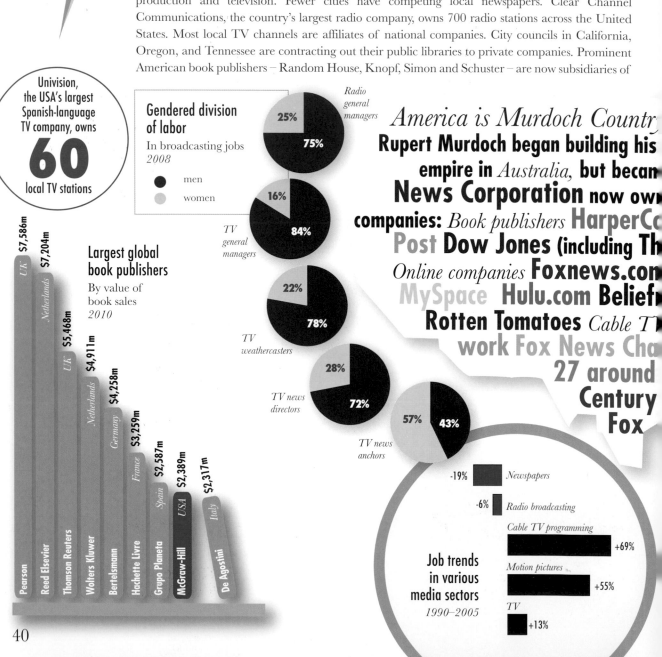

Percentage of polled public who say they do not trust the news media
September 2010

Republicans **67%**
Independents **61%**

Democrats **40%**

Univision, the USA's largest Spanish-language TV company, owns

60

local TV stations

Largest global book publishers
By value of book sales 2010

UK **$7,586m** Pearson
Netherlands **$7,204m** Reed Elsevier
UK **$5,468m** Thomson Reuters
Netherlands **$4,911m** Wolters Kluwer
Germany **$4,258m** Bertelsmann
France **$3,259m** Hachette Livre
Spain **$2,587m** Grupo Planeta
USA **$2,389m** McGraw-Hill
Italy **$2,317m** De Agostini

Gendered division of labor
In broadcasting jobs 2008

● men
● women

Radio general managers 25% / 75%

TV general managers 16% / 84%

TV weathercasters 22% / 78%

TV news directors 28% / 72%

TV news anchors 57% / 43%

America is Murdoch Country
Rupert Murdoch began building his empire in *Australia*, **but becam News Corporation now ow companies:** *Book publishers* **HarperCo Post Dow Jones (including Th** *Online companies* **Foxnews.com MySpace Hulu.com Belief Rotten Tomatoes** *Cable T* **work Fox News Cha 27 around Century Fox**

Job trends in various media sectors
1990–2005

-19% *Newspapers*
-6% *Radio broadcasting*
Cable TV programming +69%
Motion pictures +55%
TV +13%

40

global corporations. Newspaper circulation fell 9 percent between 2009 and 2010. Responding to falling advertising revenues with a binge of cost-cutting, many major newspapers – despite accelerating global interdependency – closed their overseas news bureaus.

Although 3 million Americans are employed in the communications and media sector, news outlets remain white men's enclaves. Women and people of color are rarely invited as experts on camera and/or appointed to top posts behind the scenes. Moreover, boundaries between news and entertainment have crumbled. Faced with news reporting designed chiefly to be profitable and entertaining, many distrust what they see in the media, breeding political cynicism. But ordinary Americans are not merely passive spectators in this media tale: many prefer sound-bite news and are impatient with nuanced, in-depth news coverage and extensive reporting on developments outside the USA. Journalists who don't fit criteria for celebrity are often ignored.

64%
of US newspapers shrank the space they devoted to international news
2007–09

Who's the presumed expert?

Race/ethnicity of cable news guest experts during May 2008

- White
- African American
- Hispanic
- Asian American

CNN
83%
11%
4% 2%

Fox News
88%
9%
3%

MSNBC
83%
16%
1%

Racial division of labor

In TV and radio news
2008

- White
- African American
- Hispanic
- Asian American
- Native American

TV
76%
10%
10%
3%
<1%

Radio
88%
8%
4%
<1%

media

US citizen in 1980. His
following American media
ns *Newspapers* New York
(Wall Street Journal)
ypost.com Wsj.com
AmericanIdol.com
x Business Net-
Local TV Stations
USA *Film* **20th**

Gender of guest experts on prime-time programs of three major cable news channels during May 2008

- men
- women

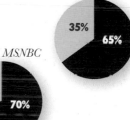

CNN
65% 35%

Fox News
65% 35%

MSNBC
70% 30%

Newspaper	Asian American	African American	Hispanic	Native American
San Francisco Chronicle	11%	3%	6%	0%
Miami Herald	3%	13%	22%	0%
Denver Post	2%	4%	11%	0%
Atlanta Journal/Constitution	2%	21%	3%	<1%
Honolulu Advertiser	54%	1%	3%	0%
Chicago Tribune	6%	9%	5%	3%
Boston Globe	8%	9%	4%	<1%
St. Louis Post-Dispatch	3%	10%	1%	0%
New York Times	6%	8%	4%	<1%

Minorities

As percentage of selected newspapers' newsroom staff *2008*

A Networked Society

A man's world

Women as percentage
of total in US
2010

CEOs in top
tech companies: **6%**

Software engineers: **22%**

Computer science graduates

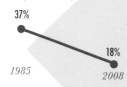

37%
1985

18%
2008

THANKS TO THE INTERNET, new verbs are cascading into our daily conversations: to text, to Google, to Tweet, to friend, to unfriend. And there's a new cast of characters striding across the land: geeks, hackers, bloggers, cyberbullies, web masters, and dot.com millionaires. There always have been rumor-mills, information leaks, and startling innovations. But today, due to the internet (and its software and hardware underpinnings), each operates at hyper-speed, spreading more widely, refined by fewer filters. As the internet's applications dash ahead of our ability to weigh their consequences, there are pressing concerns about accountability, surveillance, and privacy.

Although there are still some electronics assembly jobs left in the US, more and more electronics companies are moving their manufacturing assembly overseas. Together, the companies that produce the hardware goods driving America's internet culture – the keyboards, the smart-phones, the iPods – employ an estimated total of 3.4 million workers worldwide, most of whom are young women factory workers in China, Taiwan, Malaysia, Vietnam, the Philippines, and South Korea.

Silicon Valley

Computer software and hardware companies set up shop in an area of California in the1950s, and in 1971 the term "Silicon Valley" was coined — referring to one of the central elements in microchips. By 2000, Silicon Valley was abuzz with software engineers, internet visionaries, entrepreneurs and venture capitalists, all trying to ride the internet wave. Today, even though some of the computing giants are headquartered elsewhere, "Silicon Valley" has become popular shorthand for the entire industry.

The policies of the officials of Santa Clara county — at the heart of Silicon Valley — on housing, fair employment and environmental protection, all shape the dot.com industry, and are shaped by it.

Some of the best-known companies in Silicon Valley
Apple
Cisco Systems
Google
Hewlett Packard
Intel
Sun Microsystems
Yahoo
eBay

San Francisco

Fremont

SAN MATEO
Redwood City

Newark

Mountain View

Milipitas

Santa Clara

Sunnyvale

San Jose

Cupertino

Campbell

ALAMEDA

Morgan Hill

SANTA CRUZ

SANTA CLARA

Gilroy

Santa Cruz

Employee profile

Profile of those employed in computer and math jobs in Silicon Valley compared with US average
2006–08

Silicon Valley

African American **2%**
Hispanics **5%**

Asian and Asian American **54%**

38% *White*

US average

African American **7%**
Hispanics (of all races) **5%**

16% *Asian and Asian American*

70% *White*

Santa Clara county

Profile of population
2010

24% *Hispanics of any race*

People identifying as of other races or of two or more races

0.3% *Native Hawaiian and Pacific Islander*

3% *African American*

17%

26%

54% *White*

Asian and Asian American

eBay

Profile of employees
2005

37% *Women*

63% *Men*

African American **2%**

4% *Hispanic*

Asian and Asian American **39%**

55% *White*

Money helps to keep you connected...

Percentage of each household income group
who use the internet
2010

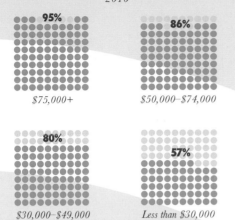

95% $75,000+

86% $50,000–$74,000

80% $30,000–$49,000

57% *Less than $30,000*

...So does education

Internet use in those aged over 18 with different educational attainment
2010

With a college degree

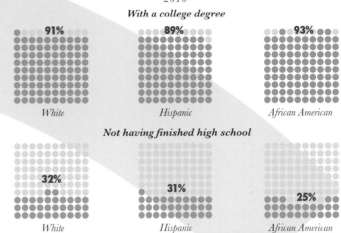

91% *White*

89% *Hispanic*

93% *African American*

Not having finished high school

32% *White*

31% *Hispanic*

25% *African American*

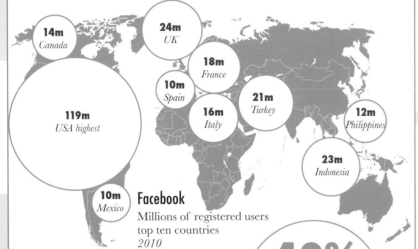

14m *Canada*

24m *UK*

18m *France*

10m *Spain*

119m *USA highest*

16m *Italy*

21m *Turkey*

12m *Philippines*

23m *Indonesia*

10m *Mexico*

Facebook
Millions of registered users
top ten countries
2010

**Percentage of Americans
who say they use this
news source**
2010

Local TV **78%**
National TV or cable **73%**

Online news **61%**
Radio news **54%**
Local newspaper **50%**

National newspaper **17%**

42%
of Americans aged
50 years or more
used the internet for
social networking
2010

70%
of Black
and Hispanic
people texted
2010

50%
of White people
texted
2010

Wikipedia's total
contributors:
87%
men
13%
women

The users

The internet has had pronounced impacts on Americans' lives — from how we shop and socialize to how we vote and get our news. Some optimists assert that the internet has become the Great Leveler: in a wireless nation, the assumption goes, everyone is equal, not held back by old-school demographics of race or age or class; as long as one has an internet connection, one can be as involved as finger agility will allow. The gritty reality may be less rosy. Not everyone can afford the latest computer or smart-phone, nor are all households wireless. Most Americans don't have influence at the corporate offices of Microsoft, Intel, Apple or Google, nor do most people have access to venture capital. The problems caused by unequal access to literacy, education, and money do not stop at the digital shoreline.

Part Three

Land of Hope and Opportunity

The Economy

Foreign direct investment (FDI)

Share of all FDI in US by home country of investor companies
2009

UK	20%
Japan	11%
Netherlands	10%
Canada	10%
Germany	9%
Switzerland	8%
France	8%
Luxembourg	6%
Other	18%

THE UNITED STATES HAS THE WORLD'S LARGEST ECONOMY. Measured by Gross Domestic Product (GDP), the value of all final goods and services produced in a given year, it has a $14 trillion economy, far exceeding its nearest rivals, China and Japan at $5 trillion each. The US economy is so big that a single state, even the smallest, is equivalent to the entire economy of other countries.

In the era of globalization, no economy stands on its own two feet. Money and goods flow across national borders at an extraordinary rate. The US is the largest investor in the rest of the world, with about $3.4 trillion of American direct investments abroad; the US is also the country most heavily invested in, with foreign direct investments into the US worth over $2 trillion.

Big movers and little shakers

States sized according to Gross Domestic Product (GDP)
2009

■ = $10 billion
GDP given where $300bn or more

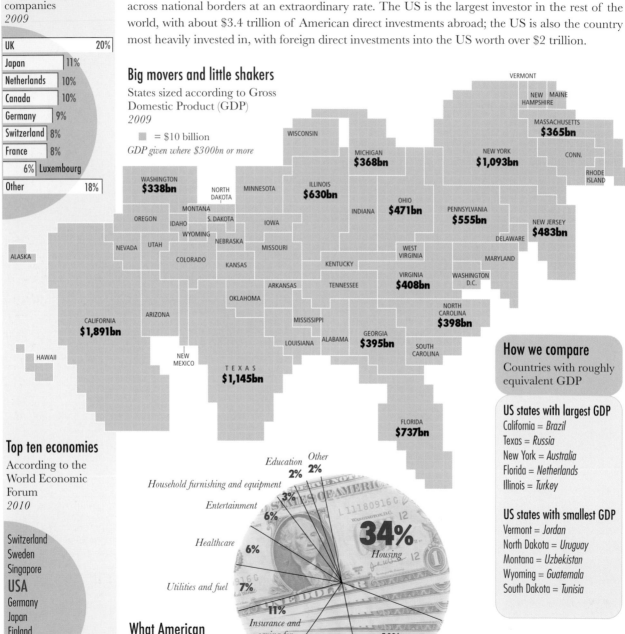

VERMONT
NEW HAMPSHIRE · MAINE
MASSACHUSETTS **$365bn**
WISCONSIN
MICHIGAN **$368bn**
NEW YORK **$1,093bn**
CONN.
RHODE ISLAND
WASHINGTON **$338bn**
NORTH DAKOTA
MINNESOTA
ILLINOIS **$630bn**
OHIO **$471bn**
PENNSYLVANIA **$555bn**
MONTANA
OREGON · IDAHO
WYOMING
S. DAKOTA
IOWA
INDIANA
NEW JERSEY **$483bn**
DELAWARE
NEVADA · UTAH
NEBRASKA
MISSOURI
WEST VIRGINIA
MARYLAND
ALASKA
COLORADO
KANSAS
KENTUCKY
VIRGINIA **$408bn**
WASHINGTON D.C.
CALIFORNIA **$1,891bn**
ARIZONA
ARKANSAS
TENNESSEE
NORTH CAROLINA **$398bn**
OKLAHOMA
MISSISSIPPI
GEORGIA **$395bn**
HAWAII
NEW MEXICO
TEXAS **$1,145bn**
LOUISIANA · ALABAMA
SOUTH CAROLINA
FLORIDA **$737bn**

How we compare

Countries with roughly equivalent GDP

US states with largest GDP
California = *Brazil*
Texas = *Russia*
New York = *Australia*
Florida = *Netherlands*
Illinois = *Turkey*

US states with smallest GDP
Vermont = *Jordan*
North Dakota = *Uruguay*
Montana = *Uzbekistan*
Wyoming = *Guatemala*
South Dakota = *Tunisia*

Top ten economies

According to the World Economic Forum
2010

Switzerland
Sweden
Singapore
USA
Germany
Japan
Finland
Netherlands
Denmark
Canada

What American households spend their money on
2009

Education **2%**
Other **2%**
Household furnishing and equipment **3%**
Entertainment **6%**
Healthcare **6%**
Utilities and fuel **7%**
Housing **34%**
Insurance and saving for retirement **11%**
Transportation **16%**
Food **13%**

Drivers of the economy

In a single snapshot, it's impossible to portray the economy as a whole. But the "lived" economy is more easily comprehended. Every year, fewer Americans work in manufacturing, and more work in the service economy, especially in the healthcare sector. The single-largest private employer in the US (and in the world) is Walmart, employing 1.4 million people in the US alone, more than 1 percent of the American workforce. The shrinkage of the manufacturing sector is a source of great nostalgia and angst for Americans, and manufacturing is a touchstone in American popular culture for how the economy is faring. In many states, the state itself is the largest employer: 22 million Americans, about 17 percent of the workforce, work in government at the local, state, or federal levels. Many economists say that consumer spending is the most potent economic driver, but fewer Americans have the capacity for discretionary spending.

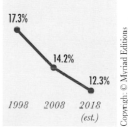

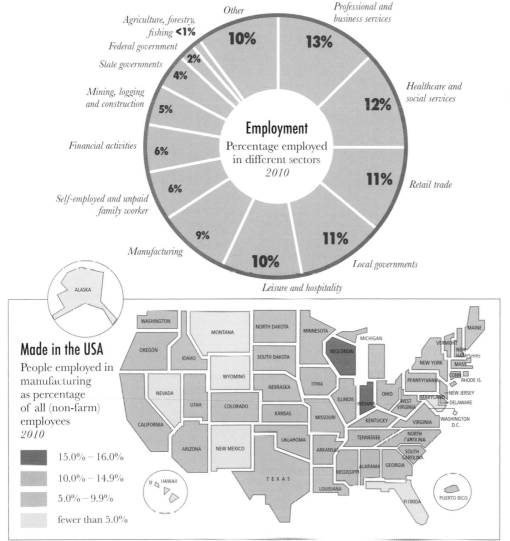

Employment
Percentage employed in different sectors
2010

- Other **10%**
- Professional and business services **13%**
- Healthcare and social services **12%**
- Retail trade **11%**
- Local governments **11%**
- Leisure and hospitality **10%**
- Manufacturing **9%**
- Self-employed and unpaid family worker **6%**
- Financial activities **6%**
- Mining, logging and construction **5%**
- State governments **4%**
- Federal government **2%**
- Agriculture, forestry, fishing **<1%**

Manufacturing
As a percentage of GDP
2008 or most recent selected countries

%	Country
34%	China
28%	Indonesia
28%	South Korea
24%	Germany
21%	Japan
19%	Mexico
16%	Canada
16%	India
14%	USA
14%	Bolivia
13%	UK

Made in the USA
People employed in manufacturing as percentage of all (non-farm) employees
2010

- 15.0% – 16.0%
- 10.0% – 14.9%
- 5.0% – 9.9%
- fewer than 5.0%

(US map with states labeled: ALASKA, WASHINGTON, OREGON, IDAHO, MONTANA, NORTH DAKOTA, MINNESOTA, MICHIGAN, MAINE, VERMONT, NEW HAMPSHIRE, NEW YORK, MASS., CONN., RHODE IS., PENNSYLVANIA, NEW JERSEY, MARYLAND, DELAWARE, WASHINGTON D.C., WEST VIRGINIA, VIRGINIA, OHIO, INDIANA, ILLINOIS, WISCONSIN, IOWA, SOUTH DAKOTA, WYOMING, NEBRASKA, NEVADA, UTAH, COLORADO, KANSAS, MISSOURI, KENTUCKY, CALIFORNIA, ARIZONA, NEW MEXICO, OKLAHOMA, TENNESSEE, NORTH CAROLINA, SOUTH CAROLINA, ARKANSAS, GEORGIA, ALABAMA, MISSISSIPPI, TEXAS, LOUISIANA, FLORIDA, HAWAII, PUERTO RICO)

Manufacturing jobs
Percentage of US workforce employed in manufacturing

- 1998: 17.3%
- 2008: 14.2%
- 2018 (est.): 12.3%

Corporate Life

SMALL BUSINESSES generate almost half of the jobs in the United States, but large corporations generate the largest share of the wealth – or, rather, the workers who work for the corporations generate the wealth; the corporations generate the profits.

Large corporations dominate the lives of Americans from birth to death. The web of everyday life is increasingly filtered through interactions with brands that shape and reflect personal and class identity: Crest toothpaste (Procter & Gamble), GM cars, Coca-Cola, Apple iPods, Budweiser beer, Heinz ketchup. We shop at Walmart, eat at McDonald's, perhaps buy groceries at Whole Foods, or more likely at Kroger's, ship packages by UPS, watch Waste Management trucks pick up our trash, and pay our mortgage to Citibank. Relatively few of us may directly encounter Corrections Corporation of America (the largest private prison corporation), but most of us encounter corporate leviathans without even knowing who they are – most students at universities can't name the food service giant that runs their food courts (most likely Chartwells, Sodexho, or Aramark); most of us can't name the corporate owner of our daily newspaper. While the public

Bailout loans

Top 10 private sector recipients of public funds ("Troubled Asset Relief Program") *2008*
Some of these loans have been repaid

AIG **$70bn**
GM **$54bn**
Citigroup **$50bn**
Bank of America **$45bn**
JP Morgan Chase, Wells Fargo **$25bn**
GMAC Financial Services **$12.5bn**
Morgan Stanley, Goldman Sachs **$10bn**
PNC Financial Services **$7.6bn**

Biggest US companies

Most employees worldwide
2010

Walmart	2,100,000
UPS	408,000
IBM	399,409
McDonald's	385,000
Target	351,000

Highest market value
2010

Exxon Mobil	$314bn
Microsoft	$260bn
Apple	$209bn
Walmart	$209bn
Berkshire Hathaway	$201bn

Largest private contractors in Iraq and Afghanistan
2004–06

KBR	$16bn
DynCorp	$2bn
Washington Group	$1bn
IAP Worldwide Services	$902m
Environmental Chemical Corp	$900m

Power centers

Cities with five or more headquarters of Fortune 500 firms
2010

7 San Francisco
5 Los Angeles
5 Englewood

Big payday for CEOs

Annual compensation for top three CEOs
2009–10

Gregory Maffel (Liberty Media Corp)
Total compensation received in *2009* **$87,493,565**
Equivalent of:
• combined salary of **218** US presidents *or*
• combined earnings of **2,730** workers on average wage *or*
• combined earnings of **5,801** workers on minimum wage

Lawrence Ellison (Oracle Corp)
Total compensation received in *2009* **$56,810,851**
Equivalent of:
• combined salary of **142** US presidents *or*
• **1,772** average workers *or*
• **3,767** minimum-wage earners

John Hammergren (McKesson Corporation)
Total compensation received in *2010* **$54,584,021**
Equivalent of:
• combined salary of **136** US presidents *or*
• **1,703** average workers *or*
• **3,619** minimum-wage earners

presence of corporations seems to be at an all-time high, thanks to the ubiquitous logos that dot every surface we see and article of clothing we wear, knowledge about them is low. Few of us understand the business practices, ownership webs, transnational sites, or policy positions of the corporations that surround us.

The scale and power of the largest corporations are almost unimaginable. Walmart's revenues are larger than the GDP of 10 states combined (Vermont, North Dakota, Montana, Wyoming, South Dakota, Alaska, Rhode Island, Maine, Idaho, and New Hampshire); Exxon Mobil's revenues are equivalent to Maryland's annual GDP. Corporations are not just neutral providers of goods and services. Corporations buy political influence and pull the levers of power with impunity; they sway public policy, from tax laws to international debates about doing business with human rights abusers; they shape public priorities; they shape popular culture and tastes. Some corporations are deemed "too big to fail," others are simply too big to regulate.

image
brand
trademark
identity
product
services
solutions
market
logistics
strategy

mission
logo
corporate

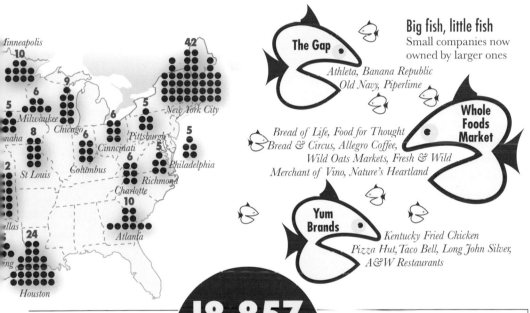

Big fish, little fish
Small companies now owned by larger ones

The Gap
Athleta, Banana Republic Old Navy, Piperlime

Whole Foods Market
Bread of Life, Food for Thought Bread & Circus, Allegro Coffee, Wild Oats Markets, Fresh & Wild Merchant of Vino, Nature's Heartland

Yum Brands
Kentucky Fried Chicken Pizza Hut, Taco Bell, Long John Silver, A&W Restaurants

Largest philanthropic foundations
Total assets 2009

Foundation	Total assets
William & Flora Hewlett Fdn	$6,869,108,000
Robert Wood Johnson Fdn	$8,490,415,783
J. Paul Getty Trust	$9,339,172,138
Ford Foundation	$10,373,847,207
Bill & Melinda Gates Foundation	$33,912,320,600

18,857
corporations are listed as being housed at one single address in the Cayman Islands

Overseas tax havens

Companies with operations overseas pay US taxes only if they bring the profits back to the US. So, many companies run profits through off-shore subsidiaries to reduce their tax burden. Of the 100 largest US companies, 83 have subsidiaries in overseas tax havens. Some are located there for legitimate business reasons; others for tax avoidance.

Zero tax

The Government Accountability Office reports that 72% of foreign corporations and 57% of US companies doing business in the US paid no federal income taxes for at least one year from 1998 to 2005. More than half of foreign companies and 42% of US companies paid no US income taxes for two or more years in that period. Some shelter their income in foreign tax havens; others report losses that reduce or eliminate their taxes.

Highest number of subsidiaries in foreign tax havens
2007

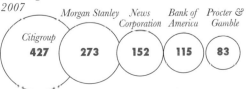

Citigroup	Morgan Stanley	News Corporation	Bank of America	Procter & Gamble
427	273	152	115	83

Top-ranking companies that paid NO federal taxes on income
2009

General Electric
Bank of America
CitiGroup
Valero

Jobs, Jobs, Jobs

> "A job is more than a job. It's where you fit in society."
> Man whose accountant wife had been unemployed for four years

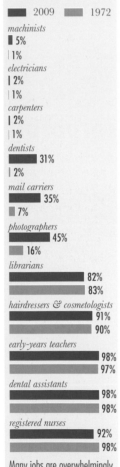

Gender segregation

Women as percentage of workers in selected occupations
1972 & 2009

■ 2009 ■ 1972

machinists
5%
1%

electricians
2%
1%

carpenters
2%
1%

dentists
31%
2%

mail carriers
35%
7%

photographers
45%
16%

librarians
82%
83%

hairdressers & cosmetologists
91%
90%

early-years teachers
98%
97%

dental assistants
98%
98%

registered nurses
92%
98%

Many jobs are overwhelmingly occupied either by women or by men. Some occupations have become less gender-segregated over the past four decades, but others have not. Many that have remained feminized – "pink collar" jobs – are also low paying.

HAVING A PAID JOB ISN'T JUST ABOUT MONEY; it's about identity and belonging. Beside the threat to one's economic security, being unemployed in America can make one feel excluded. Thus, with over 14 million Americans unemployed in 2010 – and even more underemployed – anxiety has been rife.

Behind unemployment averages are particulars. The recent Great Recession hit male-dominated construction and manufacturing industries especially hard. Despite the recession, college graduates still had much better job prospects than high-school graduates. Unemployed 19-year-olds and 50-year-olds both faced more daunting job searches than 30-year-olds. Workers in Michigan were more likely to have lost their jobs than those in Virginia. Unemployed single mothers were stymied in their job searches by the lack of affordable childcare.

Since the Great Depression of the 1930s, the federal government has woven a patchy "social safety net" – unemployment and disability insurance, retraining programs, food stamps, Medicaid, support for poor children – to provide a partial buffer against the harshness of economic cyclical downturns. But it's very partial.

In recent decades, the American jobs landscape has changed fundamentally. Women have become nearly half (49.9 percent) of the country's paid workforce, as more women have sought careers, more families need two adult incomes, and more households are headed by single women. More jobs require post-high-school education. Employers have shed full-time jobs with benefits, preferring part-timers and short-term contract workers. Many skilled manufacturing jobs have gone overseas, though jobs in service industries such as healthcare have grown.

Obtaining secure, safe, decently paid jobs can be obstructed by discrimination, sexual harassment, and workplace health hazards. Federal laws are supposed to ban gender, age, racial, ethnic, and religious discrimination in hiring and promotion, and to ensure workplace safety. They have made some occupations more diverse and some jobs safer. But many employees may not file safety or discrimination complaints for fear of employer retaliation. And today, with only 12 percent of working Americans belonging to labor unions, few working people have collective support to back them up.

4.7% of all employed Americans work multiple jobs

If the path to every occupation were without obstacles for some and grease for others, the distribution of workers by race in each occupation would be broadly similar. In reality, though, each occupation in this country has had – and still has – a distinctive relationship to the workings of race, despite laws and community efforts to "level the playing field."

Who does what job?

Racial/ethnic make-up of selected occupations
2007 or latest data available

● White   ● Asian
● Black   ● other

▢ percentage Hispanic. As an ethnic category, this can include people who identify with one or more race.

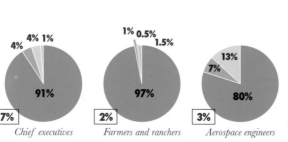

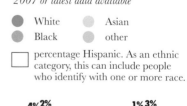

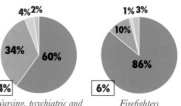

Chief executives — 91%, 4%, 4%, 1%, 7%
Farmers and ranchers — 97%, 1%, 0.5%, 1.5%, 2%
Aerospace engineers — 80%, 7%, 13%, 3%
Nursing, psychiatric and home health aides — 60%, 34%, 4%, 2%, 14%
Firefighters — 86%, 10%, 1%, 3%, 6%

Unemployment

Working age population
officially recorded as
out of work and looking for job
August 2010

- 12.5% – 15.5%
- 10.0% – 12.4%
- 7.5% – 9.9%
- 5.0% – 7.4%
- 3.7% – 4.9%

National average: 9.6%

ALASKA

WASHINGTON · *MONTANA* · *NORTH DAKOTA* · *MINNESOTA* · *MICHIGAN* · *MAINE* · *VERMONT* · *NEW HAMPSHIRE*
OREGON · *IDAHO* · *SOUTH DAKOTA* · *WISCONSIN* · *NEW YORK* · *MASS* · *CONN* · *RHODE IS.*
WYOMING · *NEBRASKA* · *IOWA* · *OHIO* · *PENNSYLVANIA* · *NEW JERSEY* · *DELAWARE*
NEVADA · *UTAH* · *COLORADO* · *ILLINOIS* · *INDIANA* · *WEST VIRGINIA* · *MARYLAND* · *WASHINGTON D.C.*
CALIFORNIA · *KANSAS* · *MISSOURI* · *KENTUCKY* · *VIRGINIA*
ARIZONA · *NEW MEXICO* · *OKLAHOMA* · *TENNESSEE* · *NORTH CAROLINA*
HAWAII · *ARKANSAS* · *ALABAMA* · *GEORGIA* · *SOUTH CAROLINA*
TEXAS · *MISSISSIPPI* · *LOUISIANA* · *FLORIDA*
PUERTO RICO

14.9 million
Americans
were unemployed
August 2010

SMALL NUMBERS MATTER

When Florida's unemployment rate inched up from 11.5% in July 2010 to 11.7% in August 2010, that meant that in one month 25,000 more Floridians had lost their jobs.

Hidden unemployed

Groups not counted in the official unemployment figures
August 2010

People who work part-time, but want full-time jobs:
8.9m

"Discouraged" workers: people who have stopped looking, but want a job:
1.1m

"For many of our families, the 40-hour week is over. They may still have a job, but they're trying to survive on reduced hours, with no benefits."
Manager of a food pantry and soup kitchen
September 2010

Who is unemployed?

Percentage of each group officially unemployed
August 2010

Adult men: 9.8%
Adult women: 8.0%

White	Black	Hispanic (of all races)	Asian
8.7%	16.3%	12.0%	7.2%

Racial/ethnic groups

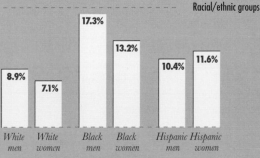

White men	White women	Black men	Black women	Hispanic men	Hispanic women	Less than high school diploma	High school graduate	Some college	BA degree or higher
8.9%	7.1%	17.3%	13.2%	10.4%	11.6%	14.0%	10.3%	8.7%	4.6%

Race and gender
People aged 20–64 years

Different educational attainment
People 25 years and older

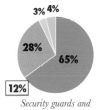
12% · 3% 4% · 28% · 65%
Security guards and gaming surveillance officers

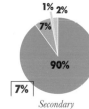
3% · 2% · 32% · 7% · 59%
Medical scientists

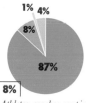
7% · 1% 2% · 7% · 90%
Secondary school teachers

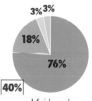
8% · 1% 4% · 8% · 87%
Athletes, coaches, umpires and related workers

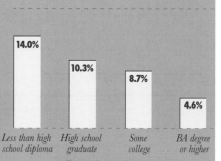
40% · 3% 3% · 18% · 76%
Maids and housekeeping cleaners

1% 1% · 98%
Tool and die makers (machinists)

Copyright © Myriad Editions

The Wage Gap

State minimum hourly wage in 2010

Lowest:
Georgia
$5.15
Highest:
Washington
$8.55

ALTHOUGH SOME AMERICANS RECEIVE INCOME from investments and pensions, most rely on weekly wages. The idea of a mandated "minimum hourly wage" emerged as part of New Deal reforms. Under the Fair Labor Standards Act (1938), Congress sets the federal minimum wage and determines who is exempted or covered by the law. Workers on small farms are excluded; non-live-in domestic workers have been covered only since 2009. Opposition in Congress to raising the federal minimum wage is always stiff. State legislatures set minimum hourly wages for workers in small companies or in non-interstate-related jobs, causing substantial differences across the country. Labor unions and social movements have demanded that employers pay not just a minimum wage, but a living wage: one that covers housing, food, heating, school, and health costs in the worker's community.

Equal pay has been a central demand of the American women's movement since the 1960s. The Equal Pay Act (1963), made any sex-based wage discrimination within the same job category illegal, but it has taken court cases to ensure the law's implementation. The Equal Employment Opportunity Commission (EEOC) enforces the Equal Pay Act. Title VII of the 1964 Civil Rights Act, enforced by the Justice Department, bans hiring and promotion discrimination against women.

Despite progress, the gender wage gap persists – and is even wider between the average wages of White men and those earned by women of color. Women who gain access to traditionally male occupations do not automatically achieve the wage equality stipulated in law. And many women continue to work in "feminized jobs," which are undervalued and lowly paid. Even in these occupations, men make, on average, more than women. Women's advocates call not just for equal pay within the same job category, but re-evaluations of the social value of feminized jobs, and for equitable pay between jobs of "comparable worth."

Only
**single,
childless women**
working in large cities
earn on average
as much as or more
than men
2010

Gender wage gap
Full-time women's weekly
earnings as a percentage
of men's
2009

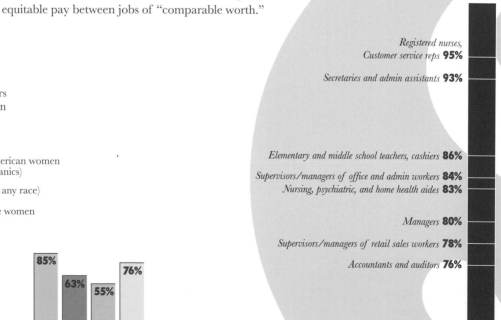

Registered nurses,
Customer service reps **95%**

Secretaries and admin assistants **93%**

Elementary and middle school teachers, cashiers **86%**

Supervisors/managers of office and admin workers **84%**
Nursing, psychiatric, and home health aides **83%**

Managers **80%**

Supervisors/managers of retail sales workers **78%**

Accountants and auditors **76%**

**In most common occupations
for women**

How race and ethnicity affects the wage gap
Median weekly earnings
of full-time women workers
compared with that of men
2009

Asian women

Black or African American women
(includes Black Hispanics)

Hispanic women (of any race)

Non-Hispanic White women

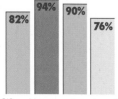

*Women's wages as percentage of
earnings of men
in same race/ethnic group*

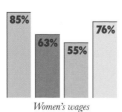

*Women's wages
as percentage of earnings
of White men*

The Department of Labor's Wages and Hours Division enforces the federal minimum wage, which covers all employees in enterprises with an annual value of at least $500,000 and every individual employee doing a job with an inter-state dimension: for example, a secretary who makes phone calls across state lines; an assembly worker whose products cross state lines. State minimum wages apply to those within a state working in small enterprises or in work unconnected to inter-state commerce. Where the federal minimum is higher, it supersedes that of the state; where the federal minimum is lower, the state's own higher minimum wage supersedes it. Some states simply adopt whatever is the current federal minimum.

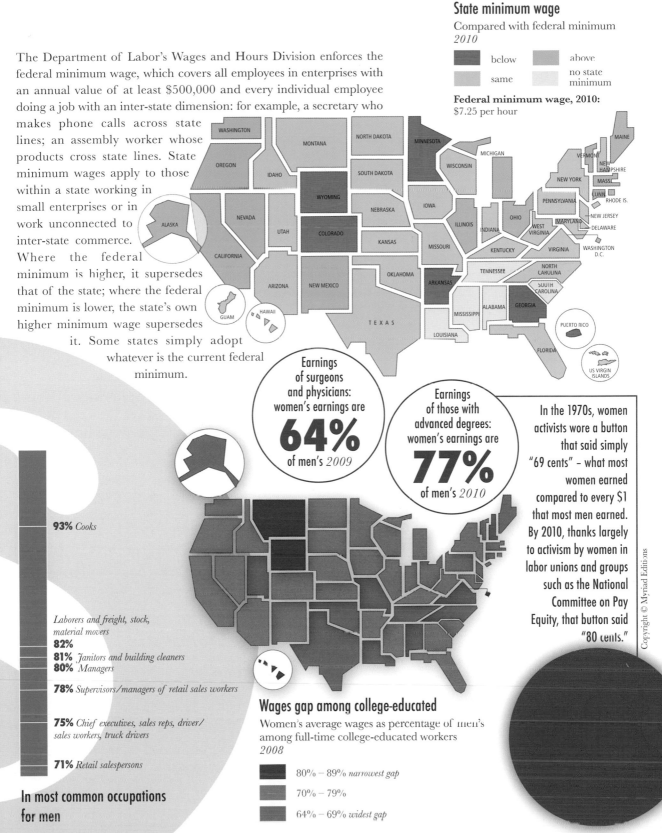

State minimum wage
Compared with federal minimum
2010

- below
- same
- above
- no state minimum

Federal minimum wage, 2010:
$7.25 per hour

Earnings of surgeons and physicians: women's earnings are

64%
of men's *2009*

Earnings of those with advanced degrees: women's earnings are

77%
of men's *2010*

In the 1970s, women activists wore a button that said simply "69 cents" – what most women earned compared to every $1 that most men earned. By 2010, thanks largely to activism by women in labor unions and groups such as the National Committee on Pay Equity, that button said "80 cents."

93% *Cooks*

Laborers and freight, stock, material movers
82%
81% *Janitors and building cleaners*
80% *Managers*

78% *Supervisors/managers of retail sales workers*

75% *Chief executives, sales reps, driver/ sales workers, truck drivers*

71% *Retail salespersons*

In most common occupations for men

Wages gap among college-educated
Women's average wages as percentage of men's among full-time college-educated workers
2008

- 80% – 89% *narrowest gap*
- 70% – 79%
- 64% – 69% *widest gap*

Poverty and Wealth

How we compare: income inequality
in OECD countries
mid-2000s
based on Gini coefficient

Greatest inequality:
Mexico
Turkey
USA
Portugal
Poland

Least inequality:
Sweden
Denmark
Luxembourg

THE UNITED STATES IS ONE OF THE WORLD'S WEALTHIEST NATIONS with one of the highest standards of living. In early 2010, it was home to 413 billionaires, with a combined net worth of $1.4 trillion, who were just the top of the pyramid of 7.8 million households with net worth of $1 million or more. At the same time, millions of Americans live in deprivation and hardship, a population that is rapidly growing in the current economic collapse. Almost a fifth of American households have an annual income of less than $20,000, and 15 percent of Americans live at or below official poverty levels. Official poverty statistics, in the US, as elsewhere in the world, underestimate poverty; some analysts suggest that the "actual" poverty rate may be closer to 30 percent. In 2008, 15 percent of households were categorized as facing "food insecurity," an increase from 11 percent the year before. More than 40 million Americans rely on food stamps.

Many more hover on the brink of poverty, and cycle in and out of the official statistics: over any 10-year period, about 40 percent of Americans fall below the official poverty line. Poverty varies widely by race and sex; in terms of broad demographics, the poorest of the poor in the US are Native Americans and single female heads of families with children.

About
14%
of adults relied on food stamps
2010

Living in poverty
Percentage of population living below official poverty threshold
2009

- 20% or more
- 15.0% – 19.9%
- 10.0% – 14.9%
- fewer than 10.0%

Highest territory: American Samoa 61%
Highest state: Mississippi 21.9%

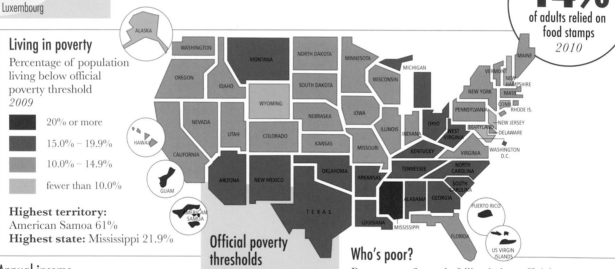

Annual income
Percentage of US households by income
2008

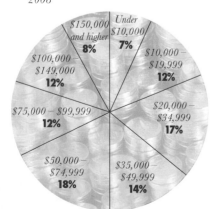

- $150,000 and higher **8%**
- Under $10,000 **7%**
- $10,000 – $19,999 **12%**
- $100,000 – $149,000 **12%**
- $75,000 – $99,999 **12%**
- $20,000 – $34,999 **17%**
- $50,000 – $74,999 **18%**
- $35,000 – $49,999 **14%**

Official poverty thresholds
Households with incomes below these levels were officially "poor" in 2009

One person 65 or over
$10,289

One person under age 65
$11,161

Two adults, no children
$14,366

One adult, one child
$14,787

One adult, two children
$17,285

Two adults, one child
$17,268

Who's poor?
Percentage of people falling below official poverty thresholds *2009*

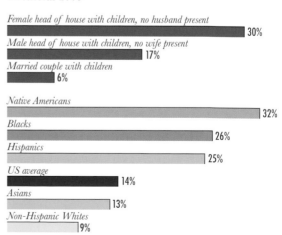

Female head of house with children, no husband present **30%**
Male head of house with children, no wife present **17%**
Married couple with children **6%**
Native Americans **32%**
Blacks **26%**
Hispanics **25%**
US average **14%**
Asians **13%**
Non-Hispanic Whites **9%**

"Wealth" is not the same as "income." It includes assets such as houses, cars, boats, savings accounts, or investments. When an individual or household loses income due to health problems, family breakup, or unemployment, it is wealth that provides a safety net. Wealth is accumulated over time, or passed on through inheritance, and is highly stratified by race and sex. For those without wealth accumulation, social disadvantage is amplified from generation to generation.

The wealth gap in the US is considerable and growing fast. The gap between the wealth of women and men, for all races, is greater than the gap in income. Unmarried minority women experience the largest wealth disadvantage.

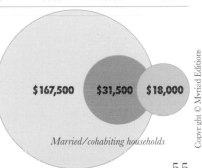

Wealthiest Americans
based on net worth
September 2010

Bill Gates (Microsoft)	$54bn
Warren Buffett (Hathaway)	$45bn
Larry Ellison (Oracle)	$27bn
Christy Walton (Walmart)	$24bn
Charles Koch (Koch Inds)	$22bn
David Koch (Koch Inds)	$22bn
Jim Walton (Walmart)	$20bn
Alice Walton (Walmart)	$20bn
Robson Walton (Walmart)	$20bn
Michael Bloomberg (Bloomberg Lp)	$18bn

Zero wealth
Percentage of households of married/cohabiting adults aged 18–64 with no or negative wealth
2007

31% *Hispanic*

28% *African American*

19% *US average*

15% *Non-Hispanic White*

Wealth distribution
Distribution of net worth among US households
2007

- percentage of households *owning*
- percentage of total wealth

Richest **1%** *own*
35% *of total wealth*

4% *own*
27%

5% *own*
11%

10% *own*
12%

40% *own*
15%

Poorest **40%** *own*
0.2% *of total wealth*

Multimillionaire households
Number of US households with net worth of $10m or above
2007

67,000 (*1983*) 190,000 (*1995*) 338,000 (*2001*) 464,000 (*2007*)

Wealth
Median wealth (excluding vehicles) held by each group
2010

- Non-Hispanic White
- African American
- Hispanic

$41,500 $100 $200
Single women

$43,800 $7,900 $9,730
Single men

$167,500 $31,500 $18,000
Married/cohabiting households

Copyright © Myriad Editions

55

Immigration and Insecurity

THE STORY OF THE UNITED STATES IS, first and foremost, the story of immigrants. Apart from the First Peoples, everyone came from somewhere else, or has recent ancestors who did. About 40 percent of European Americans have family who came through Ellis Island; the vast majority of African Americans descended from slaves, forcibly brought from Africa to ports such as Charleston; Angel Island, in San Francisco Bay, was both a port of entry and a detention center for Asian immigrants; for many Hispanics, a newly expanding US simply appropriated, bought, or won their land and their presence with it.

Americans have a long history of fearing and despising subsequent waves of immigrants. A "pull-up-the-drawbridge" mentality seems to afflict them once they've settled and claimed their new identity. The US could not have emerged as an economic and industrial power in the 20th century without the labor and entrepreneurial savvy of millions of immigrants. In the post-industrial 21st century, the economy will expand only through immigration – like most rich-world countries, natural fertility rates in the US are below replacement levels, and without immigrants the country faces economic decline and a workforce too small to pay for the benefits and security of the aging population.

But despite this dependence, or perhaps because of it, in the post-9/11, Great Recession mood of the first decade of the 21st century, anti-immigrant and anti-foreigner fervor in the US is high and heated.

In January 2010, the government **lifted** the longstanding **ban** on people with **HIV** entering or migrating to the US

30
states have laws or constitutional amendments declaring English the only official state language

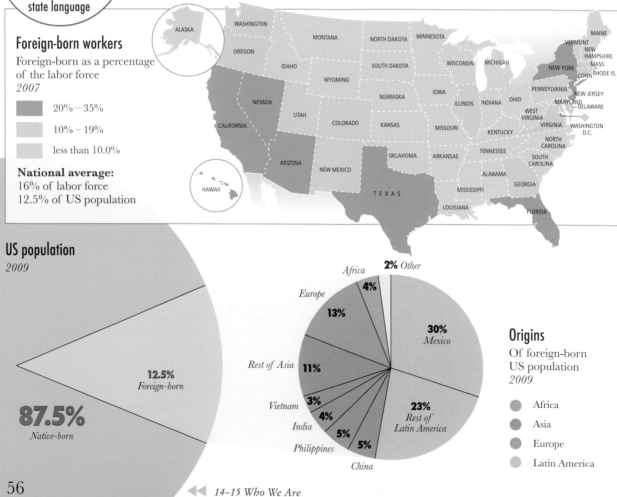

Foreign-born workers

Foreign-born as a percentage of the labor force
2007

- 20% – 35%
- 10% – 19%
- less than 10.0%

National average:
16% of labor force
12.5% of US population

US population
2009

12.5% *Foreign-born*

87.5% *Native-born*

2% *Other*

Africa 4%

Europe 13%

30% *Mexico*

Rest of Asia 11%

23% *Rest of Latin America*

Vietnam 3%

India 4%

Philippines 5%

China 5%

Origins
Of foreign-born US population *2009*

- Africa
- Asia
- Europe
- Latin America

◄◄ 14–15 Who We Are

Under scrutiny

Controlling the borders – keeping the "bad guys" out – is one of the key pillars of the post-9/11 Homeland Security regime. Tourists, visitors, outsiders are all under heightened surveillance and suspicion. A vast Homeland Security bureaucracy, too big and secret to know in its entirety, scrutinizes anyone who wants to come into the US – as well as those already here, especially immigrants and foreigners.

Local and state police departments are newly pressured into taking on federal immigration enforcement activities, running an immigration check on everyone they stop. Some police departments have refused to do so, while others have joined the effort. The Nationwide Suspicious Activity Reporting Initiative (SAR) collects hundreds of thousands of "tips" called in by neighbors and officials. SAR notes are sent to Fusion Centers (intelligence analysis offices) where operatives use a database called Guardian to sort through the millions of bits of information scooped up. The language and ideology of security has overwhelmed the language and ideology of welcome.

Predator Drones equipped with video cameras are used along the Mexican and Canadian borders by US Customs and Border Patrol – just one of **23** government organizations working alongside **154** private companies on border control.

1,271 government organizations and **1,931** private companies work on programs related to counterterrorism, homeland security and intelligence.

In Washington DC and the surrounding area, **33** building complexes for top-secret intelligence work have been built since September 2001 or are under construction. Together, they occupy about **17 million** square feet.

Closing the gate
2000–09

◯ estimated flow into the US of unauthorized immigrants

850,000
2000–05

550,000
2005–07

300,000
2007–09

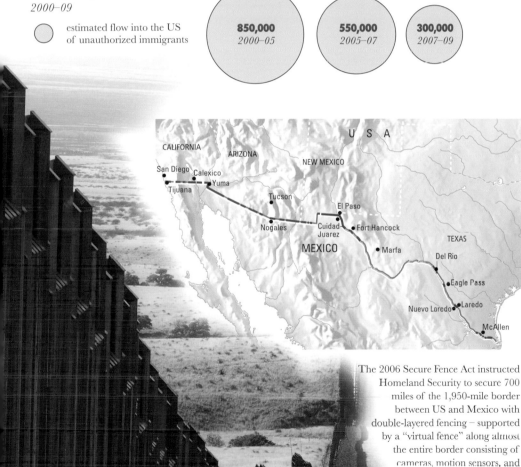

A barrier to immigration

—— existing fence
January 2009

—— no fence

Deaths on the border
2006–09

1,659 migrants
mostly from exposure and heat exhaustion as they tried to cross illegally into the US

14 migrants
shot by US border patrol agents

20 US Border Patrol agents
in the line of duty

The 2006 Secure Fence Act instructed Homeland Security to secure 700 miles of the 1,950-mile border between US and Mexico with double-layered fencing – supported by a "virtual fence" along almost the entire border consisting of cameras, motion sensors, and aerial surveillance. As of 2010, about 650 miles of the actual fence had been constructed, and in 2010 the government halted the invisible fence project.

Khaki Country

DOES A STANDING ARMY THREATEN DEMOCRACY? Is a beefed-up military worth going into national debt for? The country's founders were sharply divided on these questions, which remain unresolved today in American society. Despite a long history of peace activism, many Americans have absorbed militaristic ideas: for instance, believing that soldiering is the highest form of patriotism, that the world is full of enemies, that protecting against terrorists trumps civil rights, that men are the natural protectors of women, that jet bombers overhead make sporting events exciting, and that Commander-in-Chief is the President's most important job. Many towns' local economies depend on a nearby military base. Video war games marketed to children have become more authentically combat-like. Uniformed recruiters have gained access to many school cafeterias and classrooms.

Yet Americans are ambivalent about compulsory military service. In 1973, Congress responded to growing public discontent during the Vietnam War by ending the all-male draft. However, American men today still must register for military service when they turn 18. Of the country's 44 presidents, 27 have served in either the national military or a state militia. There are around 1.4 million Americans in the all-volunteer active-duty force, another 850,000 in the reserves. In addition, the Department of Defense has 1.5 million civilian employees.

Whom do Americans trust?

Percentage of respondents who expressed "a great deal of confidence" in each institution
February, 2010

- **59%** – Military
- **50%** – Small business
- **35%** – Major educational institutions
- **34%** – Medicine
- **31%** – Supreme Court
- **27%** – The White House
- **24%** – Courts and justice system
- **17%** – Television news
- **13%** – Press, law firms
- **8%** – Congress, Wall Street

How we compare: women in military

Women as percentage of military personnel
2010

New Zealand	17%
Latvia	17%
Australia	16%
Canada	15%
UK	14%
Germany	9%
Belgium	8%
Poland	2%
Afghanistan	0.3%

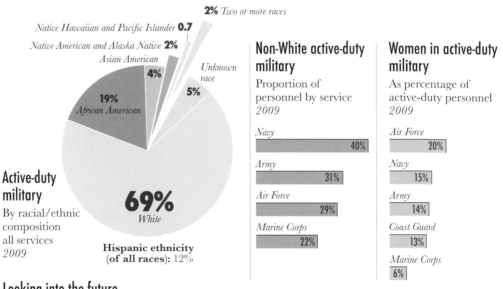

Active-duty military

By racial/ethnic composition all services *2009*

- **69%** White
- **19%** African American
- **4%** Asian American
- **2%** Native American and Alaska Native
- **0.7** Native Hawaiian and Pacific Islander
- **2%** Two or more races
- **5%** Unknown race

Hispanic ethnicity (of all races): 12%

Non-White active-duty military

Proportion of personnel by service *2009*

- Navy **40%**
- Army **31%**
- Air Force **29%**
- Marine Corps **22%**

Women in active-duty military

As percentage of active-duty personnel *2009*

- Air Force **20%**
- Navy **15%**
- Army **14%**
- Coast Guard **13%**
- Marine Corps **6%**

Looking into the future

Views of Americans asked about US military power *February 2010*

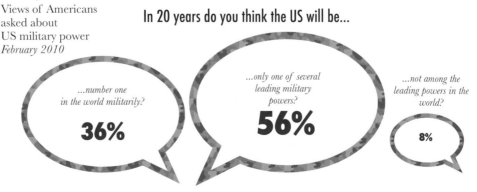

In 20 years do you think the US will be...

- ...number one in the world militarily? **36%**
- ...only one of several leading military powers? **56%**
- ...not among the leading powers in the world? **8%**

To continuously refill its ranks, the military has launched expensive ad campaigns. As a result, 521 colleges now host Reserve Officers' Training Corps (ROTC), and it has multiplied the number of young cadets in Junior ROTC – the Pentagon's goal is to have 3,500 high schools enrolled by 2011. Since 2001, the Defense Department has relied increasingly on part-time soldiers in the National Guard and Reserves, and has hired private contractors to perform many of the military's functions. To make up for the men lost when the draft ended, the Pentagon has recruited more women: during the Vietnam War only 2 percent of active duty personnel were women; today they comprise 14 percent. In December 2010, Congress repealed the "Don't Ask, Don't Tell" law that barred gay men and lesbians from openly serving in the military, and had led to 14,000 service members being discharged since 1994.

Some question, as Thomas Jefferson did, whether a large, professional force runs counter to democratic norms and is too separated from civil society. Perhaps having a non-conscript professional force has persuaded many Americans that going to war is "easy".

Recruits from South and West

As a proportion of total

65%
2009

54%
1973

Answering the call

Ratio of each state's share of new military recruits to that state's share of total US 18–24-year-old civilian population
2007

1.25 – 1.67
states over-represented among enlistees

1.00 – 1.24

1.00 = enlistees in line with state population as proportion of total US population

0.75 – 0.99

0.25 – 0.74. *states under-represented among enlistees*

Highest: Montana
Lowest: District of Columbia

WASHINGTON, ALASKA, HAWAII, MONTANA, OREGON, IDAHO, NORTH DAKOTA, MINNESOTA, WISCONSIN, MICHIGAN, MAINE, NEW HAMPSHIRE, VERMONT, MASS., NEW YORK, RHODE IS., CONN., PENNSYLVANIA, NEW JERSEY, MARYLAND, DELAWARE, WYOMING, SOUTH DAKOTA, IOWA, NEBRASKA, ILLINOIS, INDIANA, OHIO, WEST VIRGINIA, VIRGINIA, WASHINGTON D.C., NEVADA, UTAH, COLORADO, KANSAS, MISSOURI, KENTUCKY, NORTH CAROLINA, CALIFORNIA, ARIZONA, NEW MEXICO, OKLAHOMA, ARKANSAS, TENNESSEE, SOUTH CAROLINA, ALABAMA, MISSISSIPPI, GEORGIA, TEXAS, LOUISIANA, FLORIDA

Veterans in state populations
2010

7%
New York - lowest

14%
Alaska - highest

Which do you think is more likely over the next 20 years...

...the US will have combat troops actively fighting in various countries around the world on a regular basis.

67%

...there will be long periods of time in which the US does not have combat troops actively fighting in other countries.

30%

...no opinion

3%

60–61 Shock and Awe; 94–95 Arms Seller to the World; 96–97 Nuclear State

Shock and Awe

WAR IN IRAQ
The Iraqi toll

Estimated number of Iraqis who:

died from violence between 2003 and 2010

99,052 – 108,132

fled the country and were still refugees *Jan 2010*

1.8 million

were forced from their homes and still displaced within Iraq *Jan 2010*

1.6 million

Military deaths
March 2003–Nov 2010

USA: **4,429**

Other Coalition forces: **318**

THE ATTACKS ON SEPTEMBER 11, 2001 killed close to 3,000 people. Of the 19 al-Qaeda airplane hijackers, 15 were from Saudi Arabia, as is al-Qaeda's leader, Osama bin Laden. In the 1990s, he and his followers took refuge in Afghanistan, then ruled by a group of extreme Islamicist Afghan men calling themselves the Taliban.

President George W. Bush declared a "war on terror" and launched a US-led military invasion of Afghanistan in October, 2001, arguing that the Taliban – while not perpetrators of the 9/11 bombings – provided al-Qaeda with a safe haven. In this effort, the US chose as its chief Afghan ally the "Northern Alliance," a loose network of Afghan military commanders – "war lords" – who had fought against the Soviet occupation in the 1980s and against the Taliban in the 1990s, and who were known for their own oppressive, sexist practices.

In March 2003, the Bush Administration launched a military invasion of Iraq on the grounds that the country's dictatorial regime, headed by Saddam Hussein, was developing weapons of mass destruction. This later turned out not to be the case. Despite thousands demonstrating against the invasion, many Americans initially accepted the invasion as integral to the US-led international "war on terror," even though there was no evidence that Saddam Hussein's regime had participated in the 9/11 attacks. The US military employed overwhelming force against Iraq, targeting its infrastructure, in particular, with the intention of inducing a state of "shock and awe" among Iraqi troops and civilians. While the US reliance on such high-powered weaponry did topple the regime, it caused a high toll among Iraqi civilians, destroyed the country's economy, and inspired a fragmented armed insurgency that would last for years.

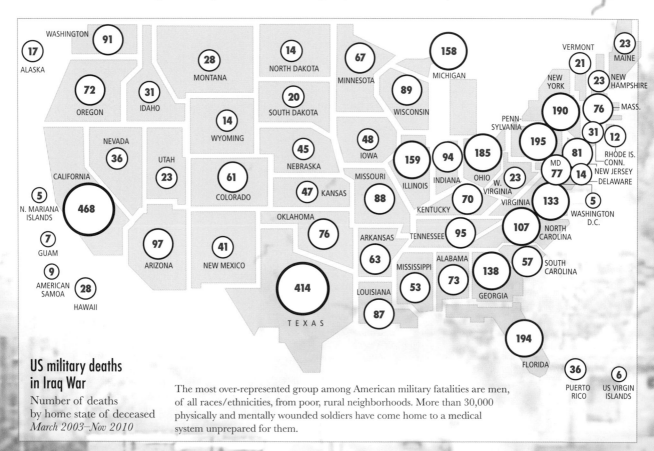

US military deaths in Iraq War

Number of deaths by home state of deceased
March 2003–Nov 2010

The most over-represented group among American military fatalities are men, of all races/ethnicities, from poor, rural neighborhoods. More than 30,000 physically and mentally wounded soldiers have come home to a medical system unprepared for them.

In the wake of 9/11, many Americans grew suspicious of recent immigrants, as well as of their fellow-US citizens who were Muslims. The government expanded surveillance at home and military operations overseas – for example in the southern Philippines. Violating constitutional guarantees of due process, as well as the 1945 Geneva Conventions and UN Convention Against Torture, the US government expanded detentions at its Guantánamo Naval Base and initiated "extraordinary renditions," secret air-lifting of suspects to CIA-run "black sites" and to foreign prisons for questioning, using forms of torture it called "enhanced interrogation techniques."

As the US waged two wars, the national debt soared, relationships with allies (Germany, Turkey, France, Japan, Canada) became strained, and popular patriotism took on a new intensity. Then, fatalities mounted. The complexities of both Iraq's and Afghanistan's own domestic politics – initially ignored – confounded most Americans. US popular enthusiasm for the wars waned; the media turned away. Still, the wars continue.

WAR IN AFGHANISTAN
The Afghan toll

Estimated number of Afghan civilians who:

were killed directly or indirectly in the war between 2001 and 2010
14,643 – 34,240

were still refugees *Jan 2010*
2.9 million

were forced from their homes and still displaced within Afghanistan *Jan 2010*
297,000

Military deaths
Oct 2001–Nov 2010

USA **2,303**
UK **345**
Canada **153**
France **50**
Germany **45**
Denmark **39**
Italy **33**
Spain **30**
Netherlands **30**

War-within-a-war

In 2008 alone, an estimated 3,000 American women soldiers were sexually assaulted by American male soldiers. Between 2007 and 2008, the number of women soldiers serving in Iraq and Afghanistan who were sexually assaulted by their male comrades rose by 25%.

US had spent **$1.15 trillion** on wars in Iraq and Afghanistan as of July 2010

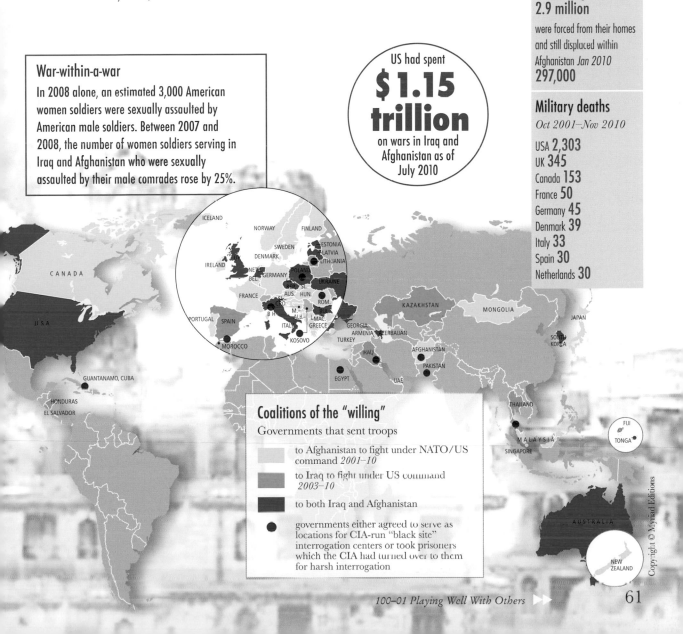

Coalitions of the "willing"
Governments that sent troops

to Afghanistan to fight under NATO/US command *2001–10*

to Iraq to fight under US command *2003–10*

to both Iraq and Afghanistan

● governments either agreed to serve as locations for CIA-run "black site" interrogation centers or took prisoners which the CIA had turned over to them for harsh interrogation

Part Four

Health and Wellbeing

Marriage and Divorce

AMERICAN ATTITUDES

Towards divorce

Divorce is morally acceptable *2008*

Republicans: **61%**

Democrats: **72%**

Independents: **74%**

2001: **59%** 2008: **70%**

Towards same-sex marriage

Support for legalization *2010*

Republicans: **28%**

Independents: **49%**

Democrats: **56%**

South: **35%**

Midwest: **40%**

East: **53%**

West: **53%**

AMERICANS' EXPERIENCES OF MARRIAGE and divorce have been, and still are, entwined with ideas and laws about property, family, sexuality, violence, race and, ultimately, first-class citizenship. African Americans' rights to marry were subverted by slavery. Until 1967, some all-white state legislatures prohibited marriages between men and women of different races. Being poor in America has made it harder both to marry and to divorce.

Presumptions that husbands had the "natural right" to control their wives meant that 19th-century married women had to organize to win control of their own property and, as recently as the 1960s, banks could refuse a loan to a married woman if her husband did not approve. The same stubborn notion that women as wives should be under their husbands' control also severely limited women's right to divorce even physically abusive husbands into the late 20th century.

State legislatures and state courts, not the federal government, control much of marital law-making. They decide how hard or easy it is to get married or divorced, who can marry whom, what benefits flow to married couples, and what constitutes grounds for divorce. This is why the currently fierce campaigns over gay marriage are being waged state by state. It matters where you live in the United States.

American ideas about marriage and divorce today are in flux. Most Americans no longer see divorce as immoral. Remarrying and creating new "blended families" is commonplace. While the debates over same-sex marriage remain heated, more Americans now say they accept gay marriage. And, as the country has become more racially diverse, and state anti-miscegenation laws have fallen, marriages between people of different races have become more common. Yet, many Americans are eschewing marriage altogether. And having a "partner" no longer automatically means being married.

11,000
marriages were performed between same-sex couples in Massachusetts
2004–08

Same-sex marriage

Legal status
2010

State has:

amended constitution to define marriage as only between man and woman

passed laws prohibiting same-sex marriage

passed restrictive marriage laws but offers strong same-sex domestic partnership protections or civil unions short of marriage

not restricted marriage laws and offers strong same-sex domestic partnership protections or civil unions short of marriage

legalized same-sex marriage

neither banned gay marriage, nor legalized it, nor passed notably strong protections for same-sex partnerships

Many states recognize versions of same-sex partnerships, but only five have legalized gay marriage. Even if gay men or lesbians are legally married in a particular state, so long as federal law does not recognize those marriages, the gay spouses are denied married persons' federal tax benefits, inheritance benefits and survivor benefits.

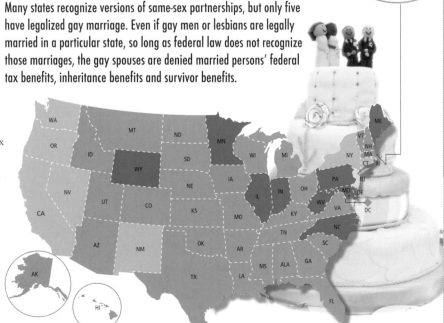

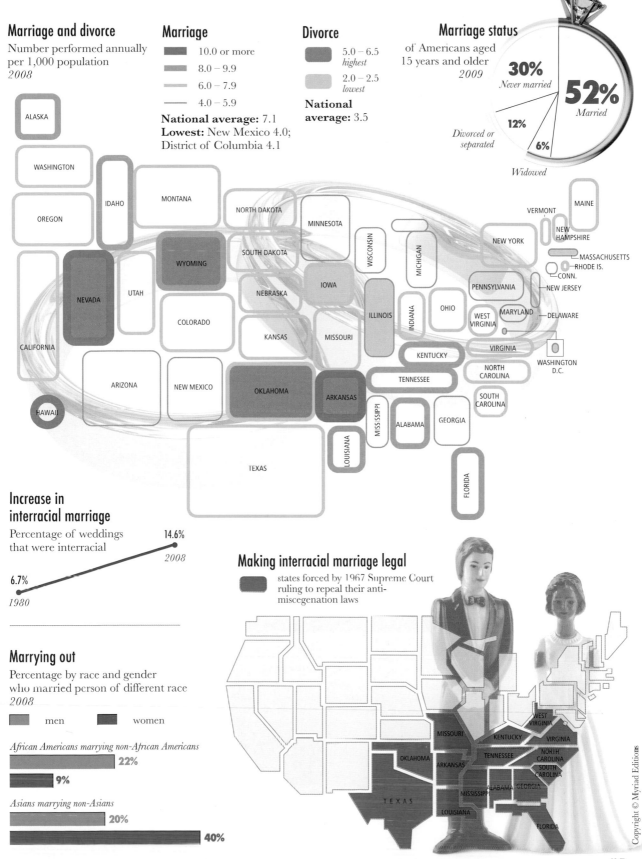

Marriage and divorce
Number performed annually per 1,000 population
2008

Marriage
- 10.0 or more
- 8.0 – 9.9
- 6.0 – 7.9
- 4.0 – 5.9

National average: 7.1
Lowest: New Mexico 4.0; District of Columbia 4.1

Divorce
- 5.0 – 6.5 highest
- 2.0 – 2.5 lowest

National average: 3.5

Marriage status
of Americans aged 15 years and older
2009

30% *Never married*
52% *Married*
12% *Divorced or separated*
6%
Widowed

ALASKA
WASHINGTON
OREGON
IDAHO
MONTANA
NORTH DAKOTA
MINNESOTA
WISCONSIN
MICHIGAN
VERMONT
MAINE
NEW HAMPSHIRE
NEW YORK
MASSACHUSETTS
RHODE IS.
CONN.
NEW JERSEY
WYOMING
SOUTH DAKOTA
IOWA
PENNSYLVANIA
DELAWARE
NEVADA
UTAH
NEBRASKA
ILLINOIS
INDIANA
OHIO
WEST VIRGINIA
MARYLAND
CALIFORNIA
COLORADO
KANSAS
MISSOURI
KENTUCKY
VIRGINIA
WASHINGTON D.C.
ARIZONA
NEW MEXICO
OKLAHOMA
ARKANSAS
TENNESSEE
NORTH CAROLINA
HAWAII
MISSISSIPPI
ALABAMA
GEORGIA
SOUTH CAROLINA
LOUISIANA
TEXAS
FLORIDA

Increase in interracial marriage
Percentage of weddings that were interracial

14.6%
2008

6.7%
1980

Marrying out
Percentage by race and gender who married person of different race
2008

- men
- women

African Americans marrying non-African Americans
22%
9%

Asians marrying non-Asians
20%
40%

Making interracial marriage legal
states forced by 1967 Supreme Court ruling to repeal their anti-miscegenation laws

MISSOURI
OKLAHOMA
ARKANSAS
KENTUCKY
TENNESSEE
WEST VIRGINIA
VIRGINIA
NORTH CAROLINA
SOUTH CAROLINA
ALABAMA
GEORGIA
MISSISSIPPI
LOUISIANA
TEXAS
FLORIDA

65

Sickness and Health

IN THE UNITED STATES, the availability of healthcare and the nature of illness vary with geography, race, age, class, and sex. Racial disparities in access to health care, treatment, disease prevalence, and survival rates are stark. While these disparities have received considerable attention over the past decade, there has been little improvement in reducing them.

Women outlive men, with an average life expectancy advantage of about six years. This is partly a result of biology, but is also attributable to health behaviors. Stereotypic masculinity is bad for men's health: almost twice as many men as women binge drink; they smoke more, eat less fruit and vegetables, and see doctors less frequently. Men are also two to four times more likely than women to die prematurely from unintentional injury, homicide, and suicide.

Poor health and poverty are mutually reinforcing. In 2009, 15 percent of the US population reported that they hadn't seen a doctor in the previous year because of cost.

How we die

Top five causes of death among those age 18 or older
2007

Women
heart disease
cancer
stroke
respiratory disease
Alzheimer's disease

Men
heart disease
cancer
unintentional injuries
respiratory disease
stroke

Single-leading cause of death
2007

Heart disease
Non-Hispanic Whites
Non-Hispanic Blacks
Hispanics
Native American/
 Alaska Native men

Cancer
Asian Americans
Native American/
 Alaska Native women

Diabetes

Prevalence of diagnosed diabetes in adults age 20 or older
2004–06

Native Americans/ Alaska Natives
16.5%

African Americans
11.4%

Hispanics
10.4%

Asian Americans
7.5%

Non-Hispanic Whites
6.6%

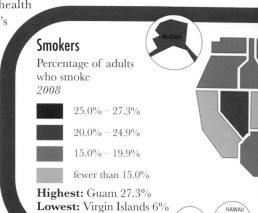

Smokers

Percentage of adults who smoke
2008

- 25.0% – 27.3%
- 20.0% – 24.9%
- 15.0% – 19.9%
- fewer than 15.0%

Highest: Guam 27.3%
Lowest: Virgin Islands 6%

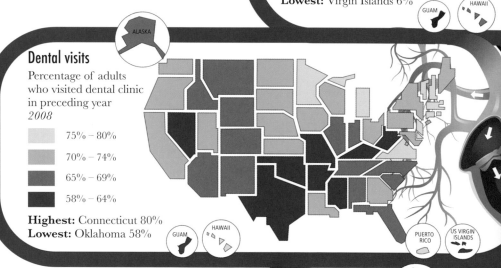

Dental visits

Percentage of adults who visited dental clinic in preceding year
2008

- 75% – 80%
- 70% – 74%
- 65% – 69%
- 58% – 64%

Highest: Connecticut 80%
Lowest: Oklahoma 58%

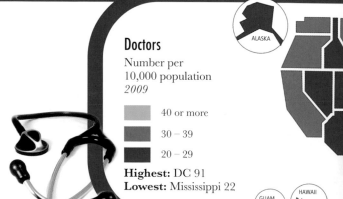

Doctors

Number per 10,000 population
2009

- 40 or more
- 30 – 39
- 20 – 29

Highest: DC 91
Lowest: Mississippi 22

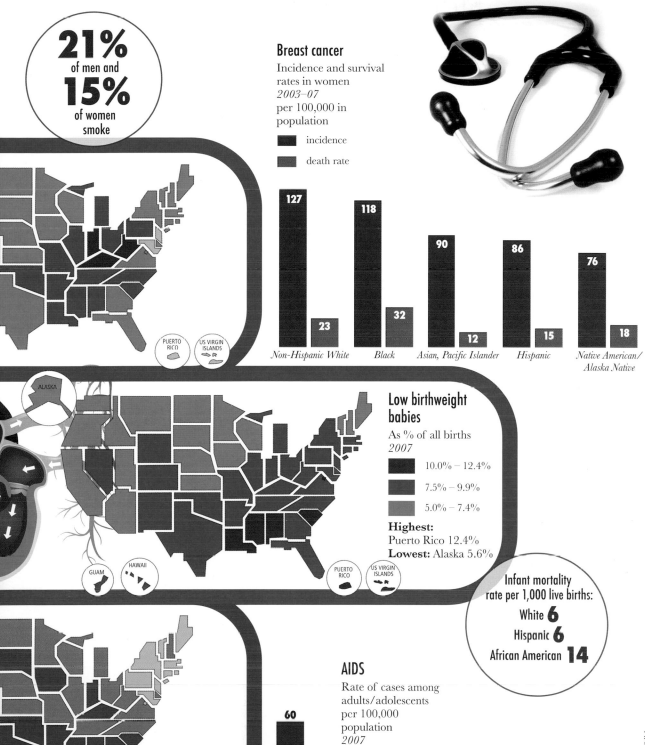

21% of men and **15%** of women smoke

Breast cancer

Incidence and survival rates in women
2003–07
per 100,000 in population

■ incidence
■ death rate

	Non-Hispanic White	Black	Asian, Pacific Islander	Hispanic	Native American/ Alaska Native
incidence	127	118	90	86	76
death rate	23	32	12	15	18

Low birthweight babies

As % of all births
2007

■ 10.0% – 12.4%
■ 7.5% – 9.9%
■ 5.0% – 7.4%

Highest: Puerto Rico 12.4%
Lowest: Alaska 5.6%

Infant mortality rate per 1,000 live births:
White **6**
Hispanic **6**
African American **14**

AIDS

Rate of cases among adults/adolescents per 100,000 population
2007

African American	Hawaiian/ Pacific Islander	Hispanic	Native American/ Alaska Native	Non-Hispanic White	Asian
60	22	20	9	6	4

Healthcare Politics

US RANKING

In comparison
to selected
OECD countries

Infant mortality

Deaths per 1,000 live
births *2005*

Turkey	23
Mexico	18
USA	**7** *3rd worst*
Hungary	6
Australia	5
Canada	5
South Korea	5
UK	5
Germany	4
Japan	3

Life expectancy

for men
2009

Poland	71
Turkey	72
Mexico	73
USA	**75**
South Korea	76
UK	77
Germany	77
Spain	78
France	78
Canada	78
Japan	79

Magnetic Resonance Imaging

Units per million
population
2009

Japan	40
USA	**26** *2nd best*
South Korea	16
Greece	13
New Zealand	9
UK	8
Germany	8
Canada	7
Australia	5

MONEY AND RELIGION play a bigger role in determining the nature of healthcare in the United States than in any other industrialized country.

The American healthcare system, from primary care services to hospitals to insurance, is mostly privatized. The US has one of the most high-tech health systems in the world, but reliance on high-cost (and, not coincidentally, high-profit) technological innovation doesn't necessarily translate into better healthcare for the population as a whole. More than 50 million Americans don't have health insurance, and an estimated 16 million more are considered "underinsured" because they have high out-of-pocket costs relative to their income. Of the 30 industrialized countries in the OECD, all but three governments provide universal or near-universal health coverage, with the US at the very bottom of the rankings. A World Health Organization study in 2000 ranked the US healthcare system as the highest in cost, the first in responsiveness, 37th in overall performance, and 72nd by overall level of health outcomes among 191 countries. Racial disparities in access to healthcare are deep and persistent. For all Americans, health quality and access to healthcare is a direct function of income and class.

There is a growing awareness of the shortcomings of the American approach to healthcare provision, but little agreement on how to solve the problems. Healthcare is big business: private insurance companies and healthcare industries lobby fiercely against any reform that might undercut their grip on healthcare provision and profits.

Fierce debates rage about the appropriate role for government in providing healthcare, and ideological battle lines seem to be hardening. Even the modest healthcare reforms passed by the Democratic-majority Congress in 2010, which still left healthcare in the hands of private interests, were met with ideologically ferocious opposition and fear-mongering about a "socialist takeover" of the American healthcare system.

Perhaps the most fraught public policy divide is over women's access to reproductive healthcare. The Religious Right has organized strenuously against provision of vaccines that protect girls from sexually transmitted diseases, against emergency contraception, and, most effectively, against access to abortions.

Health expenditure

Public and private annual
spending per capita
by selected OECD
countries
2007

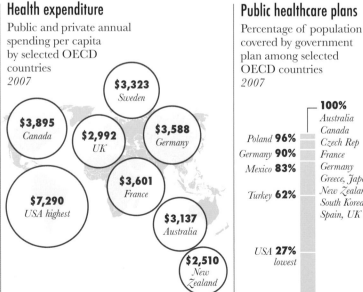

- **$3,323** *Sweden*
- **$3,895** *Canada*
- **$2,992** *UK*
- **$3,588** *Germany*
- **$3,601** *France*
- **$7,290** *USA highest*
- **$3,137** *Australia*
- **$2,510** *New Zealand*

Public healthcare plans

Percentage of population
covered by government
plan among selected
OECD countries
2007

100%
*Australia
Canada
Czech Rep
France
Germany
Greece, Japan
New Zealand
South Korea
Spain, UK*

Poland **96%**
Germany **90%**
Mexico **83%**

Turkey **62%**

USA **27%**
lowest

**People who said they
had a medical problem
but did not visit a doctor
because of cost concerns**
2010

- *USA* **22%** *highest*
- *Germany* **16%**
- *Australia* **13%**
- *New Zealand* **9%**
- *France* **6%**
- *Sweden* **5%**
- *Canada* **4%**
- *UK* **2%**

No health insurance

Percentage of population without health insurance
2008–09

■ more than 20%		■ 11% – 15%		**Highest:** Texas 26%
■ 16% – 20%		■ 10% or fewer		**Lowest:** Massachusetts 5%

ALASKA
HAWAII
GUAM
WASHINGTON
OREGON
IDAHO
MONTANA
NORTH DAKOTA
MINNESOTA
WISCONSIN
MICHIGAN
NEVADA
UTAH
WYOMING
SOUTH DAKOTA
NEBRASKA
IOWA
ILLINOIS
INDIANA
OHIO
MAINE
VERMONT
NEW HAMPSHIRE
MASS.
RHODE IS.
CONN.
NEW YORK
PENNSYLVANIA
NEW JERSEY
MARYLAND
DELAWARE
WEST VIRGINIA
VIRGINIA
WASHINGTON D.C.
CALIFORNIA
ARIZONA
COLORADO
KANSAS
MISSOURI
KENTUCKY
TENNESSEE
NORTH CAROLINA
SOUTH CAROLINA
NEW MEXICO
OKLAHOMA
ARKANSAS
MISSISSIPPI
ALABAMA
GEORGIA
TEXAS
LOUISIANA
FLORIDA
PUERTO RICO
US VIRGIN ISLANDS

Racial/ethnic difference

Percentage of non-elderly people
without health insurance
2008–09

14%	Non-Hispanic White
23%	Black
34%	Hispanic
17%	Asian
19%	**US average**

American attitudes to healthcare

Percentage who believe that it is the responsibility of federal government to make sure all Americans have healthcare coverage

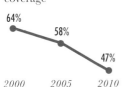

64% — 2000
58% — 2005
47% — 2010

Can't afford healthcare

Percentage of Americans who say they don't have enough money for healthcare
2010

36%
Of those earning under $24,000

16%
Of those earning $24,000–$90,000

6%
Of those earning over $90,000

Abortion

Abortion is a legal medical procedure that is increasingly being put out of reach of many women in the US by a series of state and federal prohibitions, laws, and restrictions, and by threats, violence, and obstruction.

In 2005, **87%** of all US counties and **98%** of rural counties had no abortion services.

The number of abortion providers has dropped from **2,680** in 1985 to **1,787** in 2005.

44% of medical schools offered no formal preclinical elective abortion education.

Between 1995 and 2009, states enacted **610** anti-choice measures, including **29** in 2009 alone.

32 states have laws that subject women seeking abortion services to biased counseling requirements and/or mandatory delay.

Military personnel are prohibited from obtaining coverage for abortion care through military health plans, even if a pregnancy resulted from an act of rape or incest.

The Hyde Amendment bars access to abortion care for low-income women who rely on the federal government for their healthcare.

8 states have laws that require a woman to obtain written consent from, or give notice to, her husband prior to receiving abortion care.

More than **4,000** acts of violence have been aimed at abortion clinics nationwide since 1977, including murder, arson, bombs and stalking harassment of nurses, doctors and patients.

Big business, big profits

Profits of top five US companies in each category
2009

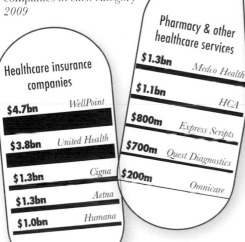

Healthcare insurance companies

$4.7bn	*WellPoint*
$3.8bn	*United Health*
$1.3bn	*Cigna*
$1.3bn	*Aetna*
$1.0bn	*Humana*

Pharmacy & other healthcare services

$1.3bn	*Medco Health*
$1.1bn	*HCA*
$800m	*Express Scripts*
$700m	*Quest Diagnostics*
$200m	*Omnicare*

Pharmaceutical companies

Merck & Co
Johnson & Johnson
Pfizer
Abbott Labs
Eli Lilly

Gun Nation

THE UNITED STATES IS A GUN-TOTING NATION. Gun ownership is seen by many as a hallmark of American identity. According to a 2010 UN survey, it has the most heavily armed civilian population in the world. With very few exceptions (such as prohibitions that apply to convicted criminals), any adult in the US can buy a gun. Nearly ubiquitous gun shops, gun shows, and online sites make access to guns easy and quick. Even Walmart sells guns.

Each state has its own system of counting and classifying guns, and many don't require registration of guns, so it is impossible to be certain of the number of guns in the US. The UN and the National Rifle Association estimate that there are between 270 million and 300 million privately owned firearms in the country, a stockpile that increases by about 4.5 million each year. Beyond these legally owned guns, the country is awash in illegal guns.

Americans die by guns in world-record numbers. Gun advocates argue that more guns, not fewer, will keep Americans safe, but the evidence suggests otherwise.

The US is also the largest global exporter of small arms – many illicit – and, with its lax gun laws and vast supply of arms, it is a dangerous neighbor. An estimated two-thirds of illicit guns seized in Canada come from the US; a 2009 US government study confirmed that about 80 percent of the firearms fueling the Mexican drug-war violence come from the US.

The fiercest public policy battles in the US are waged over guns. The Second Amendment to the Constitution is considered the bedrock of the American right to bear arms. Supreme Court decisions in 2008 and 2010 reinforced the interpretation of this amendment as protecting individual rights to arms. Fierce court battles and public policy debates have raged over issues such as the right to bear concealed weapons, the right of civilians to own semi-automatic and "military-like" weapons, and the right of states or municipalities to tighten gun laws. Not surprisingly, it is often municipal governments and police departments who most want to restrict gun ownership. The largest pro-gun lobbying organization in the US, with 4 million members and an annual income of $200 million, is the National Rifle Association (NRA).

Notable US assassinations by gun

1865:
President Abraham Lincoln
1881:
President James Garfield
1901:
President William McKinley
1934:
Senator Huey Long
1963:
President John F. Kennedy
1963:
Lee Harvey Oswald
1963:
Medgar Evers
1965:
Malcolm X
1968:
Robert Kennedy
1968:
Martin Luther King
1978:
Harvey Milk & George Moscone
1980:
John Lennon
1984:
Alan Berg
1991:
Gianni Versace
2009:
George Tiller

How we compare: civilian firearms

Countries with highest rates of ownership per 100 inhabitants
2006 or latest available

USA	89
Yemen	55
Switzerland	46
Finland	45
Serbia	38
Cyprus	36
Iraq	34
Uruguay	32
Sweden	32
Norway	31

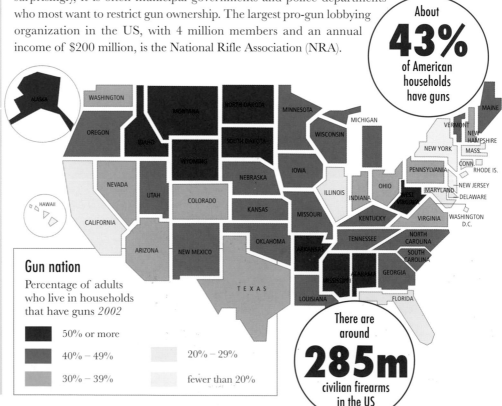

About **43%** of American households have guns

There are around **285m** civilian firearms in the US

Gun nation
Percentage of adults who live in households that have guns *2002*

- 50% or more
- 40% – 49%
- 30% – 39%
- 20% – 29%
- fewer than 20%

Deaths by guns
Rate per 100,000
2007

- 20 – 25
- 15 – 19
- 10 – 14
- fewer than 10

Mass mayhem
Mass killings
1996–2009

- ● school
- ○ non-school

Of 72
school shootings worldwide
52
occurred in the US
1996–2008

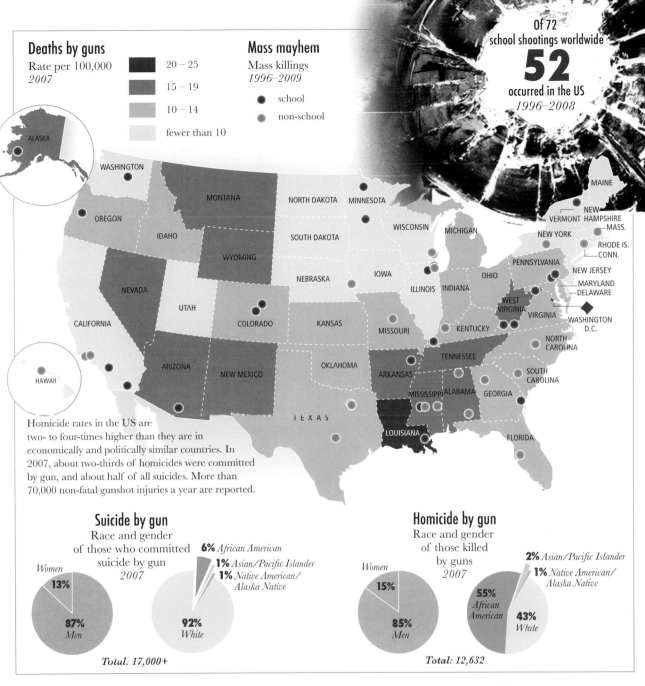

ALASKA

WASHINGTON
OREGON
IDAHO
MONTANA
NORTH DAKOTA
MINNESOTA
WISCONSIN
MICHIGAN
MAINE
VERMONT
NEW HAMPSHIRE
MASS.
NEW YORK
RHODE IS.
CONN.
PENNSYLVANIA
NEW JERSEY
MARYLAND
DELAWARE
WASHINGTON D.C.
WYOMING
SOUTH DAKOTA
NEBRASKA
IOWA
ILLINOIS
INDIANA
OHIO
WEST VIRGINIA
VIRGINIA
NEVADA
UTAH
CALIFORNIA
COLORADO
KANSAS
MISSOURI
KENTUCKY
NORTH CAROLINA
HAWAII
ARIZONA
NEW MEXICO
OKLAHOMA
ARKANSAS
TENNESSEE
SOUTH CAROLINA
MISSISSIPPI
ALABAMA
GEORGIA
TEXAS
LOUISIANA
FLORIDA

Homicide rates in the US are
two- to four-times higher than they are in
economically and politically similar countries. In
2007, about two-thirds of homicides were committed
by gun, and about half of all suicides. More than
70,000 non-fatal gunshot injuries a year are reported.

Suicide by gun
Race and gender
of those who committed
suicide by gun
2007

Women **13%**
Men **87%**

6% *African American*
1% *Asian/Pacific Islander*
1% *Native American/ Alaska Native*
92% *White*

Total: 17,000+

Homicide by gun
Race and gender
of those killed
by guns
2007

Women **15%**
Men **85%**

2% *Asian/Pacific Islander*
1% *Native American/ Alaska Native*
55% *African American*
43% *White*

Total: 12,632

Second amendment to the US Constitution

A well regulated militia being necessary to
the security of a free State, the right of the
People to keep and bear arms shall not be
infringed.

*In 2008, the Supreme Court ruled that a
Washington DC ordinance banning firearms in the
home was unconstitutional.*

*In 2010, it ruled that the City of Chicago could
not restrict the right to own guns.*

US public opinion on gun control
2009

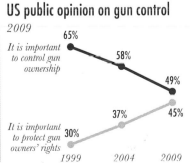

It is important
to control gun
ownership
65% → 58% → 49%

It is important
to protect gun
owners' rights
30% → 37% → 45%

1999   2004   2009

Gun laws should be more strict
Percentage who agree
2009

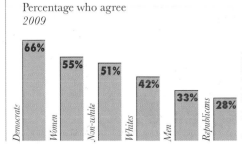

- Democrats **66%**
- Women **55%**
- Non-white **51%**
- Whites **42%**
- Men **33%**
- Republicans **28%**

Violence Against Women

Intimate-partner violence

Individuals in households reporting at least one lifetime episode of intimate-partner violence
2005

● women ● men

Average
24% 12%

Multiracial non-Hispanic households
43% 26%

American Indian/Alaska Native households
39% 19%

White non-Hispanic households
27% 16%

Black non-Hispanic households
29% 23%

Hispanic households
21% 16%

Asian households
10% 8%

ACKNOWLEDGING VIOLENCE AGAINST WOMEN disrupts treasured American myths. The American Dream has a safe home at its center. So when feminists in the 1960s started putting "domestic" together with "violence," it was disturbing; coupling "marital" with "rape," and linking "date" with "rape" was upsetting. Sex trafficking was imagined to be "over there," not here in our own communities. Many Americans say the military is the branch of government they most trust, making it hard to talk about American male soldiers sexually assaulting their female comrades. It has taken a vibrant women's movement four decades to persuade Americans that these deeply unsettling forms of violence against women are part of this nation's reality.

Most of this activism has been localized. Rape crisis centers and battered women's shelters were begun by women taking innovative action in their own local communities. By 2010, there were over 2,000 shelters for battered women across the United States, and every state had its own coalition to pool resources and share knowledge and strategies.

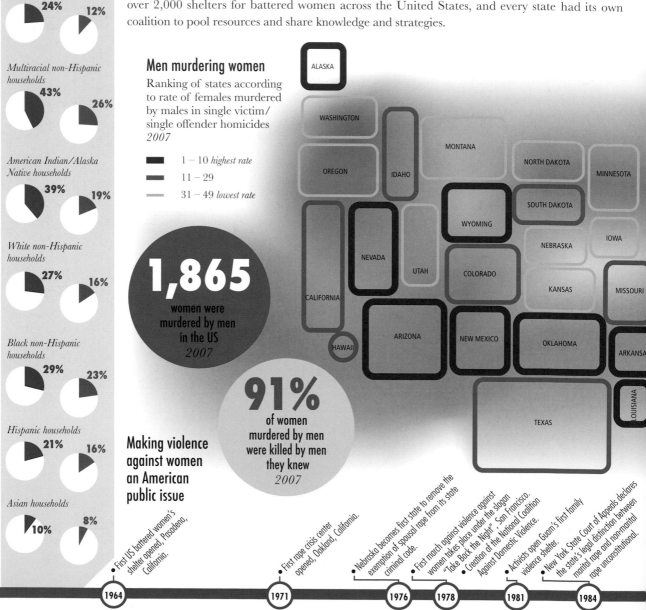

Men murdering women

Ranking of states according to rate of females murdered by males in single victim/single offender homicides
2007

■ 1 – 10 *highest rate*
■ 11 – 29
■ 31 – 49 *lowest rate*

1,865
women were murdered by men in the US
2007

91%
of women murdered by men were killed by men they knew
2007

Making violence against women an American public issue

- First US battered women's shelter opened, Pasadena, California.
- First rape crisis center opened, Oakland, California.
- Nebraska becomes first state to remove the exemption of spousal rape from its state criminal code.
- First march against violence against women takes place under the slogan "Take Back the Night", San Francisco.
- Creation of the National Coalition Against Domestic Violence.
- Activists open Guam's first family violence shelter.
- New York State Court of Appeals declares the state's legal distinction between marital rape and non-marital rape unconstitutional.

1964 1971 1976 1978 1981 1984

Anti-violence activists educated doctors, nurses, police, prosecutors, and judges, lobbied state legislators, and organized "take back the night" marches to protest street violence against women. Campaigns to end husbands' legal exemptions from marital rape charges were launched state by state. It took scores of local court cases to establish the legal reasonableness of battered women's self-defense. Only in 1994 did Congress pass a federal Violence Against Women Act, authorizing a new Office of Violence Against Women inside the Department of Justice.

Despite these advances, violence against women has become an epidemic, occurring in all income groups, all races, and all regions. Yet a woman is especially vulnerable to violence if she is poor, lives where guns are easily obtained, is nervous about her immigration status, is the target of racist stereotypes, lives in a town where affordable housing is scarce and jobs with decent pay are hard to find, where medical insurance is expensive, local governments under-fund shelters, and police don't take violence against women seriously.

SEXUAL ASSAULT

Child rape

Percentage of children in grades 9 to 12 reporting having been forced to have sexual intercourse at some point
2005

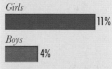

Girls 11%

Boys 4%

18%
of American women have survived a rape or an attempted rape

2,923
formal reports of sexual assault within the US military were made in 2007–08

1 in 5
women veterans seen at Veteran's Administration clinics had experienced military sexual trauma
2009

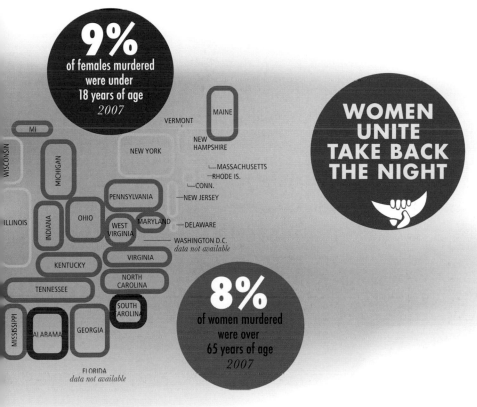

9%
of females murdered were under 18 years of age
2007

8%
of women murdered were over 65 years of age
2007

WOMEN UNITE TAKE BACK THE NIGHT

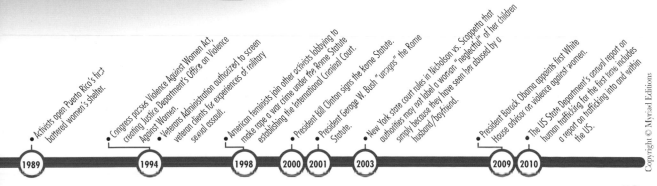

- **1989** Activists open Puerto Rico's first battered women's shelter.
- **1994** Congress passes Violence Against Women Act, creating Justice Department's Office on Violence Against Women.
- Veterans Administration authorized to screen veteran clients for experiences of military sexual assault.
- **1998** American feminists join other activists lobbying to make rape a war crime under the Rome Statute establishing the International Criminal Court.
- **2000** President Bill Clinton signs the Rome Statute.
- **2001** President George W. Bush "unsigns" the Rome Statute.
- **2003** New York state court rules in Nicholson vs. Scoppetta that authorities may not label a woman "neglectful" of her children simply because they have seen her abused by a husband/boyfriend.
- **2009** President Barack Obama appoints first White House advisor on violence against women.
- **2010** The US State Department's annual report on human trafficking for the first time includes a report on trafficking into and within the US.

Behind Bars

IN 2007, THE UNITED STATES CROSSED A THRESHOLD: one in every 100 adults was behind bars. While the prison population spiraled, long-running debates intensified. Should prisons punish or rehabilitate? Do prisons reflect the country's ideal of fairness or its history of race and class inequities? Some American prisons have become iconic: Alcatraz, San Quentin, Attica, Angola. Most go unnoticed, except by nearby townspeople, who depend on them for jobs.

There are three levels of prisons in the US: federal, state, and local. State prisons hire the most employees and hold the majority of the country's inmates. Fluctuations in prison populations don't reflect changing crime rates as much as they reflect state-by-state policy changes. During the recent recession, some money-strapped states sought to reduce their costly inmate populations – by shortening sentences, sending low-risk offenders to community care, paroling elderly inmates – while others held on tight to their "law and order" agendas. It matters *where* one is convicted of a crime in America.

For years, prison reform activists have challenged the death penalty, opposed treating juvenile offenders as adults, sought to give women prisoners access to their children, exposed racism in sentencing and sexual violence against inmates, while also supporting prisoner education and ex-convicts' voting rights.

Since the 1990s, officials at all three levels of prison have increasingly contracted out prison management to private companies such as Corrections Corporation of America and Wackenhut Corrections Corporation. State legislators want to save public money by hiring private prison companies, and to garner campaign donations from rival prison companies; prison company executives seek to gain state business, shed costly prisoner services, and keep thousands of beds filled. Observers call this relationship the "prisons-industrial complex."

Prison population

Distribution of
prisoners
mid-year 2009

Federal prisons
9%
33%
Local jails
58%
State prisons

51%

of federal inmates
were in prison for
drug offenses
2010

How we compare: incarceration

Number of inmates
per 100,000 residents
2008

USA	**750**
Russia	628
Georgia	401
Poland	236
Azerbaijan	202
England & Wales	148
Turkey	112
Germany	93
France	85
Denmark, Italy	67

Who is most likely to be behind bars?

Percentage of men in
each racial/ethnic
group
2007

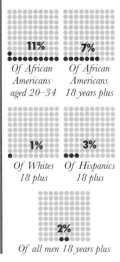

11%
Of African Americans aged 20–34

7%
Of African Americans 18 years plus

1%
Of Whites 18 plus

3%
Of Hispanics 18 plus

2%
Of all men 18 years plus

Who is behind bars?

Gender and race of
prisoners in state and
federal prisons
2008

- Black
- White
- Hispanic
- other

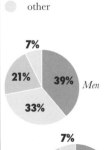

7%
21%
39% *Men*
33%

7%
17% **28%**
Women
48%

Prisons mean jobs

Total employed in correctional
institutions in 2008:

454,000

Racial/ethnic breakdown of corrections employees

2007

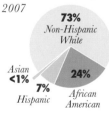

73%
Non-Hispanic White

24%
African American

Asian **<1%**
7%
Hispanic

9% increase in corrections
jobs predicted 2008–18
due to increase in prison
inmates.

Private federal prisons

12% of federal prisoners
were in privately operated
facilities mid-2009.

Texas had **5** of the **13**
federal prisons that were
contracted out to private
companies in 2010.

Privatized state prisons

Texas had **11** of the **60**
prisons nationwide contracted
to Corrections Corporation of
America in 2010.

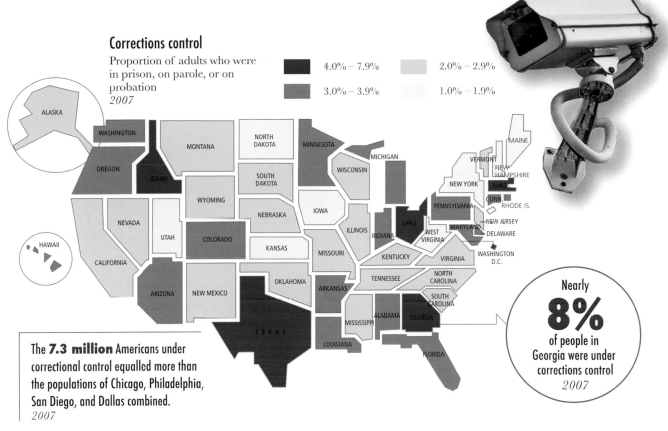

Corrections control

Proportion of adults who were in prison, on parole, or on probation
2007

- 4.0% – 7.9%
- 3.0% – 3.9%
- 2.0% – 2.9%
- 1.0% – 1.9%

Nearly **8%** of people in Georgia were under corrections control
2007

The **7.3 million** Americans under correctional control equalled more than the populations of Chicago, Philadelphia, San Diego, and Dallas combined. *2007*

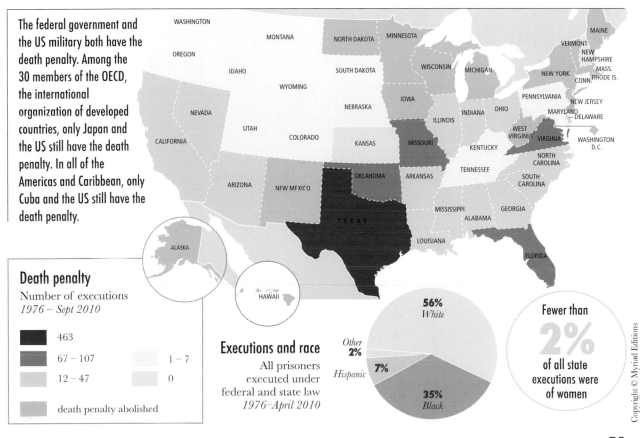

The federal government and the US military both have the death penalty. Among the 30 members of the OECD, the international organization of developed countries, only Japan and the US still have the death penalty. In all of the Americas and Caribbean, only Cuba and the US still have the death penalty.

Death penalty

Number of executions
1976 – Sept 2010

- 463
- 67 – 107
- 12 – 47
- 1 – 7
- 0
- death penalty abolished

Executions and race

All prisoners executed under federal and state law
1976–April 2010

- 56% *White*
- Other 2%
- *Hispanic* 7%
- 35% *Black*

Fewer than **2%** of all state executions were of women

Degrees and Dropouts

Academic comparison

US ranking among OECD countries *2006 and 2007*

- **university admission rate** — **9th**
  Top: Australia
- **reading literacy** *2003*
  Top: Germany
- **university graduation rate** — **15th**
  Top: Iceland
- **high school graduation rate** — **20th**
  Top: Germany
- **scientific literacy** — **21st**
  Top: Finland
- **math literacy** — **25th**
  Top: Finland

ABOUT 85 PERCENT OF AMERICAN ADULTS over age 25 have at least a high school diploma, double the proportion in 1960. About 25 percent have a Bachelor's degree or higher, up from 8 percent in 1960. This half-century of quite remarkable progress masks substantial racial, income, geographic, and sex differences in educational attainment rates. The rising tide of education has not lifted all boats.

The cost of being left behind is considerable. People without a high school diploma earn, on average, 28 percent less than those who have a high school diploma; median earnings for workers with bachelor degrees are 74 percent higher than for workers with only a high school diploma. In 2008, among 16 to 24 year olds, the unemployment rate for high school graduates was 16 percent, while for those without a high school degree it was 26 percent; for African American youth, the unemployment rate was 24 percent for high school graduates, and an extraordinary 40 percent for high school dropouts.

The cost of education itself is also considerable. The combined expenditure of federal, state and local governments on public education was just over $1 trillion in 2010. Despite this, public trust in the quality of public primary and secondary education institutions is waning, and families that can afford to do so are increasingly paying for private education for their children through high school. At the college level, about 40 percent of all students studying for a four-year degree were enrolled in private colleges, at an average cost of just under $37,000 a year (for those living on campus). These extraordinary costs leave students and families mired in debt for years after they leave school.

11% of students in kindergarten through grade 12 are in private schools

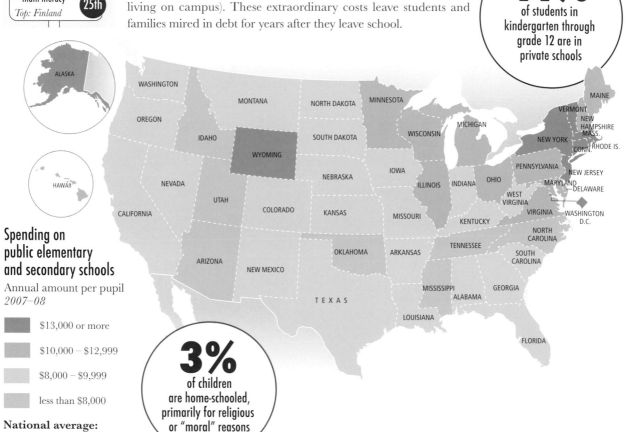

Spending on public elementary and secondary schools

Annual amount per pupil
2007–08

- $13,000 or more
- $10,000 – $12,999
- $8,000 – $9,999
- less than $8,000

National average: $10,259

3% of children are home-schooled, primarily for religious or "moral" reasons

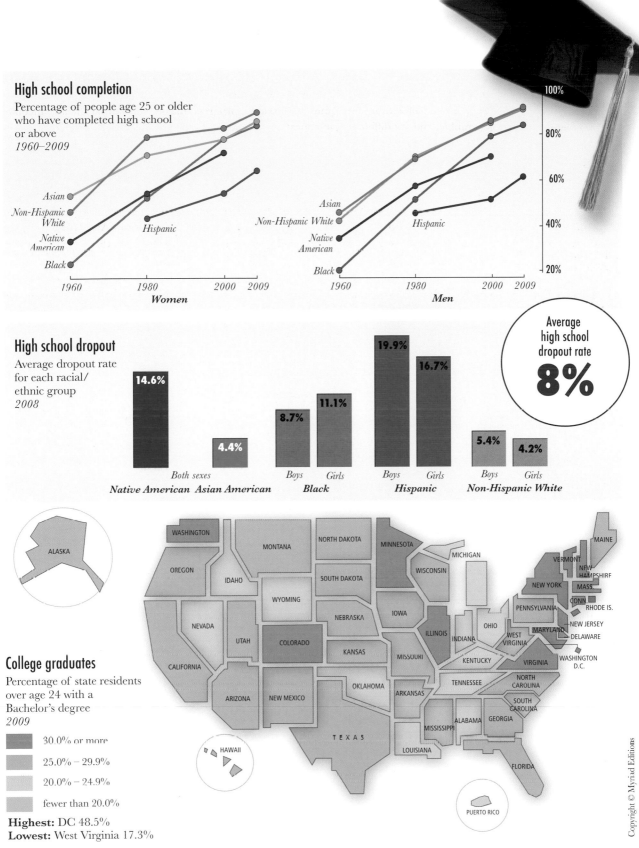

High school completion

Percentage of people age 25 or older who have completed high school or above
1960–2009

Asian
Non-Hispanic White
Native American
Hispanic
Black

100%
80%
60%
40%
20%

1960   1980   2000   2009
Women

1960   1980   2000   2009
Men

High school dropout

Average dropout rate for each racial/ethnic group
2008

Average high school dropout rate
8%

14.6%
4.4%
8.7%
11.1%
19.9%
16.7%
5.4%
4.2%

Both sexes
Native American   **Asian American**

Boys   *Girls*
Black

Boys   *Girls*
Hispanic

Boys   *Girls*
Non-Hispanic White

College graduates

Percentage of state residents over age 24 with a Bachelor's degree
2009

- 30.0% or more
- 25.0% – 29.9%
- 20.0% – 24.9%
- fewer than 20.0%

Highest: DC 48.5%
Lowest: West Virginia 17.3%

ALASKA

WASHINGTON · MONTANA · NORTH DAKOTA · MINNESOTA · MICHIGAN · MAINE · VERMONT · NEW HAMPSHIRE
OREGON · IDAHO · SOUTH DAKOTA · WISCONSIN · NEW YORK · MASS. · CONN. · RHODE IS.
WYOMING · NEBRASKA · IOWA · PENNSYLVANIA · NEW JERSEY · DELAWARE
NEVADA · UTAH · COLORADO · KANSAS · MISSOURI · ILLINOIS · INDIANA · OHIO · WEST VIRGINIA · MARYLAND · WASHINGTON D.C.
CALIFORNIA · ARIZONA · NEW MEXICO · OKLAHOMA · ARKANSAS · KENTUCKY · VIRGINIA · NORTH CAROLINA
TENNESSEE · SOUTH CAROLINA
TEXAS · MISSISSIPPI · ALABAMA · GEORGIA
HAWAII · LOUISIANA · FLORIDA
PUERTO RICO

Part Five

Consumer of the World

Sᴜsᴛᴀɪɴɪɴɢ ᴛʜᴇ "Aᴍᴇʀɪᴄᴀɴ ᴡᴀʏ ᴏꜰ ʟɪꜰᴇ" exacts a terrible environmental toll. The United States is the world's largest consumer in absolute terms of products such as corn, oil, copper, aluminum, and cocaine, and the world's largest per capita consumer of many others, from meat to paper to water. The typical American lifestyle puts enormous strain on environmental resources, at all scales from local to global. China overtook the US as the world's largest energy consumer in 2009, and is quickly catching up or surpassing the US in consumption of minerals and food. As more and more countries aspire to the "supersized" American lifestyle, the planet is put at greater and greater jeopardy.

The flip side of consumption is production, and here, too, the US excels – both at production and pollution. In some parts of the country, industrial and military activities have so polluted the air, water, and land that simply living there is a risk. The "national priorities list" identifies sites from which hazardous substances are already being released or are at high risk of being released.

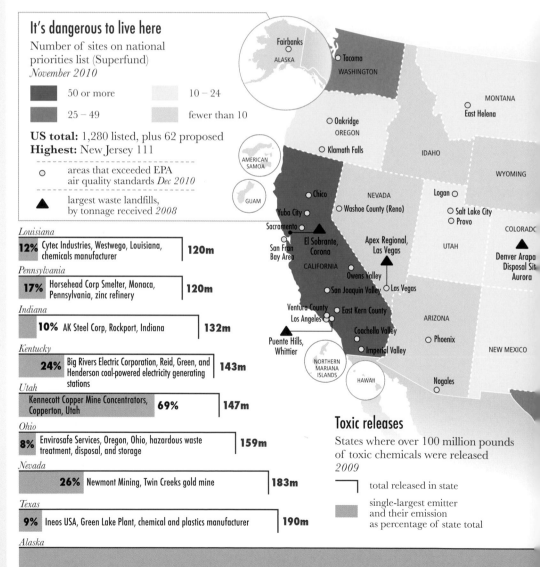

It's dangerous to live here

Number of sites on national priorities list (Superfund)
November 2010

- 50 or more
- 25 – 49
- 10 – 24
- fewer than 10

US total: 1,280 listed, plus 62 proposed
Highest: New Jersey 111

- ○ areas that exceeded EPA air quality standards *Dec 2010*
- ▲ largest waste landfills, by tonnage received *2008*

Louisiana
12% Cytec Industries, Westwego, Louisiana, chemicals manufacturer **120m**

Pennsylvania
17% Horsehead Corp Smelter, Monaca, Pennsylvania, zinc refinery **120m**

Indiana
10% AK Steel Corp, Rockport, Indiana **132m**

Kentucky
24% Big Rivers Electric Corporation, Reid, Green, and Henderson coal-powered electricity generating stations **143m**

Utah
Kennecott Copper Mine Concentrators, Copperton, Utah **69%** **147m**

Ohio
8% Envirosafe Services, Oregon, Ohio, hazardous waste treatment, disposal, and storage **159m**

Nevada
26% Newmont Mining, Twin Creeks gold mine **183m**

Texas
9% Ineos USA, Green Lake Plant, chemical and plastics manufacturer **190m**

Alaska

Toxic releases

States where over 100 million pounds of toxic chemicals were released *2009*

- total released in state
- single-largest emitter and their emission as percentage of state total

These places (formerly called "Superfund sites") threaten environmental and public health. 12 percent are federal facilities; most of those military.

Federal facilities and private industries that use any of around 600 chemicals are required to report the amount of chemical pollution they release each year. The biggest toxic releases come from chemical, mining, paper, oil, and gas industries. Areas where air pollution levels persistently exceed the national air quality standards are designated "nonattainment areas" by the EPA.

The 2011 budget for the Environmental Protection Agency was $11 billion dollars, a substantial amount that suggests the high priority given to environmental concerns. However, when compared with the Homeland Security budget of $44 billion, it is arguably still the case that the security of the nation, in the US as elsewhere, is defined primarily as protecting against external enemies rather than protecting the environment.

85%

say they reduced their energy use in the past year
2010

SMALL STEPS FORWARD

61%

of Americans said they were active in, or sympathetic to, the environmental movement
2010

Recycling cities

Percentage of waste recycled
2008

69%	*San Francisco*
62%	*Los Angeles*
55%	*Chicago, San Diego*
38%	*Philadelphia*
34%	*New York*
32%	*National average*
22%	*Phoenix*
12%	*Dallas*
3%	*Houston*

Red Dog Mining Operations, zinc-lead mine	92%	696m

Big Food

As American as Cheez Whiz...

American food inventions and date introduced to public

1848: Chewing gum
1853: Potato chips
1876: Root beer
1886: Coca Cola
1895: Peanut butter
1896: Cracker Jack popcorn
1897: Jello
1906: Corn Flakes
1923: Popsicle
1927: Kool Aid
1930: Chocolate chip cookies
1933: Twinkies
1953: Cheez Whiz
1955: Microwave oven
1959: Tang
1966: Doritos chips
1993: rBGH: recombinant bovine growth hormone

THE AMERICAN WAY OF FOOD IS ABOUT BIG: big eating, big business, and increasingly big bodies. For decades, health professionals have been telling us that American food habits are unhealthy; environmentalists have been pointing out the terrible environmental costs of our high-pesticide, high-fertilizer, animal-based diet. But these cautionary notes have made only a minor impact on the American way of food production and consumption.

In large measure, this is because of the economics of food. At an individual or household level, high-calorie, highly processed foods are generally plentiful and cheap; many low-income people live in "food deserts," with no nearby quality grocery store. Research also shows that mothers restrict their food intake during periods of food insufficiency in order to protect their children from hunger; these chronic ups and downs in food intake contribute to obesity among low-income women. High-quality foods cost more, and take more planning to procure, store, and cook. As incomes rise, so does quality of diet.

Government commodity policies play an important role in explaining the food system. For example, corn production is highly subsidized by the federal government, keeping prices low and leading to overproduction of corn products such as high fructose corn syrup. Overall, food is big business: the American food stream is controlled by fewer and fewer companies, operating bigger and bigger food production enterprises. Increasingly, animal foods are produced on massive factory farms, or "confined animal feedlot operations." These are pollution hotspots and sites of unremitting animal suffering, with tens of thousands of animals confined in small spaces. Most consumers have no idea who is responsible for the food they eat.

The scale of American food production is staggering: more than 9 billion animals a year are slaughtered for food. The US is the world's largest producer of beef and poultry, the second-largest egg producer, the third-largest pork producer. Over 1 billion pounds of pesticides are applied to food commodities each year. Americans also hold the record as the world's highest calorie consumers. And it shows.

Top US food and beverage producers

Value of sales
2008

5 retailers accounted for

48%

of US food retail market
2006

Nestlé USA & Nestlé Canada
$26.5 trillion

Tyson Foods Inc.
$26.3 trillion

Pepsico Inc.
$25.3 trillion

Kraft Foods Inc.
$24.0 trillion

Anheuser-Busch
$15.6 trillion

Making food, making money

Concentration of production in the food industry
most recent since 2006

10 companies
44%
of production

4 companies
66%
of production

4 companies
84%
of production

Eggs   **Pork**   **Beef**

Hog factory farms

States with more than 1 million hogs
2008

Highest:
Iowa 20 million

Meat farming

Number of animals slaughtered annually for food
2009

900.000
Cattle and calves

113.7m
Hogs

8.7billion

Broiler chickens

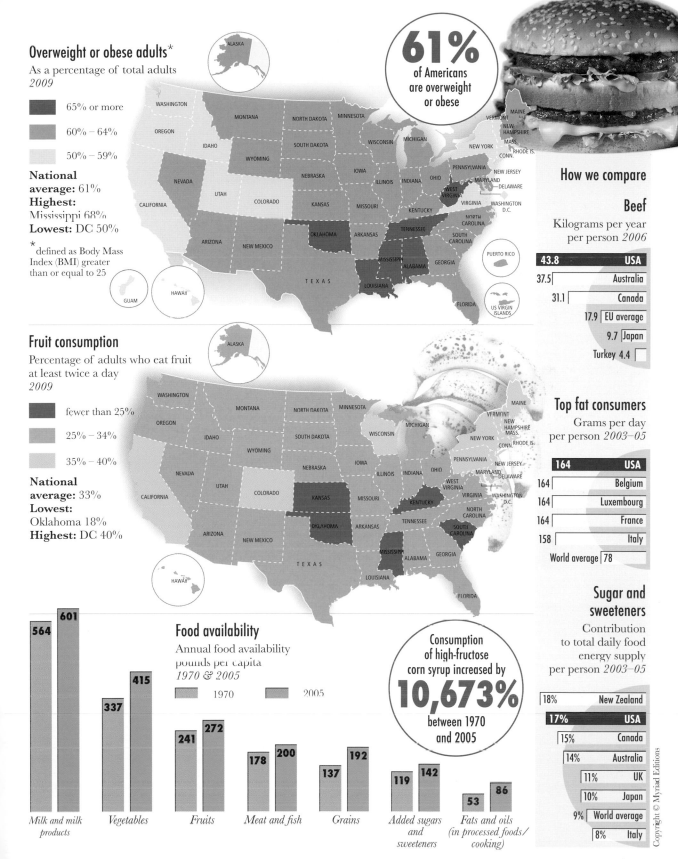

Overweight or obese adults*

As a percentage of total adults
2009

- 65% or more
- 60% – 64%
- 50% – 59%

National average: 61%
Highest: Mississippi 68%
Lowest: DC 50%

* defined as Body Mass Index (BMI) greater than or equal to 25

61% of Americans are overweight or obese

How we compare

Beef
Kilograms per year per person 2006

43.8	USA
37.5	Australia
31.1	Canada
17.9	EU average
9.7	Japan
Turkey 4.4	

Fruit consumption

Percentage of adults who eat fruit at least twice a day
2009

- fewer than 25%
- 25% – 34%
- 35% – 40%

National average: 33%
Lowest: Oklahoma 18%
Highest: DC 40%

Top fat consumers
Grams per day per person 2003–05

164	USA
164	Belgium
164	Luxembourg
164	France
158	Italy
World average 78	

Food availability
Annual food availability pounds per capita
1970 & 2005

- 1970
- 2005

Category	1970	2005
Milk and milk products	564	601
Vegetables	337	415
Fruits	241	272
Meat and fish	178	200
Grains	137	192
Added sugars and sweeteners	119	142
Fats and oils (in processed foods/cooking)	53	86

Consumption of high-fructose corn syrup increased by **10,673%** between 1970 and 2005

Sugar and sweeteners
Contribution to total daily food energy supply per person 2003–05

18%	New Zealand
17%	USA
15%	Canada
14%	Australia
11%	UK
10%	Japan
9%	World average
8%	Italy

Highest paid players

Contracted annual salary *2009*

Major League Baseball

Alex Rodriguez • New York Yankees
$33m

Mark Teixeira • New York Yankees
$25m

CC Sabathia • New York Yankees
$23m

Derek Jeter • New York Yankees
$20m

Barry Zito • San Francisco Giants
$19m

NBA

Kevin Garnett • Boston Celtics
$25m

Allen Iverson • Philadelphia 76ers
$22m

Kobe Bryant • Los Angeles Lakers
$21m

Shaquille O'Neal • Cleveland Cavaliers
$20m

LeBron James • Cleveland Cavaliers
$14m

NFL

Max Schaub • Houston Texans
$17m

Julius Peppers • Carolina Panthers
$17m

Dwight Freeney • Indianapolis Colts
$16m

Peyton Manning • Indianapolis Colts
$15m

Tom Brady • New England Patriots
$8m

Maximum salary for experienced woman player on a WNBA team in 2010:
$101,500

Base salary for a rookie male player in the NBA:
$428,163

Total made by LeBron James from salary plus endorsements in 2009:
$42m

AMERICANS EAT, SLEEP, AND BREATHE SPORTS. If you're a Chicagoan, you're either a White Sox or a Cubs fan. If you're the mother of a young daughter, you probably drive her to girls' soccer games. If you're Barack Obama, you squeeze pick-up basketball games in between national crises. Even if your tastes tend more toward music than exercise, you still routinely use sports phrases such as "end run" and "slam dunk."

Sports aren't just popular pastimes; they have become big business in America. Sports today are calculated in terms of markets, contracts and profits. Cities float bonds to subsidize the building of elaborate stadiums. Team owners yearn to relocate to more lucrative markets. Star athletes advertise sneakers, cars, and soft drinks.

American university athletics also have adopted the business model. Some head coaches are paid more than college presidents; schools' athletic budgets are rising faster than their academic budgets. For select schools, a Nike contract is worth millions.

Race, class, and gender shape who profits from sports and who is allowed to compete. Until Jackie Robinson broke the color bar in 1947, major league baseball was a white man's game. The outstanding African American ballplayers of the Negro League only recently have been given their due. Golf and tennis clubs were upper-class, white-only (and often Christian-only) enclaves. Women college athletes had to make do with the dregs of their schools' athletic budgets, while women professional athletes were left to compete for paltry prize money. If today one sees an African American on a tennis court or a girls' college team getting prime practice time on the court, it's not happenstance: it is the result of fresh ideas, legislation, court cases and political organizing. Yet even these transformations have not dislodged the business model of American sports.

In 2010, only six of the NFL's 32 teams were led by African American coaches, while 75% of the players were African American.

The big money

Five professional teams with highest revenue in each sport
2009

$1.6bn
Value of Dallas Cowboys American football franchise *2010*

New England Patriots $302m
New York Giants $230m
New York Jets $227m
USA
Dallas Cowboys $280m
Washington Redskins $345m

National Football League

Boston Red Sox $266m
USA
Chicago Cubs $246m
New York Yankees $441m
Los Angeles Dodgers $247m
New York Mets $268m

Major League Baseball

Detroit Pistons $171m
Chicago Bulls $168m
New York Knicks $202m
USA
Los Angeles Lakers $209m
Houston Rockets $160m

National Basketball Association

CANADA
Vancouver Canucks $109m
Toronto Maple Leafs $168m
Montreal Canadiens $130m
USA
Detroit Red Wings $130m
New York Rangers $139m

National Hockey League

Rival companies compete for contracts with colleges and universities that have major athletic programs. Those whose games get extensive television coverage receive millions of dollars. In return, schools agree to use the company's products, to prominently display its logo, and to avoid criticizing company policies. In addition, some well-known university coaches are paid directly by the companies. In public universities with Division I football programs, the president sometimes makes only half as much as the school's head football coach. The total compensation of the University of Southern California's head football coach in 2007 was $4.4 million.

Big Ten Athletic Conference Sponsors

- University of Illinois • Nike
- Indiana University • Adidas
- University of Iowa • Nike
- University of Michigan • Adidas
- Michigan State University • Nike
- University of Minnesota • Nike
- Northwestern University • Adidas
- Ohio State University • Nike
- Pennsylvania State University • Nike
- Purdue University, IN • Nike
- University of Wisconsin • Adidas

Pacific Athletic Conference Sponsors

- University of Arizona • Nike
- Arizona State University • Nike
- University of California, Berkeley • Nike
- University of California, LA • Adidas
- University of Oregon • Nike
- Oregon State University • Nike
- Stanford University, CA • Nike
- University of Southern California • Nike
- University of Washington • Nike
- Washington State University • Nike

$60m
Amount Adidas is paying University of Michigan between 2008 and 2016

Deals
Number of colleges and universities with contracts
2010

1 *New Balance*
6 *Russell*
8 *Under Armour*
88 *Nike*
32 *Adidas*

The racial gap
2010

Failing Five
Colleges where fewer than **30%** of Black male basketball players graduate on time compared with **100%** of White players:
Baylor University, TX
University of Kentucky
University of Missouri
University of Nevada, Las Vegas
New Mexico State University

Successful Six
Colleges where **100%** of both White and Black male basketball players graduate on time:
Brigham Young University, UT
Marquette University, WI
Notre Dame University, IN
Utah State University
University of Vermont
Wake Forest University, AL

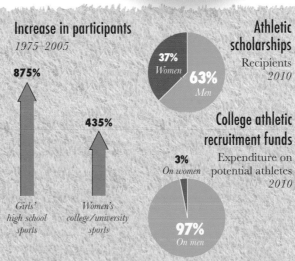

AN INCOMPLETE REVOLUTION
Title IX, a section of the Education Act Amendments of 1972, compels high schools, colleges, and universities receiving federal funding to achieve equity between men's and women's athletics. It led to the rise of girls' soccer, more athletic scholarships for college women, better equipped and coached women's athletics and the creation of the Women's National Basketball Association. Title IX is opposed by many, while women activists push for full enforcement by the Department of Education.

Increase in participants
1975–2005

875%
Girls' high school sports

435%
Women's college/university sports

Athletic scholarships
Recipients
2010

37% *Women*
63% *Men*

College athletic recruitment funds
Expenditure on potential athletes
2010

3% *On women*
97% *On men*

Copyright © Myriad Editions

Auto Nation

THE CULT OF THE CAR is mapped onto American mythologies of individualism and freedom. Car culture is highly masculinized, but in 2005 women passed a benchmark, becoming the majority of licensed drivers.

Americans' love of the car reflects not only an ideological proclivity but a necessity. Public transit is remarkably underdeveloped in the United States, and most communities offer few alternatives to driving. To the extent that public transportation systems exist, they are primarily urban; suburban and rural communities seldom have good – or any – public transportation. Public policies privilege the car: American legislators are notoriously uninterested in funding public transit. The US gasoline tax is among the lowest in the world, encouraging Americans to think that driving is cheap. Commuting to work by walking or public transit has declined in the past 30 years.

The low cost of gas and the ubiquity of cars mask the costs of auto dependence. City, state, and federal budgets are stretched to the breaking point by automobile-related infrastructure demands; $193 billion was spent on highways in 2008. The enormous environmental costs of roads, gasoline consumption, and air pollution are hard to tally, but locally the impacts are often devastating, and American cars have a globally significant impact.

Automobile production and related activities have long been a mainstay of the American economy, and in the Midwest–Great Lakes manufacturing belt the automobile has driven the economy. The recession hit the auto industry hardest: in 2008, more than 900 auto dealerships closed; auto sales in that year alone plunged 18 percent; and the "Big Three" manufacturers (Ford, GM and Chrysler) received billions of dollars in bailout funds from the federal government.

26%
of those employed in motor vehicle manufacturing are women
2009

How we compare

Number of vehicles
Per 1,000 people
2008

USA	842
Brazil	140
China	36
Indonesia	35
India	13

Gasoline tax
Value of tax in cents per gallon of gasoline 2008

USA	39
Japan	268
UK	436
France	456
Germany	485
Netherlands	518

US share of global motor vehicle manufacturing
By vehicles produced
1999–2009

2009	9%
2007	15%
2005	18%
2003	20%
2001	20%
1999	23%

The US dropped from **first** to **third** in the world between 2005 and 2009.

Anatomy of a typical auto
Weight of materials in pounds 2003

- rubber: 145
- aluminum: 256
- iron: 345
- glass: 98
- zinc: 11
- steel: 1,781
- copper & brass: 46
- plastics: 253

Employment in motor manufacturing
Number of workers employed in motor vehicle and parts manufacturing
2006

- 100,000 – 214,000
- 30,000 – 99,999
- 10,000 – 29,999
- 3,000 – 9,999
- fewer than 3,000

Consumption of resources
Motor vehicle manufacturing as percentage of total US resource use
2003

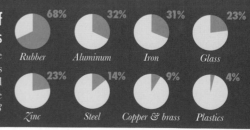

68% Rubber	32% Aluminum	31% Iron	23% Glass
23% Zinc	14% Steel	9% Copper & brass	4% Plastics

Well-travelled

Vehicle-miles of travel per state per capita
2008

- 17,735
- 12,750 – 14,999
- 10,000 – 12,749
- 7,500 – 9,999
- fewer than 7,500

ALASKA

WASHINGTON
OREGON
MONTANA
NORTH DAKOTA
MINNESOTA
IDAHO
SOUTH DAKOTA
WISCONSIN
MICHIGAN
MAINE
VERMONT
NEW HAMPSHIRE
NEW YORK
MASS.
CONN.
RHODE IS.
WYOMING
NEBRASKA
IOWA
PENNSYLVANIA
NEVADA
ILLINOIS
OHIO
NEW JERSEY
UTAH
COLORADO
KANSAS
INDIANA
WEST VIRGINIA
MARYLAND
DELAWARE
CALIFORNIA
MISSOURI
KENTUCKY
VIRGINIA
WASHINGTON D.C.
HAWAII
ARIZONA
NEW MEXICO
OKLAHOMA
TENNESSEE
NORTH CAROLINA
ARKANSAS
SOUTH CAROLINA
ALABAMA
GEORGIA
MISSISSIPPI
PUERTO RICO
TEXAS
LOUISIANA
FLORIDA

Americans drove
3.6%
fewer miles in 2008 than in 2007

OBJECTS IN MIRROR ARE CLOSER THAN THEY APPEAR

Responsibility for roads

- Federal Government **3%**
- Other **2%**
- **19%** State Governments
- **76%** Local Governments

Around
40,000
people are killed each year in vehicle accidents

Fuel consumption
Total gallons by all vehicles

- 92bn — 1970
- 181bn — 2007
- 175bn — 2008

Vehicle ownership

Distribution of different levels of ownership by household
2008

- No vehicles **9%**
- **20%** Three or more vehicles
- **33%** One vehicle
- **38%** Two vehicles

Licensed to drive

Percentage of driving-age population who hold driver's license

- 57% — 1950
- 87% — 2008

Mode of travel
on all trips
2008

- **83%** Passenger vehicle
- **11%** Walking
- Other **4%**
- **2%** Public transportation

Mode of travel for getting to work

- — walking
- — public transit

- 10% / 9% — 1970
- 5% / 3% — 2000

Alternative commutes

Cities with highest rates of alternative work commutes *2007*

Public transit
- **55%** New York City
- **5%** National average

Bike
- **4%** Portland, OR
- **<1%** National average

Walking
- **14%** Boston
- **3%** National average

Car Pooling
- **17%** Mesa, AZ
- **10%** National average

Hybrids

Hybrid gas/electric vehicles were
2.8%
of US car sales
2009

Political identification of hybrid drivers

Democrat	38%
Independent	34%
14%	Republican

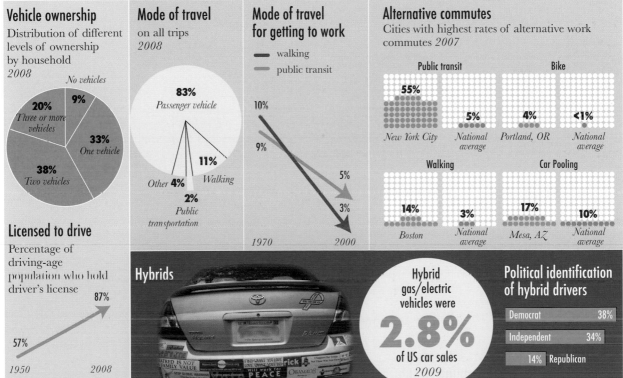

Money Comes, Money Goes

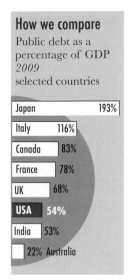

How we compare

Public debt as a
percentage of GDP
2009
selected countries

Japan	193%
Italy	116%
Canada	83%
France	78%
UK	68%
USA	54%
India	53%
	22% Australia

MOST GOVERNMENTS OF INDUSTRIALIZED COUNTRIES, and most people living in industrialized economies, are drowning in debt. The US government, with its big economy and vast military spending, is at an all-time high in deficit spending, and is coming close to historically high debt levels.

It is surprisingly difficult to come to terms with what the federal budget is and how it is spent. For example, official figures peg military spending at about 20 percent of the total US budget. Alternative estimates, which count the costs of Veterans Affairs, Homeland Security, and the chain of military spending and debt that includes past wars, puts the amount at closer to 50 percent of real spending. Then, there are fierce controversies about whether Social Security taxes collected should be "counted" as part of the budget, or should be "off-budget" since the funds are supposed to go directly into a dedicated tax fund and are not legally part of general revenues. Counting social security revenues as part of the general revenue stream shrinks the reported deficit.

But, no matter how the numbers are massaged, the US government is now unmistakably running in the red. From 1998 to 2001, the US government budget had a surplus. But the combined effects of more than $1 trillion spent on the wars in Iraq and Afghanistan since 2001, the Bush administration's deep tax cuts, and the global recession leaves the US federal government spending more each day than it takes in.

Where federal government money comes from

Counting social security contributions as part of the stream

Corporate income taxes **7%**
Other **7%**
3% *Excise taxes*
40% *Social insurance taxes*
43% *Individual taxes*

Federal budget, FY2010: $2.2 trillion

The deficit trendline

Federal budgets
1980–2010

1980 **$74bn** *deficit*
1985 **$212 billion** *deficit*
1990 **$221 billion** *deficit*
1995 **$164 billion** *deficit*
$236 billion *surplus*
2000
2004 **$413 billion** *deficit*
2008 **$459 billion** *deficit*
2010 **$1.5 trillion** *deficit*

The deficit is the budget gap in any given year between revenues and spending. Debt is the cumulative figure of all money owed by the government. Some of this debt is owed by one branch of the government to another. But more than half the total debt is owed to the public in various forms, including bonds and other promissory notes. Economists and public policy analysts debate the tipping point for debt – when it becomes a destabilizing danger to the economy. Many fear that the US is approaching that point.

US national gross debt
$14 trillion
Nov 2010

Where federal government money goes to

Official government account

Interest on national debt **6%**
21% *Medicare, Medicaid, CHIP*
Social safety-net spending (e.g. food stamps, home heating assistance, supplemental social security) **14%**
"Program areas" (e.g. science & technology; education, environment; transportation infrastructure, food safety, CDC) **20%**
20% *Social security benefits*
20% *Defense and security-related activities, including the war operations in Iraq and Afghanistan*

Federal government spending, FY2010: $3.6 trillion

Governments can roll over debt. Households and individuals can't, or not for long. Individuals in the US are piling up debt at an astonishing rate, far outpacing the rate of disposable income growth. Americans lead the world in credit card use – and debt. Bankruptcies are at an all-time high and, in tandem with the foreclosure crisis, we are now witnessing a bankruptcy crisis.

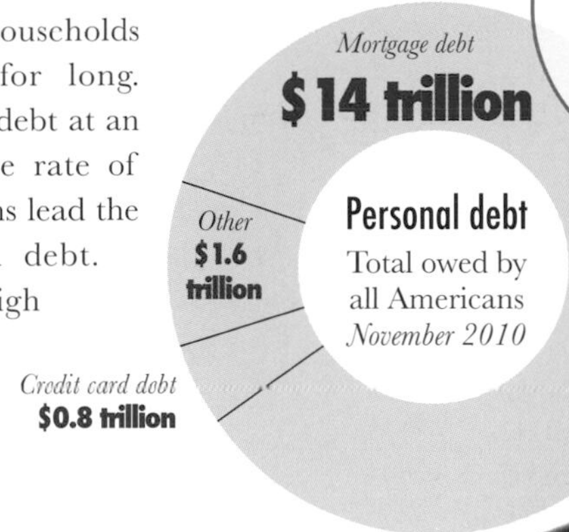

26%
of adults admit to not paying bills on time

Personal debt
Total owed by all Americans
November 2010

Mortgage debt
$14 trillion

Other
$1.6 trillion

Credit card debt
$0.8 trillion

Company profits
2009

| VISA | $2.5bn |
| Mastercard | $1.5bn |

Number of credit cards
2009
Total: 577m

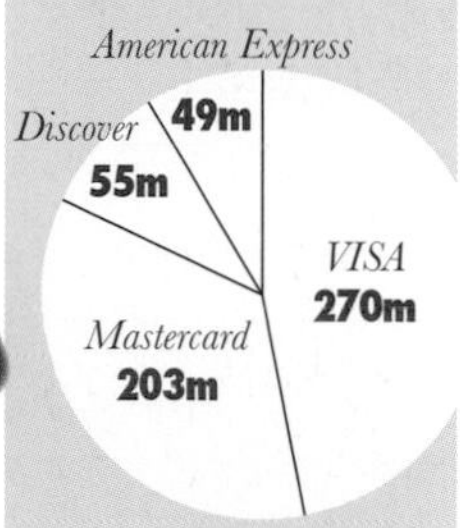

American Express **49m**
Discover **55m**
VISA **270m**
Mastercard **203m**

Average statistics
2010

Number of credit cards per person: **3.5**

Debt per household: **$16,000**

Interest rate charged Nov 2010: **16.77%**

Percentage of households with credit card debt, *2004*

| White | 54% |
| African American | 84% |

Use of credit card debt
As reported by users
2004

Basic living expenses: more than **33%**

Some medical expenses: **52%** of low and middle-income households

How the Other Half Banks
Payday lending – among the highest risk subsets of subprime lending – is characterized by small-dollar, short-term lending to borrowers typically experiencing cash flow difficulties. These loans are meant to cover a borrower's expenses until the next payday; interest rates are the annual equivalent of 400% or much higher. The economic recession has fueled the growth of these lenders.

Value of loans
Made by payday lenders

2004	2006	2008	2009
$5.2 billion	$6.8 billion	$8.2 billion	$8.1 billion

Personal bankruptcy filings
Rate per 1,000 people
2009

- 7.5– 11.3
- 5.0 – 7.4
- 2.5 – 4.9
- below 2.5

Highest: Nevada 11.3
Lowest: Northern Mariana Islands 0.1
US average: 4.7

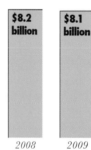

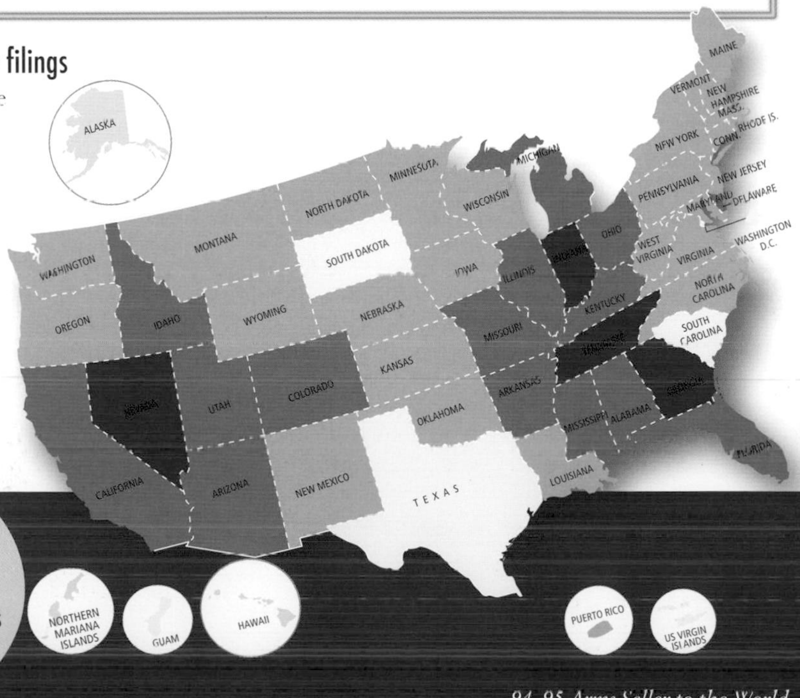

There was a 14% increase in non-business bankruptcy filings *2009–10*

Part Six

Leader of the World

Exporting Democracy

Number of overseas bases or installations
2009

716

121

In US-owned territories

In foreign countries

WE AMERICANS can't make up our collective mind: do we want to venture out into the world spreading democracy or stay comfortably at home, pulling up the drawbridge? In the wake of the horrors of World War I, President Woodrow Wilson promoted the new League of Nations as a vehicle for advancing a democratic peace worldwide, but Congress refused to let the United States join. Four decades later, during the Cold War, most Americans didn't blink when their government engineered coups against elected governments in Guatemala, Iran, and Chile. And yet Americans joined the rest of the world in celebrating the fall of the Berlin Wall and the end of apartheid in South Africa.

Today, the US has hundreds of overseas military bases and installations, far more than any other country. Each base is founded on a bi-lateral government-to-government Status of Forces Agreement. These far-flung bases are imagined to be ensuring not just American security, but protecting democracy and "freedom" in general. Yet each "SOFA" is kept secret, and most Americans are not curious about what local people in the host societies think about these bases, and would struggle to find places such as Guam, Okinawa, Bosnia-Herzegovina, Kyrgyzstan, and Diego Garcia on a map.

Many Americans like to think of themselves as "the most generous people on earth," and in private giving they are. They point to their outpouring of donations to people in Haiti, Indonesia, and Sri Lanka after natural disasters. On a larger scale, they point to the Peace Corps, whose thousands of American volunteers have dug wells and staffed rural health clinics from Morocco to Nepal. Foreign aid is a different matter, however. Americans imagine that the US government gives exceptional amounts of foreign aid to countries in need, whereas, proportionately, US foreign aid pales compared with that given by other countries. And the recipients of the largest amounts of US foreign aid are not necessarily those most in need, nor those with the firmest democratic credentials, but, rather, those countries whose governments US policy-makers believe matter most to US national security.

200,000
Peace Corps Volunteers have served
1961–2010

US military presence

Countries and US territories hosting US military bases or installations, including US-run NATO bases
2009

★ countries hosting major US bases

GREENLAND

ICELAND

UK
DENMARK
NETH.
BEL.
GERMANY
LUX.
BOSNIA-HERZEGOVINA
PORTUGAL SPAIN
ITALY
—Kosovo
GREECE
TURKEY
KYRGYZSTAN
JAPAN
SOUTH KOREA.
IRAQ
KUWAIT
AFGHANISTAN
Okinawa
EGYPT
BAHRAIN
OMAN

BAHAMAS
Guantánamo
PUERTO RICO
VIRGIN IS. (US)
ANTIGUA & BARBUDA
ARUBA

ECUADOR
PERU

DJIBOUTI

KENYA

SINGAPORE

DIEGO GARCIA

INDONESIA

★ WAKE IS.
N. MARIANA IS.
GUAM
MARSHALL ISLANDS

AMERICAN SAMOA

AUSTRALIA

MEXICO
ANTIG
BARE
DOMINICAN
REP. ST KITTS
JAMAICA HAITI & NEVI
BELIZE
GUATEMALA HONDURAS
DOMINICA
ST LUCIA
EL SALVADOR
NICARAGUA ST VINCENT & GRENADINES
GRENADA
COSTA RICA
BARE
PANAMA
VENEZUELA
GUYAN
COLOMBIA
SURIN

ECUADOR

PERU
BRAZ

BOLIV

PAR

CHILE AR

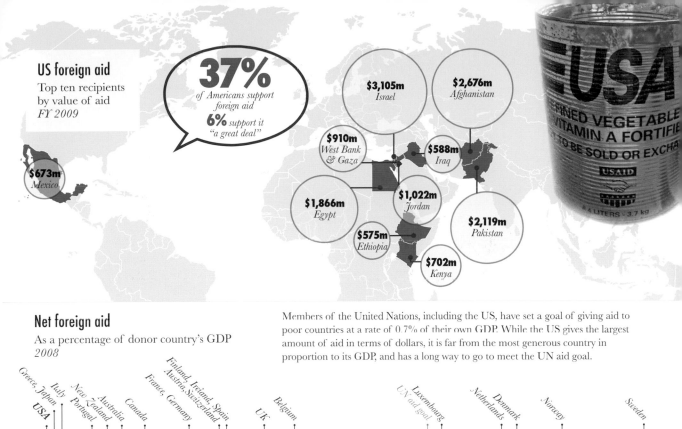

US foreign aid

Top ten recipients by value of aid
FY 2009

37% of Americans support foreign aid
6% support it *"a great deal"*

$673m *Mexico*

$910m *West Bank & Gaza*

$3,105m *Israel*

$2,676m *Afghanistan*

$588m *Iraq*

$1,866m *Egypt*

$1,022m *Jordan*

$2,119m *Pakistan*

$575m *Ethiopia*

$702m *Kenya*

Net foreign aid

As a percentage of donor country's GDP
2008

Members of the United Nations, including the US, have set a goal of giving aid to poor countries at a rate of 0.7% of their own GDP. While the US gives the largest amount of aid in terms of dollars, it is far from the most generous country in proportion to its GDP, and has a long way to go to meet the UN aid goal.

USA 0.19
Greece, Japan 0.20
Italy 0.21
New Zealand, Portugal 0.25
Australia 0.27
Canada 0.29
France, Germany 0.32
Finland, Ireland, Spain, Austria, Switzerland 0.38
0.42 0.43
UK 0.48
Belgium 0.52
UN aid goal 0.70
Luxembourg 0.72
Netherlands 0.80
Denmark 0.82
Norway 0.88
Sweden 0.99

Peace Corps

Countries to which volunteers have been sent at some time
1961–2010

37% of Peace Corps Volunteers serve in Africa

Arms Seller to the World

THE UNITED STATES IS the world's number one arms seller. Fighter planes, warships, armored vehicles roll off the assembly lines, headed not just to American soldiers, but to those of other countries. Russia runs a fairly close second; Germany, France, UK, Netherlands, and Italy are also players, though they trail far behind the US.

International arms sales appear to be recession proof. Worldwide, governments remain eager to build up their arsenals, and the US remains eager to fill them. Today, China is seen as a tantalizing future arms customer; the US also is eager to replace Russia as arms supplier to India and Algeria. In addition to sales of arms, the US gives military equipment and services to favored governments in the form of aid.

Democratic and Republican administrations share dual beliefs: firstly, that selling US-made weapons abroad keeps American arms companies profitable and in business, ready to provide arms when the US government needs them; second, that giving and selling arms binds foreign allies closely to the US, or wins over others who are wavering. The result has been to militarize US relations with many countries, to exacerbate regional tensions, and to make weapons manufacturers among the most politically powerful and profitable companies in American society.

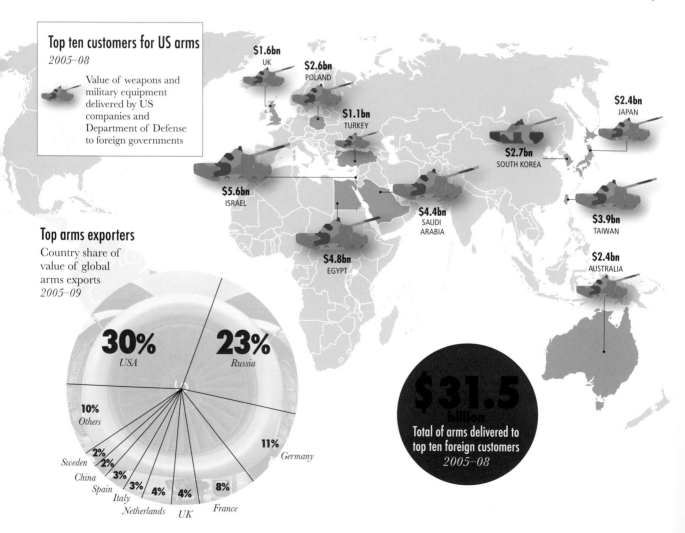

Top ten customers for US arms
2005–08

Value of weapons and military equipment delivered by US companies and Department of Defense to foreign governments

$1.6bn UK
$2.6bn POLAND
$1.1bn TURKEY
$2.4bn JAPAN
$2.7bn SOUTH KOREA
$5.6bn ISRAEL
$4.4bn SAUDI ARABIA
$3.9bn TAIWAN
$4.8bn EGYPT
$2.4bn AUSTRALIA

Top arms exporters
Country share of value of global arms exports 2005–09

30% USA
23% Russia
10% Others
11% Germany
2% Sweden
2% China
3% Spain
3% Italy
4% Netherlands
4% UK
8% France

$31.5 billion
Total of arms delivered to top ten foreign customers
2005–08

While sharing the desire for ever-expanding arms sales, weapons makers are fierce rivals. As a result of mergers, a handful of companies now dominates the US field. Their executives – former Pentagon civilian officials, retired generals and ex-members of Congress – have ready access to Washington decision-makers, their political clout enhanced by the fact that their companies and subcontractors employ people across the country. Many workers and town officials may question the rampant US global arms selling, yet worry that their own economic security depends on it.

In 2008, for the first time in 20 years, a non-US company ranked first among the world's arms corporations. However, the new top dog, the UK-based BAE, only reached the arms-selling pinnacle by making the US Defense Department one of its major customers.

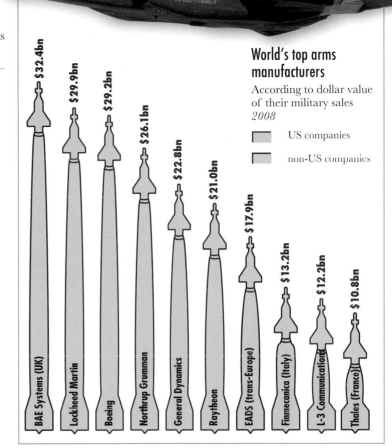

World's top arms manufacturers

According to dollar value of their military sales
2008

US companies	
non-US companies	

- $32.4bn — BAE Systems (UK)
- $29.9bn — Lockheed Martin
- $29.2bn — Boeing
- $26.1bn — Northrup Grumman
- $22.8bn — General Dynamics
- $21.0bn — Raytheon
- $17.9bn — EADS (trans-Europe)
- $13.2bn — Finmecanica (Italy)
- $12.2bn — L-3 Communications
- $10.8bn — Thales (France)

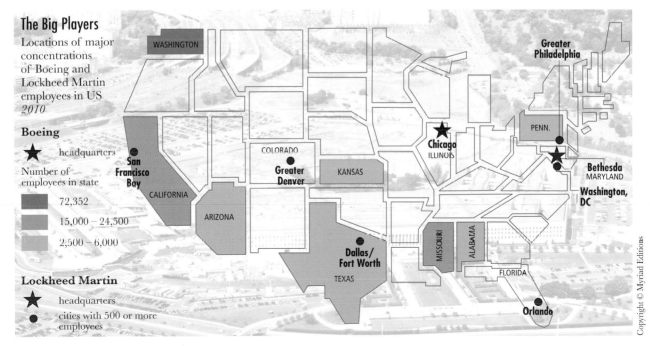

The Big Players

Locations of major concentrations of Boeing and Lockheed Martin employees in US
2010

Boeing

★ headquarters

Number of employees in state
- 72,352
- 15,000 – 24,500
- 2,500 – 6,000

Lockheed Martin

★ headquarters

● cities with 500 or more employees

WASHINGTON
San Francisco Bay
CALIFORNIA
ARIZONA
COLORADO
Greater Denver
KANSAS
Dallas/Fort Worth
TEXAS
MISSOURI
ALABAMA
FLORIDA
Orlando
Chicago
ILLINOIS
PENN.
Greater Philadelphia
Bethesda
MARYLAND
Washington, DC

Nuclear State

THE UNITED STATES WAS THE FIRST to develop a functional nuclear bomb, and the first to use it. It remains one of two nuclear superpowers in the world. The race to build nuclear arsenals started in World War II and peaked in the Cold War, when the Soviet Union and the US were in a frenzied race to achieve nuclear superiority. In the post-Cold War era, despite a program of reduction that has been in place since the START treaty was first signed in 1991, Russia and the US still maintain thousands of nuclear warheads, more than enough to destroy almost all life on the planet.

The US is the only country to have used nuclear weapons in war, when it bombed Hiroshima and Nagasaki in 1945, killing tens of thousands of Japanese and wounding thousands more. The debate about the military necessity and moral imperative of those bombings continues, but concerns are now shifting to the stability and reliability of new nuclear states, such as Pakistan and India, or aspirational nuclear states such as Iran. There is also considerable concern about safeguarding the vast stockpiles of weapons-usable nuclear materials that sit at hundreds of sites around the world; the US government will spend almost $3 billion in 2011 to help secure or transfer these stores.

The Cold War race to produce nuclear weapons was cloaked in secrecy and conducted beyond the reach of public scrutiny and accountability. The production, testing, and storing of nuclear weapons has proven to be an environmental and health calamity; its presumed imperatives superseding considerations of public protection. Every nuclear weapons production and storage site is a hazard; many sites are now being decontaminated, and others are permanently quarantined.

The truth about radioactive releases, inadequate storage of radioactive materials, contamination of public water supplies, and, in some cases, intentional contamination of civilians, is slowly being wrested into view. From 1945 to 1962, the US conducted a series of aboveground atomic weapons tests that produced "downwind" deaths and disease, the scope of which is just now being revealed. Test explosions in the Pacific vaporized several islands, left others uninhabitable, dislocated native Pacific Islander communities, and exposed thousands to radiation. Within the US, many of the tests took place on Native American lands. This was also the case with much of the uranium mining; the toll from "yellowcake" mining is just now becoming apparent. Vast stores of nuclear waste from weapons production are scattered across the US; there is no known safe means of disposing of nuclear wastes.

Stockpiles of nuclear warheads

Estimated figures, including those that are not operational
2010

<10	North Korea
60 – 80	India
70 – 90	Pakistan
80	Israel
225	UK
240	China
300	France
9,600	USA
12,000	Russia

American attitudes to nuclear weapons
2010

It is likely that the US will become involved in a nuclear war in the next decade.
38%

No country including the US should be allowed to have nuclear weapons
62%

WASHINGTON

OREGON

IDAH[O]

over 900 explosions

Fallon

NEVADA

Central Nevada Test Area

CALIFORNIA

Navajo Reservation
More than 1,000 open-pit and underground uranium mines on the reservation are abandoned, unreclaimed, and highly radioactive

Eastern Pacific

Nuclear doctrine milestones

Mutually Assured Destruction
MAD was a military doctrine of massive nuclear retaliation against any first user of nuclear weapons that prevailed until the 1970s. It was believed that nuclear deterrence was best ensured by having a massive number of nuclear weapons. MAD propelled the arms race.

1950s

Nuclear landscape

ALASKA
Amchitka Is

Legend:
- test site 1945–92
- nuclear weapons accident
- uranium mining
- nuclear weapons production and storage

Total number of US nuclear weapons tests 1945–92:
1,030
(1,125 nuclear devices detonated; 24 additional joint tests with Great Britain)

Number of US nuclear bombs lost in accidents and never recovered:
11

MONTANA
NORTH DAKOTA
SOUTH DAKOTA
WYOMING
Black Hills

MAINE
• Montreal
1950 scattered uranium
VERMONT
NEW HAMPSHIRE
MASSACHUSETTS
NEW YORK
RHODE ISLAND
CONNECTICUT
PENNSYLVANIA
NEW JERSEY
DELAWARE
MARYLAND
WASHINGTON D.C.
WEST VIRGINIA
VIRGINIA

Green Valley
UTAH
Rifle
COLORADO
ARIZONA
Farmington
NEW MEXICO
Trinity, first atomic bomb tested, 1945
Carlsbad

NEBRASKA
ILLINOIS
INDIANA
OHIO
KANSAS
MISSOURI
KENTUCKY
TENNESSEE
OKLAHOMA
ARKANSAS
TEXAS
MISSISSIPPI
ALABAMA
GEORGIA
SOUTH CAROLINA
NORTH CAROLINA
1961 – buried pieces and components of bomb

LOUISIANA
Hattiesburg
1958 missing bomb
FLORIDA

PACIFIC OCEAN
Bikini
Eniwetok
Rongelap Atoll
MARSHALL ISLANDS

NORTH PACIFIC OCEAN
Johnson Island

INDIAN OCEAN
Christmas Is. Kiribati

SOUTH ATLANTIC OCEAN
FALKLAND ISLANDS

Radiation Exposure Compensation Act (RECA)

To make partial restitution to individuals for hardships associated with radiation exposure, the RECA was enacted in 1990. From 1992 through June 2007, payments totaling $1.2 billion were authorized for 18,110 claims, almost half of which was paid to those who lived downwind of the Nevada Test Site.

Limited Test Ban Treaty
This prohibited nuclear weapons tests, or any other nuclear explosion in the atmosphere, in outer space, and under water.
1963

Nuclear Nonproliferation Treaty
Under the NPT, established by China, France, the UK, USA, and USSR as the designated "Nuclear-Weapon States," Non-Nuclear Weapon States were prohibited from possessing, manufacturing, or acquiring nuclear weapons or other nuclear explosives.
1968

Strategic Arms Limitation Treaty
SALT I froze the number of strategic ballistic missile launchers at the current level.
1972

Strategic Arms Reduction Treaty
START I reduced the number of US and Soviet long-range missiles and nuclear warheads that could be deployed from 10,000 per side to 6,000 per side.
1991

Climate Change

American Perceptions

Percentage who agreed with statement

Political differences

2009 & 2010

— Democrats
— Independents
— Republicans

Global warming is happening

81%
57%
47%

Am not at all worried by it

34%
20%
7%

The US should join other countries to set standards to address climate change

66%
53%
47%

Gender differences

2001–08

— women
— men

Percentage who said they believed that:

Human activities are the cause of climate change

64%
56%

Climate change will threaten our way of life

37%
28%

THE OVERWHELMING INTERNATIONAL SCIENTIFIC CONSENSUS is that the planet is warming and its climate is changing, that the consequences will range from disruptive to catastrophic, and that the cause is human-produced greenhouse gases (carbon dioxide primarily, but also methane and other minor gases). The US Global Change Research Program, the coordinating federal body for climate change research, echoes these findings in its 2009 report, which unambiguously concludes that: evidence of global warming is unequivocal and is primarily human-induced; climate-related changes are already underway; and widespread climate-related impacts are already occurring and will get worse, some of them rapidly.

Industrialized countries in general, and the US in particular, bear the largest share of responsibility for greenhouse gas emissions through massive burning of fossil fuels for power and transportation. Some developing countries, notably China, are now becoming major greenhouse gas emitters in their own right as they emulate the western model of economic growth and model their consumption habits on American and European norms.

Key climate change impacts in the USA

Those already underway and key predictions of the US Global Change Research Project *2009*

NORTHWEST

• declining snowpack and water supply • increasing wildfires • salmon threatened by rising water temperatures • land loss due to sea-level rises

HAWAII

• reduced freshwater availability • sea-level rise • storms intensify • coastal and marine ecosystems severely disrupted

ALASKA

• hotter, drier summers • wildfires and insect problems increase • permafrost thawing • shifts in marine species • lakes decline in area • sea-level rise

SOUTHWEST

• water supplies scarce • increasing drought and wildfires • invasive species increase • increased flooding • unique tourist and recreational sites deteriorated • unique ecosystems threatened

---

Greenhouse gases

Emitted by the US *2008*

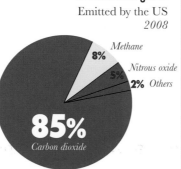

85% Carbon dioxide
8% Methane
5% Nitrous oxide
2% Others

Major sources of emissions

In the US *2008*

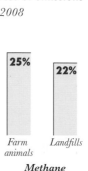

40% Electricity production
30% Transportation

Carbon dioxide

25% Farm animals
22% Landfills

Methane

21
Australia

A peculiar climate change denial movement has been forged in the past decade in the US. A few key conservative financiers and energy companies, along with right-wing popularizers, have launched ambitious campaigns to produce uncertainty and doubt in the minds of many Americans about climate change and our responsibility for it. This seems to be having some effect: the proportion of Americans who believe that climate change is occurring and that humans are the cause has dropped significantly in recent years.

At the policy level, the US has been a poor partner to its industrial allies in crafting international solutions to climate change. While governments in Germany, Japan, and Spain, for example, have put ambitious greenhouse gas control plans into motion, the US official policy response has been timid and tepid at best, and obstructionist at worst.

Climate-change deniers

Koch Industries
Gave $24.9 million from 2005–08 to promote climate change denial organizations.

EXXONMOBIL
$10 million to denial organizations 2005–08.

Americans for Prosperity
Sponsors conferences and promotes a No Climate Tax Pledge.

Institute for Energy Research
Pro-oil, anti-carbon taxes.

ClimateDepot.com, and its parent organization, the **Committee for a Constructive Tomorrow**
Main purpose to "debunk" climate change, and fight "junk global warming science."

Heartland Institute
"Fighting global warming extremism."

Heritage Foundation
"The only consensus over the threat of climate change that seems to exist these days is that there is no consensus."

Atlas Economic Research Foundation
Funds climate change denial overseas.

Cato Institute
"Protecting the environment without sacrificing economic liberty."

George Marshall Institute
Debunking 'bad' climate science

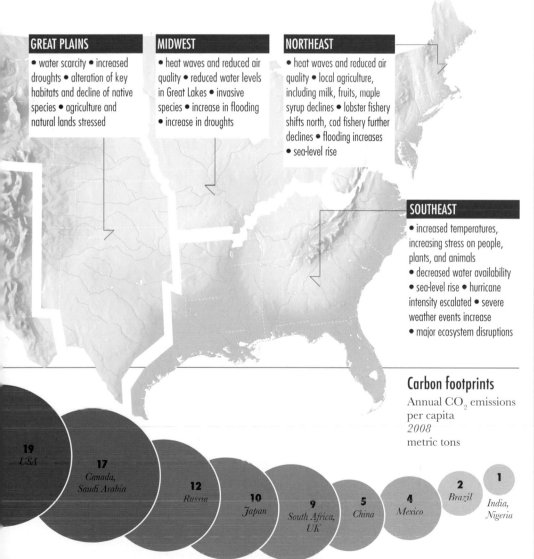

GREAT PLAINS
• water scarcity • increased droughts • alteration of key habitats and decline of native species • agriculture and natural lands stressed

MIDWEST
• heat waves and reduced air quality • reduced water levels in Great Lakes • invasive species • increase in flooding • increase in droughts

NORTHEAST
• heat waves and reduced air quality • local agriculture, including milk, fruits, maple syrup declines • lobster fishery shifts north, cod fishery further declines • flooding increases • sea-level rise

SOUTHEAST
• increased temperatures, increasing stress on people, plants, and animals • decreased water availability • sea-level rise • hurricane intensity escalated • severe weather events increase • major ecosystem disruptions

Carbon footprints
Annual CO_2 emissions per capita
2008
metric tons

19 *USA*

17 *Canada, Saudi Arabia*

12 *Russia*

10 *Japan*

9 *South Africa, UK*

5 *China*

4 *Mexico*

2 *Brazil*

1 *India, Nigeria*

Playing Well With Others

ALL OF US INHABITING THIS SMALL PLANET are more than ever interdependent. Scientists from the United States routinely collaborate with colleagues in Germany and India. American baseball scouts look to the Dominican Republic, Venezuela, and Japan for promising rookies. Public health officials have to think globally. American college students study abroad thanks to agreements between colleges in the United States, Mexico, Spain, and the UK, among dozens of others.

There is a growing recognition that few problems can be effectively tackled by any country acting in isolation. Protecting whales, preventing toxic dumping, promoting air safety and sustainable agriculture, halting the sex trafficking of women, rolling back the devastation of AIDS – each requires intense webs of awareness, information, cooperation, enforcement, and accountability. The result has been a burgeoning number of international agencies, treaties, and social movements. Each has been a work-in-progress, and the US is seen as a key player.

Most favored countries

Percentage of Americans who have a favorable view of each country
2009

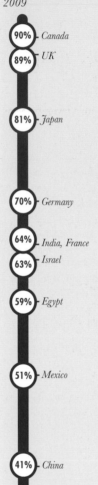

- 90% – Canada
- 89% – UK
- 81% – Japan
- 70% – Germany
- 64% – India, France
- 63% – Israel
- 59% – Egypt
- 51% – Mexico
- 41% – China

Where is that?

Percentage of Americans aged 18 to 24 years who could not find these countries on a map
2009

Afghanistan: **88%**

Iraq: **63%**

Major international organizations of which USA is a member

United Nations Security Council

With five permanent and 10 rotating member governments, its mandate is to prevent conflicts that endanger international security.

Permanent members, who have power of veto

China
France
Russia
UK
USA

The US contributes **22%** of the UN's budget – the most of any member

North Atlantic Treaty Organization (NATO)

Originally a military alliance to defend Europe against the USSR, NATO, headquartered in Brussels, has now grown to 28 members.

Albania
Belgium
Bulgaria
Canada
Croatia
Czech Republic
Denmark
Estonia
France
Germany
Greece
Hungary
Iceland
Italy
Latvia
Lithuania
Luxembourg
Netherlands
Norway
Poland
Portugal
Romania
Slovakia
Slovenia
Spain
Turkey
UK
USA

International Monetary Fund (IMF)

Established in 1945, its 187 member states monitor the international economy and make loans with stringent conditions to those governments with weak economies.

Those members with more than 1% voting rights

Australia
Belgium
Brazil
Canada
China
France
Germany
India
Italy
South Korea
Mexico
Netherlands
Russia
Saudi Arabia
Spain
Sweden
Switzerland
UK
USA
Venezuela

Group of 8 (G8)

With no official staff or authority, the heads of these leading industrialized countries meet informally to discuss international issues such as energy, finance and trade.

Germany
France
Italy
UK
Japan
Canada
Russia
USA
a representative of the European Union

Group of 20 (G20)

The finance ministers and central bankers from 20 wealthy countries meet annually to foster international economic and financial cooperation.

Countries in G8, plus

Argentina
Australia
Brazil
China
India
Indonesia
Mexico
Saudi Arabia
South Africa
South Korea
Turkey
the EU

The US government was one of the founders of the post-World War II triad of institutions designed to prevent a third world war: the United Nations, the International Monetary Fund, and the World Bank. It has been especially supportive of inter-governmental efforts to ensure competitive markets, to end the hunting of whales, and to stop sex trafficking of women. It is now among the largest public donors to global anti-HIV/AIDS campaigns.

And yet, many Americans remain wary of their country joining any international organization or ratifying any multi-government agreement in which the US government doesn't call the shots. Thus, while most Americans take for granted that US membership in the military alliance the North Atlantic Treaty Organization (NATO) serves their self-interest, they have not pressed Washington to join the new permanent war crimes tribunal, the International Criminal Court (ICC). This wary attitude towards multilateral action dismays and puzzles people in other countries – people who admire Americans for many of their values and actions, but see them today as obstructing genuine efforts to grapple with urgent global challenges.

International treaties

Under the US Constitution, an international treaty is ratified only when it has been signed by the President and ratified by a two-thirds majority of the Senate. Bilateral treaties, between the US and one other country, have been far easier to pass than more complicated, multilateral treaties, the terms of which have been hammered out by a number of governments.

Before 2000, the US ratified a number of multilateral treaties, among them the Geneva Conventions on the treatment of prisoners of war, the Convention Against Torture, and the Worldwide Chemical Weapons Convention. But since 2000, the only multilateral treaty to have been signed and ratified by the US has been the International Convention on Cybercrime, in 2006.

Some international treaties NOT ratified by the US 2010	Number of countries that have ratified treaty 2010	Other notable countries that have also not ratified	
The Convention on the Elimination of All Forms of Discrimination Against Women (1979)	**186**	Iran Somalia	Sudan
The Convention on the Rights of the Child (1989)	**192**	Somalia	
The Convention on the Prohibition of the Use, Stockpiling, Production and Transfer of Anti-Personnel Mines and on their Destruction (1997)	**156**	China India North Korea	Russia Saudi Arabia South Korea
The Rome Statute creating the International Criminal Court (1998)	**111**	Cuba China Egypt Iran Iraq Israel	Russia Rwanda Somalia Sudan Syria Vietnam

How others see the US

Percentage of those with a favorable view of the US
2010

94% – Kenya

81% – Nigeria

79% – South Korea

74% – Poland

73% – France

66% – India, Japan

65% – UK

62% – Brazil

58% – China

57% – Russia

56% – Mexico

42% – Argentina

21% – Jordan

17% – Egypt, Pakistan, Turkey

Culture Abroad

GLOBALIZATION ISN'T NEW TO AMERICA. Americans were shipping cotton, cod, and tobacco overseas before the colonies became a nation. What is new is the far-flung reach of American products, their market dominance, and their multiplicity: TV talk-show host Oprah has devoted fans in Australia and Saudi Arabia; Starbucks supplies a haven for coffee drinkers in Tokyo; Hollywood produces "world films" with lots of action and minimal dialogue to attract movie-goers in non-English-speaking countries.

The allure of such an array of American popular culture products is indeed a tribute to the country's entrepreneurial energy, marketing savvy, and perpetual innovation. Americans traveling abroad may be comforted by the sight of brands that surround them back home. Spotting a McDonald's in Santiago or seeing local teenagers in Moscow wearing Levis confirms a sense of US prominence, even though their local consumers may actually infuse them with their own meanings; people all over the world don baseball caps without caring about balls and strikes. Similarly, Americans import as well as export products that shape our collective taste: pizza, after all, did not originate in the US; yoga has its roots in India; Agatha Christie, the Beatles, and Harry Potter are among Britain's gifts to Americans.

A Hollywood film, *The Chronicles of Narnia: The Voyage of the Dawn Treader*, was simultaneously the top box-office gross earner in

35

countries
during the week of
December 5–12, 2010

Starbucks *2010*

200 stores in mainland China, which account for

70% of all Chinese coffee shop sales

McDonald's *2010*

32,000 restaurants
117 countries
1.7m employees

The very success that aggressive American commercial companies have in promoting their products on a massive scale in other countries, pushing aside local competitors, generates not just admiration and desire, but also anxiety and resentment. Mexicans may shop at the new Walmart, but don't want their own shopkeepers to go bankrupt. French and Canadian movie-goers might enjoy the latest Hollywood blockbuster, but remain committed to the continued vitality of their own film makers.

Global trade today is not conducted on a level playing field. American producers not only have more capital at their disposal than do those in most other countries, they have the potent backing of the US government. It pushes hard to ensure that other countries accept American products, even if that acceptance jeopardizes locally valued commercial and artistic sectors. Thus, when we see a Burger King opening in Shanghai or re-runs of *The Sopranos* playing on foreign TV channels, we should pause and wonder whether we are witnessing the newest steps on the road to progress, or the next bricks in the wall of cultural homogenization.

Barbies

The number owned by the average girl aged 3 to 11 years *2007*

10

7

5

USA   Italy, UK   France, Germany

Since 1959

1 billion
Barbies
have been sold
in over 150 countries

The world drinks Cola

Consumption of beverages produced by Coca Cola
2009
number of servings (8 fl oz) per capita per year

over 400

301 – 400

201 – 300

101 – 200

1 – 99

Highest: Mexico 665

Walmart

Number of stores owned by company in country or region
2009

☐ 100 stores
☐ 10 stores

Canada **318**

USA **4,258**

Mexico **1,197**

Puerto Rico **56**

Central America **502**

Chile **197**

Argentina **28**

Brazil **345**

UK **358**

China **243**

Japan **371**

Walmart's

2.1m
workers make it
the world's largest
employer

103

ALASKA

WASHINGTON

OREGON

IDAHO

MONTANA

NORTH
DAKOTA

SOUTH DAKOTA

WYOMING

NEBRASKA

NEVADA

UTAH

COLORADO

KANSAS

CALIFORNIA

ARIZONA

NEW MEXICO

OKLAHOMA

TEXAS

NORTHERN
MARIANA
ISLANDS

GUAM

AMERICAN
SAMOA

MICRONESIA

HAWAII

State Profiles

Federal spending

Federal spending per capita
Fiscal Year 2009

$12,000 – $20,351	
$10,000 – $11,999	
$8,000 – $9,999	
$4,690 – $7,999	

National average: $10,396
Highest: Alaska $20,351
Lowest state: Nevada $7,148
Lowest territory: Micronesia $2,530

The United States is a political federation, a collection of states tenuously united by a national purpose and a federal government. Tensions between states' rights and federalism have shaped the US since the earliest days of its founding. Ironically, some of the strongest advocates of the rights of states are from states that are the most dependent on federal support. More than 30 states receive more money from federal government expenditures than they send to the federal government in tax revenues. New Mexico, Mississippi and Alaska are the top winners in this exchange: they receive about $2 in federal spending for every $1 in taxes they send to the federal government.

About 30% of federal expenditure in the states is distributed using census population and income data as a guide. Medicaid funding, for example, is allocated to states based on the size of their poor populations and their Medicaid income limits. The other 70% comes in special allotments, wages of federal employees, earmarks, grants, support to businesses, subsidies, including agricultural, transportation, and research & development subsidies, funds flowing through federal agencies that perform their work in the states including military facilities, highway building, housing support, and emergency assistance.

PUERTO RICO   US VIRGIN ISLANDS

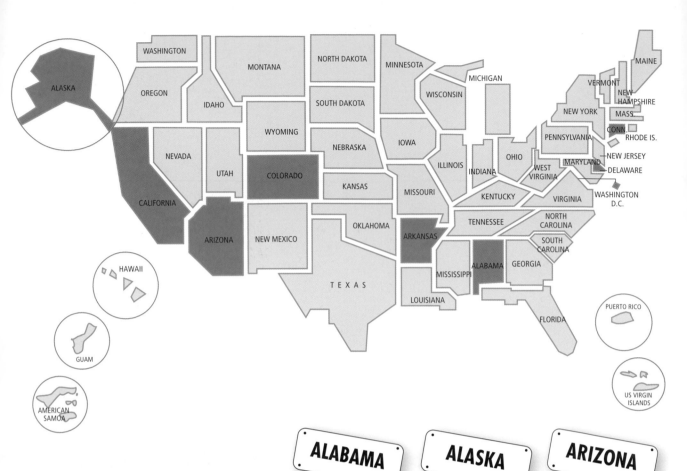

	ALABAMA	ALASKA	ARIZONA
Land area	**52,419** sq miles	**663,267** sq miles	**113,998** sq miles
Total GDP	**$169.9** billion	**$45.7** billion	**$256.4** billion
Total population	**4,779,736**	**710,231**	**6,392,017**
White, not Hispanic or Latino	**67.9**%	**65.0**%	**57.1**%
Black alone	**26.1**%	**3.9**%	**3.9**%
American Indian and Alaska Native alone	**0.5**%	**13.2**%	**4.5**%
Asian alone	**1.1**%	**4.8**%	**2.5**%
Native Hawaiian and other Pacific Islander alone	**0.0**%	**0.8**%	**0.2**%
Hispanic or Latino origin	**2.9**%	**6.1**%	**30.1**%
Percentage of people over age 65	**13.8**%	**7.4**%	**13.1**%
Median household income	**$40,489**	**$66,953**	**$48,745**
Poverty rate (official)	**17.5**%	**9.0**%	**16.5**%
Physicians (nonfederal) per 10,000 people	**27**	**26**	**29**
High school completion rate	**82**%	**91**%	**84**%
People under correctional control	**3.09**%	**2.77**%	**3.03**%
People living in households with guns	**57**%	**61**%	**36**%
Women as representatives in state legislature	**12**%	**20**%	**31**%
Walmart Supercenters	**92**	**6**	**71**
Starbucks (company-operated and licensed)	**63**	**38**	**387**
Farmland	**8,950,000** acres	**890,000** acres	**26,100,000** acres
Hogs	**175,000**	**900**	**165,000**

	ARKANSAS	CALIFORNIA	COLORADO
Land area	53,179 sq miles	163,696 sq miles	104,094 sq miles
Total GDP	$101.8 billion	$1.9 trillion	$252.7 billion
Total population	2,915,918	37,253,956	5,029,196
White, not Hispanic or Latino	75.0%	41.5%	70.5%
Black alone	15.5%	6.1%	3.9%
American Indian and Alaska Native alone	0.6%	0.8%	1.0%
Asian alone	1.1%	12.5%	2.6%
Native Hawaiian and other Pacific Islander alone	0.1%	0.4%	0.1%
Hispanic or Latino origin	5.6%	36.6%	20.2%
Percentage of people over age 65	14.3%	11.2%	10.4%
Median household income	$37,823	$58,931	$55,430
Poverty rate (official)	18.8%	14.2%	12.9%
Physicians (nonfederal) per 10,000 people	25	34	33
High school completion rate	82%	81%	89%
People under correctional control	3.41%	2.76%	3.46%
People living in households with guns	58%	20%	35%
Women as representatives in state legislature	24%	28%	37%
Walmart Supercenters	68	76	60
Starbucks (company-operated and licensed)	34	2394	409
Farmland	13,700,000 acres	25,400,000 acres	31,300,000 acres
Hogs	280,000	80,000	730,000

	CONNECTICUT	DELAWARE	DISTRICT OF COLUMBIA
Land area	5,543 sq miles	2,489 sq miles	68 sq miles
Total GDP	$227.4 billion	$60.6 billion	$99.1 billion
Total population	3,574,097	897,934	601,723
White, not Hispanic or Latino	72.8%	67.4%	33.3%
Black alone	9.6%	20.8%	53.2%
American Indian and Alaska Native alone	0.3%	0.3%	0.3%
Asian alone	3.5%	3.1%	2.9%
Native Hawaiian and other Pacific Islander alone	0.0%	0.0%	0.1%
Hispanic or Latino origin	12.0%	6.8%	8.6%
Percentage of people aged over age 65	13.8%	14.2%	11.7%
Median household income	$67,034	$56,860	$59,290
Poverty rate (official)	9.4%	10.8%	18.4%
Physicians (nonfederal) per 10,000 people	47	33	91
High school completion rate	89%	87%	87%
People under correctional control	3.07%	3.77%	4.82%
People living in households with guns	16%	27%	5%
Women as representatives in state legislature	32%	24%	23%
Walmart Supercenters	5	5	0
Starbucks (company-operated and licensed)	109	21	78
Farmland	400,000 acres	500,000 acres	0 acres
Hogs	3,100	9,000	0

	FLORIDA	GEORGIA	HAWAII
Land area	65,755 sq miles	59,425 sq miles	10,931 sq miles
Total GDP	$737.0 billion	$395.2 billion	$66.4 billion
Total population	18,801,310	9,687,653	1,360,301
White, not Hispanic or Latino	59.3%	57.3%	24.9%
Black alone	15.6%	30.0%	2.3%
American Indian and Alaska Native alone	0.3%	0.2%	0.3%
Asian alone	2.4%	3.0%	37.1%
Native Hawaiian and other Pacific Islander alone	0.0%	0.1%	8.8%
Hispanic or Latino origin	21.0%	8.0%	8.7%
Percentage of people over age 65	17.3%	10.3%	14.7%
Median household income	$44,736	$47,590	$64,098
Poverty rate (official)	14.9%	16.5%	10.4%
Physicians (nonfederal) per 10,000 people	35	26	39
High school completion rate	85%	84%	90%
People under correctional control	3.22%	7.92%	3.15%
People living in households with guns	26%	41%	10%
Women as representatives in state legislature	24%	19%	33%
Walmart Supercenters	174	132	0
Starbucks (company-operated and licensed)	583	268	93
Farmland	9,250,000 acres	10,400,000 acres	1,110,000 acres
Hogs	20,000	230,000	13,000

	IDAHO	ILLINOIS	INDIANA
Land area	83,570 sq miles	57,914 sq miles	36,418 sq miles
Total GDP	$54.0 billion	$630.4 billion	$262.6 billion
Total population	1,567,582	12,830,632	6,483,802
White, not Hispanic or Latino	84.4%	64.4%	82.6%
Black alone	0.7%	14.5%	8.8%
American Indian and Alaska Native alone	1.5%	0.2%	0.2%
Asian alone	1.1%	4.4%	1.4%
Native Hawaiian and other Pacific Islander alone	0.1%	0.0%	0.0%
Hispanic or Latino origin	10.2%	15.2%	5.2%
Percentage of people over age 65	12.0%	12.4%	12.9%
Median household income	$44,926	$53,966	$45,424
Poverty rate (official)	14.3%	13.3%	14.4%
Physicians (nonfederal) per 10,000 people	23	35	28
High school completion rate	88%	86%	87%
People under correctional control	5.71%	2.61%	3.80%
People living in households with guns	57%	20%	39%
Women as representatives in state legislature	25%	28%	21%
Walmart Supercenters	19	106	87
Starbucks (company-operated and licensed)	52	539	186
Farmland	11,400,000 acres	26,700,000 acres	14,800,000 acres
Hogs	33,000	4,350,000	3,550,000

	IOWA	KANSAS	KENTUCKY
Land area	56,272 sq miles	82,277 sq miles	40,409 sq miles
Total GDP	$142.3 billion	$124.9 billion	$156.6 billion
Total population	3,046,355	2,853,118	4,339,367
White, not Hispanic or Latino	89.9%	79.8%	87.2%
Black alone	2.5%	5.6%	7.5%
American Indian and Alaska Native alone	0.4%	0.8%	0.2%
Asian alone	1.5%	2.2%	1.0%
Native Hawaiian and other Pacific Islander alone	0.0%	0.1%	0.0%
Hispanic or Latino origin	4.2%	9.1%	2.4%
Percentage of people over age 65	14.8%	13.0%	13.2%
Median household income	$48,044	$47,817	$40,072
Poverty rate (official)	11.8%	13.4%	18.6%
Physicians (nonfederal) per 10,000 people	28	30	29
High school completion rate	91%	90%	82%
People under correctional control	1.85%	1.88%	2.83%
People living in households with guns	44%	44%	48%
Women as representatives in state legislature	23%	29%	15%
Walmart Supercenters	49	53	74
Starbucks (company-operated and licensed)	51	68	85
Farmland	30,800,000 acres	46,200,000 acres	14,000,000 acres
Hogs	19,900,000	1,740,000	350,000

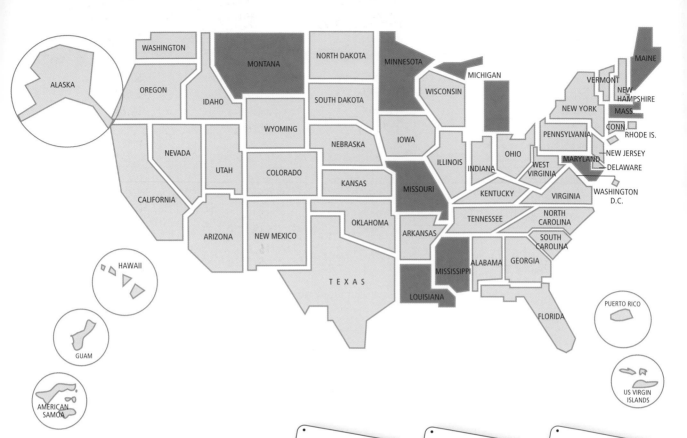

	LOUISIANA	MAINE	MARYLAND
Land area	51,840 sq miles	35,385 sq miles	12,407 sq miles
Total GDP	$208.4 billion	$51.3 billion	$286.8 billion
Total population	4,533,372	1,328,361	5,773,552
White, not Hispanic or Latino	61.3%	94.2%	56.6%
Black alone	32.0%	1.3%	29.0%
American Indian and Alaska Native alone	0.5%	0.5%	0.3%
Asian alone	1.5%	0.9%	5.1%
Native Hawaiian and other Pacific Islander alone	0.0%	0.0%	0.0%
Hispanic or Latino origin	3.4%	1.3%	6.7%
Percentage of people over age 65	12.3%	15.5%	12.1%
Median household income	$42,492	$45,734	$69,272
Poverty rate (official)	17.3%	12.3%	9.1%
Physicians (nonfederal) per 10,000 people	31	41	48
High school completion rate	82%	90%	88%
People under correctional control	3.89%	1.23%	3.67%
People living in households with guns	46%	41%	22%
Women as representatives in state legislature	15%	29%	31%
Walmart Supercenters	80	16	15
Starbucks (company-operated and licensed)	68	27	216
Farmland	8,050,000 acres	1,350,000 acres	2,050,000 acres
Hogs	11,000	4,400	31,000

	MASSACHUSETTS	MICHIGAN	MINNESOTA
Land area	10,555 sq miles	96,716 sq miles	86,939 sq miles
Total GDP	$365.2 billion	$368.4 billion	$260.7 billion
Total population	6,547,629	9,883,640	5,303,925
White, not Hispanic or Latino	78.2%	77.3%	84.7%
Black alone	6.3%	13.9%	4.4%
American Indian and Alaska Native alone	0.1%	0.5%	1.0%
Asian alone	5.0%	2.4%	3.7%
Native Hawaiian and other Pacific Islander alone	0.0%	0.0%	0.1%
Hispanic or Latino origin	8.6%	4.1%	4.1%
Percentage of people over age 65	13.6%	13.4%	12.7%
Median household income	$64,081	$45,255	$55,616
Poverty rate (official)	10.3%	16.2%	11.0%
Physicians (nonfederal) per 10,000 people	57	37	36
High school completion rate	89%	88%	92%
People under correctional control	4.10%	3.65%	3.85%
People living in households with guns	13%	40%	45%
Women as representatives in state legislature	26%	25%	35%
Walmart Supercenters	11	78	48
Starbucks (company-operated and licensed)	203	220	123
Farmland	510,000 acres	10,000,000 acres	26,900,000 acres
Hogs	10,000	980,000	7,500,000

	MISSISSIPPI	MISSOURI	MONTANA
Land area	48,430 sq miles	69,704 sq miles	147,042 sq miles
Total GDP	$95.9 billion	$239.8 billion	$36.0 billion
Total population	2,967,297	5,988,927	989,415
White, not Hispanic or Latino	58.2%	81.8%	87.6%
Black alone	37.1%	11.2%	0.3%
American Indian and Alaska Native alone	0.5%	0.3%	6.7%
Asian alone	0.8%	1.5%	0.5%
Native Hawaiian and other Pacific Islander alone	0.0%	0.1%	0.0%
Hispanic or Latino origin	2.2%	3.2%	3.0%
Percentage of people over age 65	12.7%	13.7%	14.5%
Median household income	$36,646	$45,229	$42,322
Poverty rate (official)	21.9%	14.6%	15.1%
Physicians (nonfederal) per 10,000 people	22	33	30
High school completion rate	80%	87%	91%
People under correctional control	2.61%	2.81%	2.28%
People living in households with guns	54%	45%	61%
Women as representatives in state legislature	14%	21%	26%
Walmart Supercenters	60	102	11
Starbucks (company-operated and licensed)	23	145	19
Farmland	11,000,000 acres	29,100,000 acres	60,800,000 acres
Hogs	375,000	3,150,000	175,000

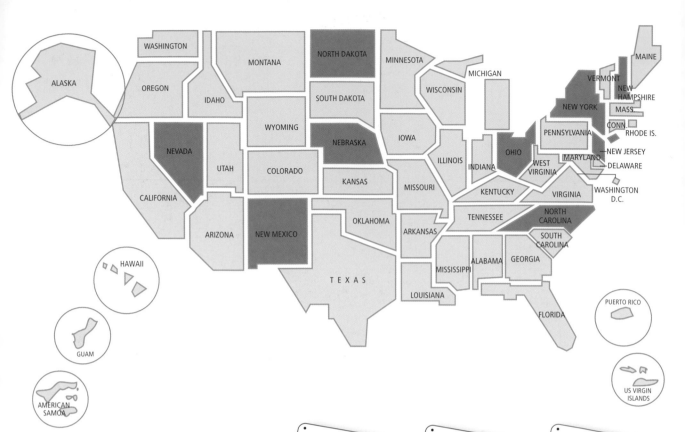

	NEBRASKA	NEVADA	NEW HAMPSHIRE
Land area	77,354 sq miles	110,561 sq miles	9,350 sq miles
Total GDP	$86.4 billion	$126.5 billion	$59.4 billion
Total population	1,826,341	2,700,551	1,316,470
White, not Hispanic or Latino	83.3%	55.6%	92.7%
Black alone	4.3%	7.7%	1.3%
American Indian and Alaska Native alone	0.9%	1.2%	0.2%
Asian alone	1.7%	6.6%	1.9%
Native Hawaiian and other Pacific Islander alone	0.1%	0.5%	0.0%
Hispanic or Latino origin	7.9%	25.7%	2.6%
Percentage of people over age 65	13.4%	11.6%	13.5%
Median household income	$47,357	$53,341	$60,567
Poverty rate (official)	12.3%	12.4%	8.5%
Physicians (nonfederal) per 10,000 people	31	25	38
High school completion rate	90%	84%	91%
People under correctional control	2.26%	2.07%	1.14%
People living in households with guns	42%	32%	31%
Women as representatives in state legislature	20%	32%	37%
Walmart Supercenters	31	28	12
Starbucks (company-operated and licensed)	41	228	23
Farmland	45,600,000 acres	5,900,000 acres	470,000 acres
Hogs	3,350,000	3,500	2,800

	NEW JERSEY	NEW MEXICO	NEW YORK
Land area	8,721 sq miles	121,589 sq miles	54,556 sq miles
Total GDP	$483.0 billion	$74.8 billion	$1.1 trillion
Total population	8,791,894	2,059,179	19,378,102
White, not Hispanic or Latino	60.9%	41.0%	59.7%
Black alone	13.7%	2.2%	15.7%
American Indian and Alaska Native alone	0.3%	9.4%	0.3%
Asian alone	7.8%	1.4%	7.0%
Native Hawaiian and other Pacific Islander alone	0.0%	0.1%	0.0%
Hispanic or Latino origin	16.3%	44.9%	16.7%
Percentage of people over age 65	13.4%	13.2%	13.4%
Median household income	$68,342	$43,028	$54,659
Poverty rate (official)	9.4%	18.0%	14.2%
Physicians (nonfederal) per 10,000 people	41	30	49
High school completion rate	87%	83%	85%
People under correctional control	2.88%	2.85%	1.89%
People living in households with guns	11%	40%	18%
Women as representatives in state legislature	31%	30%	25%
Walmart Supercenters	12	32	65
Starbucks (company-operated and licensed)	208	61	507
Farmland	730,000 acres	43,000,000 acres	7,100,000 acres
Hogs	8,000	2,000	95,000

	NORTH CAROLINA	NORTH DAKOTA	OHIO
Land area	53,819 sq miles	70,700 sq miles	44,825 sq miles
Total GDP	$398.0 billion	$31.9 billion	$471.3 billion
Total population	9,535,483	672,591	11,536,504
White, not Hispanic or Latino	66.7%	89.1%	82.1%
Black alone	21.0%	1.1%	11.8%
American Indian and Alaska Native alone	1.1%	5.7%	0.2%
Asian alone	2.0%	0.8%	1.6%
Native Hawaiian and other Pacific Islander alone	0.0%	0.0%	0.0%
Hispanic or Latino origin	7.4%	2.1%	2.6%
Percentage of people over age 65	12.7%	14.7%	13.9%
Median household income	$43,674	$47,827	$45,395
Poverty rate (official)	16.3%	11.7%	15.2%
Physicians (nonfederal) per 10,000 people	31	30	36
High school completion rate	84%	84%	88%
People under correctional control	2.62%	1.58%	4.03%
People living in households with guns	41%	54%	32%
Women as representatives in state legislature	26%	16%	21%
Walmart Supercenters	123	11	127
Starbucks (company-operated and licensed)	227	10	295
Farmland	8,600,000 acres	39,600,000 acres	13,900,000 acres
Hogs	9,700,000	151,000	1,940,000

	OKLAHOMA	OREGON	PENNSYLVANIA
Land area	69,898 sq miles	98,381 sq miles	46,055 sq miles
Total GDP	$153.8 billion	$165.6 billion	$554.8 billion
Total population	3,751,351	3,831,074	12,702,379
White, not Hispanic or Latino	70.7%	79.4%	80.7%
Black alone	7.3%	1.8%	10.5%
American Indian and Alaska Native alone	6.1%	1.3%	0.1%
Asian alone	1.6%	3.6%	2.5%
Native Hawaiian and other Pacific Islander alone	0.1%	0.4%	0.0%
Hispanic or Latino origin	7.6%	11.0%	4.8%
Percentage of people over age 65	13.4%	13.5%	15.4%
Median household income	$41,664	$48,457	$49,520
Poverty rate (official)	16.2%	14.3%	12.5%
Physicians (nonfederal) per 10,000 people	26	36	42
High school completion rate	86%	89%	88%
People under correctional control	2.41%	3.08%	3.58%
People living in households with guns	45%	40%	37%
Women as representatives in state legislature	11%	28%	15%
Walmart Supercenters	76	17	93
Starbucks (company-operated and licensed)	73	326	285
Farmland	35,100,000 acres	16,400,000 acres	7,750,000 acres
Hogs	2,400,000	20,000	1,120,000

	RHODE ISLAND	SOUTH CAROLINA	SOUTH DAKOTA
Land area	1,545 sq miles	32,020 sq miles	77,116 sq miles
Total GDP	$47.8 billion	$159.6 billion	$38.3 billion
Total population	1,052,567	4,625,364	814,180
White, not Hispanic or Latino	77.7%	64.8%	85.1%
Black alone	6.0%	27.9%	1.0%
American Indian and Alaska Native alone	0.4%	0.3%	8.6%
Asian alone	3.0%	1.3%	1.0%
Native Hawaiian and other Pacific Islander alone	0.0%	0.1%	0.0%
Hispanic or Latino origin	11.6%	4.1%	2.6%
Percentage of people over age 65	14.4%	13.6%	14.4%
Median household income	$54,119	$42,442	$45,043
Poverty rate (official)	11.5%	17.1%	14.2%
Physicians (nonfederal) per 10,000 people	47	28	28
High school completion rate	85%	84%	90%
People under correctional control	3.79%	2.61%	2.52%
People living in households with guns	13%	45%	60%
Women as representatives in state legislature	22%	10%	19%
Walmart Supercenters	2	72	12
Starbucks (company-operated and licensed)	23	74	22
Farmland	70,000 acres	4,900,000 acres	43,700,000 acres
Hogs	1,800	240,000	1,280,000

	TENNESSEE	TEXAS	UTAH
Land area	42,143 sq miles	268,581 sq miles	84,899 sq miles
Total GDP	$244.5 billion	$1.1 trillion	$112.9 billion
Total population	6,346,105	25,145,561	2,763,885
White, not Hispanic or Latino	76.5%	46.6%	81.1%
Black alone	16.5%	11.5%	1.2%
American Indian and Alaska Native alone	0.2%	0.6%	1.1%
Asian alone	1.4%	3.6%	2.0%
Native Hawaiian and other Pacific Islander alone	0.0%	0.1%	0.8%
Hispanic or Latino origin	3.7%	36.5%	12.0%
Percentage of people over age 65	13.3%	10.2%	9.0%
Median household income	$41,725	$48,259	$55,117
Poverty rate (official)	17.1%	17.2%	11.5%
Physicians (nonfederal) per 10,000 people	32	26	26
High school completion rate	83%	80%	90%
People under correctional control	2.49%	4.56%	1.57%
People living in households with guns	46%	36%	45%
Women as representatives in state legislature	18%	24%	22%
Walmart Supercenters	107	305	35
Starbucks (company-operated and licensed)	139	831	57
Farmland	10,900,000 acres	130,400,000 acres	11,100,000 acres
Hogs	205,000	1,120,000	740,000

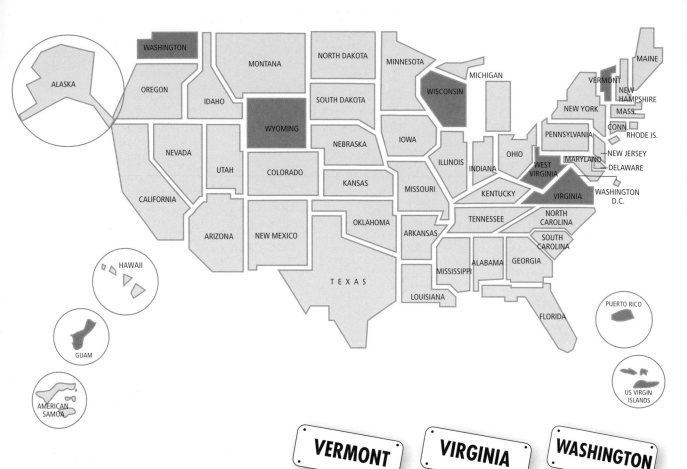

	VERMONT	VIRGINIA	WASHINGTON
Land area	9,614 sq miles	42,774 sq miles	71,300 sq miles
Total GDP	$25.4 billion	$408.4 billion	$338.3 billion
Total population	625,741	8,001,024	6,724,540
White, not Hispanic or Latino	94.8%	66.1%	74.4%
Black alone	0.8%	19.6%	3.4%
American Indian and Alaska Native alone	0.3%	0.3%	1.3%
Asian alone	1.0%	5.0%	6.6%
Native Hawaiian and other Pacific Islander alone	0.0%	0.1%	0.4%
Hispanic or Latino origin	1.4%	6.8%	9.8%
Percentage of people over age 65	14.4%	12.1%	12.0%
Median household income	$51,618	$59,330	$56,548
Poverty rate (official)	11.4%	10.5%	12.3%
Physicians (nonfederal) per 10,000 people	48	33	34
High school completion rate	91%	87%	90%
People under correctional control	2.16%	2.19%	3.33%
People living in households with guns	46%	36%	36%
Women as representatives in state legislature	37%	17%	33%
Walmart Supercenters	0	84	36
Starbucks (company-operated and licensed)	5	368	674
Farmland	1,220,000 acres	8,000,000 acres	14,800,000 acres
Hogs	2,600	350,000	25,000

	WEST VIRGINIA	WISCONSIN	WYOMING
Land area	24,230 sq miles	65,498 sq miles	97,814 sq miles
Total GDP	$63.3 billion	$244.4 billion	$37.5 billion
Total population	1,852,994	5,686,986	563,626
White, not Hispanic or Latino	93.4%	84.5%	86.1%
Black alone	3.1%	6.0%	0.9%
American Indian and Alaska Native alone	0.2%	0.9%	2.6%
Asian alone	0.6%	2.1%	0.7%
Native Hawaiian and other Pacific Islander alone	0.0%	0.0%	0.1%
Hispanic or Latino origin	1.1%	5.1%	7.7%
Percentage of people over age 65	15.8%	13.4%	12.2%
Median household income	$37,435	$49,993	$52,664
Poverty rate (official)	17.7%	12.4%	9.8%
Physicians (nonfederal) per 10,000 people	32	33	25
High school completion rate	83%	90%	92%
People under correctional control	1.48%	2.57%	2.65%
People living in households with guns	58%	44%	63%
Women as representatives in state legislature	16%	22%	18%
Walmart Supercenters	37	65	10
Starbucks (company-operated and licensed)	21	116	15
Farmland	3,700,000 acres	15,200,000 acres	30,100,000 acres
Hogs	7,000	360,000	89,000

	GUAM	PUERTO RICO	US VIRGIN ISLANDS
Land area	212 sq miles	5,325 sq miles	134 sq miles
Total GDP	$2.5 billion	$64.8 billion	$1.6 billion
Total population	180,865	3,725,789	109,750
White, not Hispanic or Latino	0.0%	1.0%	0.0%
Black alone	1.0%	7.1%	76.2%
American Indian and Alaska Native alone	0.0%	0.2%	0.0%
Asian alone	32.5%	0.3%	0.0%
Native Hawaiian and other Pacific Islander alone	44.6%	0.0%	0.0%
Hispanic or Latino origin		74.9%	14.0%
Percentage of people over age 65	7.0%	14.1%	13.6%
Median household income	$41,821	$18,314	$26,925
Poverty rate (official)	0.2%	45.0%	32.0%
Physicians (nonfederal) per 10,000 people		32	
High school completion rate	32%	60%	61%
People under correctional control			0.0%
People living in households with guns		0%	
Women as representatives in state legislature	27%	24%	7%
Walmart Supercenters	0	7	0
Starbucks (company-operated and licensed)	n/a	3	
Farmland	1,000 acres	470,000 acres	5,881 acres
Hogs	635	69,892	1,125

Sources

14–15 Who We Are
Vital statistics
US Census 2009, American Community Survey, Tables BO2001; C02005; B01001; B03001. www.census.gov
Who we live with
US Census 2009, American Community Survey, Table C09016. www.census.gov
Racial/ethnic segregation
 Black-White residential segregation
 Racial/ethnic breakdown
New Racial Segregation Measures for States and Large Metropolitan Areas: Analysis of the 2005–2009 American Community Survey. censusscope.org
A country of citizens
US Census 2009, American Community Survey, Table C05001. www.census.gov
Well-being
Gallup-Healthways Index. www.well-beingindex.com [accessed Dec 20, 2010]
Are you gay?
National Gay & Lesbian Task Force, How Big is the LGBT Community? April 2010. www.thetaskforce.org
What class we think we are
ABC News, The Comeback: New Poll Shows Concerns of American Middle Class; March 15, 2010. abcnews.go.com
38% of Americans consider themselves…
Lydia Saad, Ideologically, Where is the US Moving? Nearly 4 in 10 Americans Say Their Views Have Grown More Conservative. Gallup Poll; July 6, 2009. www.gallup.com
Ancestry
US Census 2009, American Community Survey, Table B04003. www.census.gov

16–17 Indian Country
Number of Americans…
US Census Bureau. www.census.gov
Percentage of Native Americans…
Stella U. Ogunwole, We The People: American Indians and Alaska Natives in the United States. US Census Bureau; Feb 2006. www.census.gov
Indigenous peoples
American Samoa
US Department of the Interior, Office of Insular Affairs. www.doi.gov
Alaska
US Census Bureau, State & County QuickFacts. quickfacts.census.gov
Alaska Department of Natural Resources, Fact Sheet: Land Ownership in Alaska; March 2000. dnr.alaska.gov
What Percentage of Land in Alaska Does the Government Own? www.answerbag.com
Guam
CIA, The World Factbook, 2011. www.cia.gov
2004 Guam Statistical Yearbook. www.spc.int
Hawaii
Gale Courey Toensing, US Supremes Rule Against Native Hawaiians' Land Claims; April 5, 2009. www.indiancountrytoday.com
US Census Bureau. State & County QuickFacts. quickfacts.census.gov
Northern Mariana Islands
Edward Pangelinan, Covenant Provision on Land Alienation Restriction in NMI. Saipan Tribune; Dec 11, 2009. www.saipantribune.com
US Department of the Interior, Office of Insular Affairs. www.doi.gov
Puerto Rico
The Puerto Rico Encyclopedia. www.encyclopediapr.org
US Virgin Islands
US Virgin Islands, New World Encyclopedia. www.newworldencyclopedia.org
Land Loss
Francis Paul Prucha, Atlas of American Indian Affairs.

Lincoln, NE: University of Nebraska Press; 1990. pp. 22–30.
What's left
Indian Reservations in the Continental United States. www.nps.gov
US Census Bureau, Cartographic Boundary Files, American Indian Reservations and American Indian Off-ReservationTrust Lands. www.census.gov

18–19 American Empire
Population
CIA World Factbook, 2010. www.cia.gov
The US overseas
US Department of State, Dependencies and Areas of Special Sovereignty Fact Sheet. Bureau of Intelligence and Research, Washington, DC; Dec 18, 2007. www.state.gov
US Department of the Interior, Office of Insular Affairs. www.doi.gov
US Fish & Wildlife Service. www.fws.gov
CIA World Factbook, 2010. www.cia.gov
Jana Lipman, Guantanamo: A Working-Class History Between Empire and Revolution. Princeton: Princeton University Press; 2009.
Pacific Remote Islands National Wildlife Refuge Complex. www.fws.gov
Baker Island National Wildlife Refuge, Draft Comprehensive Conservation Plan and Environmental Assessment; 2007. www.fws.gov
Ronald Reagan Ballistic Missile Defense Test Site. www.smdc.army.mil
Interagency Group on Insular Areas, 2007 Annual Report. Office of Insular Affairs, US Department of Interior, Washington, DC; 2007. www.doi.gov
Interagency Group on Insular Affairs, 2008 Annual Report. Office of Insular Affairs, US Department of Interior, Washington, DC; 2008. www.doi.gov
GAO, US Insular Areas: Application of the US Constitution. Report to the Committee of Resources, House of Representatives; 1997.
Websites of the governments of American Samoa, Guam, Commonwealth of Northern Mariana Islands (CNMI), US Virgin Islands, and the Commonwealth of Puerto Rico.
David Vine, Island of Shame: the Secret History of the US Military Base on Diego Garcia. Princeton: Princeton University Press; 2009.

20–21 This Land is Our Land
Mark Sigmon, Hunting and Posting on Private Land in America. Duke Law Journal, 54: 549; 2004.
Land use in USA
Who owns America?
Economic Research Service, US Department of Agriculture, Major Uses of Land in the United States; 2002. www.ers.usda.gov
Public lands
Natural Resources Council of Maine, Public Land Ownership by State. www.nrcm.org
Map based on a design by Big Think. bigthink.com/ideas/21343
The Land Report, America's Top 100 Landowners; Fall 2010. www.landreport.com
What Percentage of Land in Alaska Does the Government Own? www.answerbag.com
Making a killing
Where hunters hunt
Top 5 hunting states
US Fish & Wildlife Service, 2006 National Survey of Fishing, Hunting, and Wildlife-Associated Recreation.
Public land, private profit: Mining
GAO, Hardrock Mining: Information on Abandoned Mines and Value and Coverage of Financial Assurances on BLM Land; March 12, 2008. www.gao.org

PEW Campaign for Responsible Mining, Reforming the US Hardrock Mining Law of 1872; 2008. www.pewminingreform.org
Public land, private profit: Grazing
GAO, Livestock grazing: federal expenditures and receipts vary, depending on the agency and the purpose of the fee charged; 2005. www.gao.org

24–25 A Land of Homeowners
Dedrick Muhammad et al, The State of the Dream 2004. Boston: United for a Fair Economy. www.faireconomy.org
George S. Masnick, Homeownership Trends and Racial Inequality in the United States in the 20th Century. Cambridge, MA: Joint Center for Housing Studies, Harvard University; Feb 2001. www.jchs.harvard.edu
William J. Collins, Race and Twentieth-Century American Economic History. National Bureau of Economic Research; Winter 2006. www.nber.org
American attitudes to home ownership
2010 Fannie Mae National Housing Survey. www.fanniemae.com
State of housing
US Census Bureau, Characteristics of Housing, Plumbing Facilities. www.census.gov
12% of Native American houses…
Housing Assistance Council. www.ruralhome.org
How we compare
US National Association of Home Builders. www.nahb.com/
Fionnuala Earley, What Explains the Differences in Home Ownership Rates in Europe? Housing Finance International; Sept 2004. www.housingfinance.org
Soula Proxenos, Homeownership Rates: A Global Perspective. Housing Finance International; Dec, 2004. www.housingfinance.org
Statistics Canada, 2006, 2008 Census: Changing patterns in Canadian Home Ownership and Shelter Costs. www.statcan.gc.ca
Japan Statistical Yearbook 2005. www.stat.go.jp
Most likely to own
US Census Bureau, Housing Vacancy Survey; 2010. Table 15. www.census.gov
How Americans are housed
Dreams come true
US Census Bureau, American Housing Survey; 2007. www.census.gov
Dream on
US Census Bureau, Housing Vacancy Survey; 2010. www.census.gov
Race and homeownership
Urban Institute. www.urban.org

26–27 Dreams Foreclosed
1 in 78 housing units…
1.65 Million Properties Receive Foreclosure Filings in First Half of 2010. www.realtytrac.com
Delinquencies
US Department of Housing & Urban Development, US Housing Market Conditions. www.huduser.org
Triggers
Homeownership Preservation Foundation. www.995hope.org
US Census Bureau, American Housing Survey; 2010. Tables 3–15. www.census.gov
US Census Bureau, 2010 Statistical Abstract. www.census.gov
Foreclosures
Center for Responsible Lending, Foreclosures by Race & Ethnicity: Demographics of a Crisis; June 2010. www.responsiblelending.org
Foreclosures (map)
1.65 Million Properties Receive Foreclosure Filings in First Half of 2010. www.realtytrac.com
75 Percent of Nation's Top Metro Areas Post Increasing Foreclosure Activity in First Half of 2010.

www.realtytrac.com

Who were sold the subprimes?
Allen J. Fishbein Patrick Woodall, *Women are Disproportionately Represented in High-Cost Mortgage Market.* Consumer Federation of America; Dec 2006. www.consumerfed.org

Increase in severely cost-burdened households
The State of the Nation's Housing 2010. Joint Center for Housing Studies, Cambridge, MA: Harvard University; 2010. www.jchs.harvard.edu

Top 10 in trouble
US Census Bureau, American Community Survey, 2010. www.census.org

46% of those renting...
Bureau of Labor, Consumer Expenditure Survey. www.bls.gov

28–29 Homelessness
Who are the homeless?
People seeking shelter services
39% of homeless...
Odds on homelessness
US Department of Housing and Urban Development Office of Community Planning and Development, *The 2009 Annual Homeless Assessment Report;* June 2010. www.hudhre.info
National Law Center on Homelessness & Poverty. www.nlchp.org

Extent of homelessness
National Coalition for the Homeless & National Law Center on Poverty and Homelessness, Homes Not Handcuffs: The Criminalization of Homelessness in US Cities. www.nationalhomeless.org

Public opinion
Lydia Saad and Linda Lyons, Are Women Hardwired for Worry? Gallup Poll; May 10, 2005. www.gallup.com
Linda Lyons, Nation's Hunger, Homelessness Trouble Americans. Gallup Poll; April 12, 2005. www.gallup.com

Assistance for homeless
Nancy Gonter, Number of homeless in hotels decreasing, but Massachusetts still spending close to $1 million a month; April 18, 2010. www.masslive.com
City spending for runaway and homeless youth grows. New York City Independent Budget Office; 2010. www.ibo.nyc.ny.us
US Department of Housing & Urban Development, *Costs Associated with First-Time Homelessness for families and individuals;* March 2010. www.hud.gov

30–31 Religious Identities
Religious identification among racial/ethnic groups
Barry A. Kosmin and Ariela Keysar, *American Religious Identification Survey.* Hartford, Connecticut: Trinity College; 2008. www.americanreligionsurvey-aris.org

Importance of religion
Jeffrey Jones, Asian-Americans Lean Left. Gallup Poll; Feb 3, 2010. www.gallup.com

Religious identification
Kosmin and Keysar, *American Religious Identification Survey.* Op cit.
The PEW Forum on Religion and Public Life, The US Religious Landscape Survey; 2008. pewforum.org

Prejudice towards religious groups
Gallup Center for Muslim Studies, In US, Religious Prejudice Stronger Against Muslims; Jan 21, 2010. www.gallup.com

Dominant religion
Map courtesy of Jon T. Kilpinen, Valparaiso University, US.

Islam
US Government, Bureau of International Information Programs, Muslims in America – A Statistical

Portrait? 2008. www.america.gov [accessed June 12, 2010]

Jews
Jeffrey Jones, Tracking Religious Affiliation, State by State. Gallup Poll; June 24, 2004. www.gallup.com
Kosmin and Keysar, *American Religious Identification Survey.* Op cit.
PEW Forum, The US Religious Landscape Survey. Op cit.

The rise of the "Nones"
Frank Newport, In US, Increasing Number Have No Religious Identity. Gallup Poll; May 21, 2010. www.gallup.com

32–33 God and Politics
The secular state?
Religious beliefs
68% of Americans believed in...
The PEW Forum on Religion and Public Life, The US Religious Landscape Survey; 2008. pewforum.org
Jennifer Robison, The Devil and Demographic Details. Gallup Poll; Feb 23, 2003. www.gallup.com
Frank Newport, On Darwin's Birthday only 4 in 10 believe in Evolution. Gallup Poll; Feb 11, 2009. www.gallup.com
Frank Newport, Republicans, Democrats Differ on Creationism. Gallup Poll; June 20, 2008. www.gallup.com

The great solution
Frank Newport, In US, Increasing Number Have No Religious Identity. Gallup Poll; May 21, 2010. www.gallup.com

Importance of religion
How we compare
Frank Newport, State of the States: Importance of Religion. Gallup Poll; Jan 28, 2009. www.gallup.com
Steve Crabtree and Brett Pelham, What Alabamians and Iranians have in Common. Gallup Poll; Feb 9, 2009. www.gallup.com

34% of Americans described themselves as...
Barry A. Kosmin and Ariela Keysar, *American Religious Identification Survey.* Hartford. Connecticut: Trinity College; 2008. www.americanreligionsurvey-aris.org

Women are more religious
The Pew Forum on Religion & Public Life, The Stronger Sex – Spiritually Speaking. Feb 26, 2009. pewforum.org

Megachurches
Hartford Institute for Religion Research, Profile of Total US Megachurches; 2008. hirr.hartsem.edu
Karl Taro Greenfeld, God Wants Me to Be Rich. *Portfolio.com;* July 15, 2008. www.portfolio.com

Big players in the religious right
Americans United for Separation of Church and State. www.au.org

Political ideology
Frank Newport, Mormons Most Conservative Major Religious Group in the US. Gallup Poll; Jan 11, 2010. www.gallup.com

The sex of faith
The PEW Forum on Religion and Public Life, The US Religious Landscape Survey; 2008. pewforum.org

34–35 The Road to Suffrage
Voting Rights and Citizenship, City University of New York. www1.cuny.edu
Civil Rights Movement Veterans, Voting Rights History: Two Centuries of Struggle. www.crmvet.org
Irene M. Franck and David M. Brownstone, *Women's World: A Timeline of Women in History.* New York: Harper Collins; 1995.
The Sentencing Project, Expanding the Vote: State Felony Disenfranchisement Reform 1997–2008; 2008. www.sentencingproject.org
The Native Vote Alliance of Minnesota. www.nativevotemn.org

Charles A. Kromkowski, African-American Suffrage, in Stanley Kutler, editor, *Dictionary of American History.* New York: Charles Scribner's Sons; 2002.
National Coalition for the Homeless. www.nationalhomeless.org
National Health Care for the Homeless Council. www.nhchc.org
Cesar J. Ayala and Rafael Bernabe, *Puerto Rico in the American Century.* Chapel Hill: University of North Carolina Press; 2007.

36–37 Representatives
Under-representation in state legislatures
National Conference of State Legislatures, Women in State Legislatures: 2009 Legislative Season. www.ncsl.org
National Conference of State Legislatures, Number of Asian American Legislators: 2007–2008 Legislative Season. www.ncsl.org
National Conference of State Legislatures, 2009 Latino Legislators. www.ncsl.org
National Conference of State Legislatures, Number of Native American Legislators: 2009 Legislative Season. www.ncsl.org
National Conference of State Legislatures, Legislator Demographics: State-by-State. www.ncsl.org

Ahead of the curve
National Conference of State Legislatures, Women in State Legislatures: 2009 Legislative Season. www.ncsl.org

People of colour in the Senate and House of Representatives
65 of the 90 women ...
Congressional Quarterly, *Roll Call;* Nov 4, 2010. innovation.cq.com
112th United States Congress. en.wikipedia.org

Let the redistricting begin
Winners and Losers in Census 2010 Appointment; Dec 21, 2010. thatsmycongress.com

Gerrymanders
Gerrymandered districts at www.google.com/images

38–39 Yes We Can!
Gender gap
Center for American Women and Politics, The Gender Gap: Voting Choices in Presidential Elections. Eagleton Institute of Politics, Rutgers University; Dec 2008. www.cawp.rutgers.edu

Turnout
Curtis Gans, African-Americans, Anger, Fear and Youth Propel Turnout to Highest Level Since 1964. *AU News,* American University; Dec 17, 2008. hotlineblog.nationaljournal.com

Turnout according to gender and race/ethnicity
Center for American Women and Politics, Gender Differences in Voter Turn-Out. Eagleton Institute of Politics, Rutgers University; Nov 2009. www.cawp.rutgers.edu

Who voted?
Votes cast
Center for the Study of the American Electorate, American University, Washington DC. www1.american.edu

2008 Presidential Election
Map created by Myriad based on data published in *The Washington Post,* Nov 2008. www.washingtonpost.com

Voting patterns by family income
Voting patterns according to age
Voting patterns by gender and race/ethnicity
National Exit Polls Table. *The New York Times;* Nov 5, 2008. elections.nytimes.com/2008

40–41 Media
Percentage of polled public...
Lymari Morales, Distrust in US Media Edges up to

Record High. Gallup Poll; Sept 29, 2010. www.gallup.com

Univision, the USA's largest...
Pew Project for Excellence in Journalism, Who Owns the News Media? 2010. www.stateofthemedia.org

Largest global book publishers
Philip Jones, Pearson stays on top as world's largest book publisher. *The Bookseller*; June 21, 2010. www.thebookseller.com

Gendered division of labor
Racial division of labor
Bob Papper, 2008 Women and Minorities Survey. Radio Television Digital News Association/Hoftra University; 2008. rtnda.org

Job trends in various media sectors
Institute for Women's Policy Research, *Jobs and Diversity in the Communications and Media Sector*; Aug 2006. www.iwpr.org

64% of US newspapers shrank...
Pew Research Center's Project for Excellence in Journalism, The Changing Newsroom: Changing Content; July 21, 2008. www.journalism.org

Minorities
American Society of Newspaper Editors, ASNE Newsroom Census; 2009. asne.org

Who's the presumed expert?
Media Matters for America, Gender and Ethnic Diversity in Prime-time Cable News; 2008. mediamatters.org

42–43 A Networked Society
Jonathan Adams and Kathleen E. McLaughlin, Silicon Sweatshops. *Global Post*; Nov 17, 2009. www.globalpost.com

A man's world
Claire Cain Miller, Out of the Loop in Silicon Valley. *New York Times*; April 17, 2010. www.nytimes.com

Silicon Valley; Santa Clara county
California County Map. www.counties.org
Santa Clara County. www.sccgov.org
Santa Clara County, California. en.wikipedia.org

Employee profile; eBay
Mike Swift, Blacks, Latinos and Women Lose Ground at Silicon Valley Tech Companies. *San Jose Mercury*; Feb 13, 2010. www.mercurynews.com

Of Wikipedia's total contributors...
Noam Cohen, Define Gender Gap? Look Up Wikipedia's Contributor List, *New York Times*, Jan 31, 2011. www.nytimes.com

Money helps to keep you connected...
Jim Jansen, Use of the Internet in Higher-Income Households. Pew Internet and American Life Project; Nov 24, 2010. www.pewinternet.org

...So does education
Susannah Fox and Gretchen Livingston, Latinos Online. Pew Hispanic Center and Pew Internet and American Life Project; March 27, 2007. www.pewinternet.org

Facebook
Norimitsu Onishi, Internet Grows in Indonesia, as Does a Debate on its Limits. *New York Times*; April 20, 2010. www.nytimes.com

Percentage of Americans who say...
Kristen Purcell, et al., Understanding the Participatory News Consumer. Project for Excellence in Journalism, Pew Research Center; March 1, 2010. www.pewinternet.org

70% of Blacks...
50% of Whites...
Aaron Smith, Technology Trends Among People of Color. Pew Internet and American Life Project; Sept 17, 2010. www.pewinternet.org

42% of Americans...
Mary Madden, Older Adults and Social Media. Pew Internet and American Life Project; Aug 27, 2010. www.pewinternet.org

46–47 The Economy
Foreign direct investment
Marilyn Ibarra-Caton, Direct Investment Positions for 2009 Country and Industry Detail. US Department of Commerce, Bureau of Economic Analysis; July 2010.

Top ten economies
Manufacturing
World Economic Forum, *Global Competitiveness Report 2010-2011*. www.weforum.com

Big movers and little shakers
US Department of Commerce, Bureau of Economic Analysis. www.bea.gov
World Bank Indicators Database; Dec 15, 2010. data.worldbank.org

What American households spend their money on
Consumer Expenditure Survey 2009, Table 48. www.bls.gov

Employment
Bureau of Labor Statistics, Nonfarm Payrolls by Industry Sector. data.bls.gov
Bureau of Labor Statistics, Employment by Industry Sector. www.bls.gov

Made in the USA
Bureau of Labor Statistics, news release: Regional and State Unemployment; Dec 17, 2010. Table 6. www.bls.gov

Manufacturing jobs
Bureau of Labor Statistics, Employment by Industry Sector. Op cit.

48–49 Corporate Life
Bailout loans
Matthew Ericson, Elaine He and Amy Schoenfeld, Tracking the $700 Billion Bailout. *The New York Times*. www.nytimes.com

Most employees
Highest market value
Power centers
Forbes Magazine/CNN, Fortune 500; 2010. money.cnn.com

Largest private contracts in Iraq and Afghanistan
Top Ten Private Contractors in Iraq and Afghanistan 2004–2006. *Boston Globe*. www.boston.com

Big payday for CEOs
AFL-CIO, CEO Pay Database. www.aflcio.org

Overseas tax havens
GAO, GAO-09-157: Large US Corporations with Foreign Subsidiaries; Dec 2008. www.gao.gov

Zero tax
GAO, GAO-08-957, Tax Administration: Comparison of the Reported Tax Liabilities of Foreign- and US-Controlled Corporations; July 2008. www.gao.gov
Forbes.com, What the Top 25 Companies Pay in Taxes; 2010. www.forbes.com

Largest philanthropic foundations
The Foundation Center, Top Funders. foundationcenter.org [accessed Dec 20, 2010]

50–51 Jobs, Jobs, Jobs
"A job is more than a job..."
"For many of our families..."
Bob Herbert, We Haven't Hit Bottom Yet. *New York Times*; Sept 25, 2010. www.nytimes.com
Motoko Rich, For the Unemployed Over 50, Fears of Never Working Again. *New York Times*; Sept 20, 2010. www.nytimes.com

Gender segregation
Ariane Hegewisch, Hannah Liepmann, Jeffrey Hayes, et al., *Separate and Not Equal? Gender Segregation in the Labor Market and the Gender Wage Gap*. Institute for Women's Policy Research; Sept, 2010. www.iwpr

4.7% of all employed...

Unemployment
Who is unemployed?
Hidden unemployed
Bureau of Labor Statistics, news release: The Employment Situation; Sept, 2010 www.bls.gov

Who does what job?
US Bureau of Labor Statistics, *Labor Force Characteristics by Race and Ethnicity 2007*; Sept 2008. Table 5. www.bls.gov

52–53 The Wage Gap
State minimum hourly wage
State minimum wage
US Department of Labor, Wage and Hour Division, Minimum Wage Laws in the States; July 1, 2010. www.dol.gov

Only single, childless women...
Earnings of those with advanced...
Alexandria McMahon and Katie Johnson Chase, Are We There Yet? *Boston Globe*; Oct 24, 2010. www.boston.com

How race and ethnicity affects the wage gap
Gender wage gap
Earnings of surgeons...
Institute for Women's Policy Research, Fact Sheet #C350a; updated April 2010. www.iwpr.org

Wages gap among college-educated
Judy Goldberg Day and Catherine Hill, *Behind the Pay Gap*. American Association of University Women. Table 2. aauw.org

54–55 Poverty and Wealth
How we compare
OECD. StatExtracts, Income Distribution – Inequality. stats.oecd.org

About 14% of adults...
USDA, Economic Research Service, Food Security in the United States: Key Statistics and Graphics. www.ers.usda.gov

Living in poverty
Official poverty thresholds
US Census Bureau, Income, Poverty and Health Insurance in the United States: 2009, Tables and Figures. www.census.gov

Annual income
US Census Bureau, Population Survey 2009, Annual Social and Economic Supplement; Table HINC-01. www.census.gov

Who's poor?
US Census Bureau, 2009 and 2010 Annual Social and Economic Supplements. www.census.gov

Wealthiest Americans
Forbes Magazine, Forbes 400: The Richest People in America. www.forbes.com
Gawker.com, The Forbes 400: A Demographic Background. gawker.com

Zero wealth
Wealth
Insight Center, *Lifting as we Climb: Women of Color, Wealth, and America's Future*; Spring 2010. www.insightcced.org
Edward N. Wolff, *Recent Trends in Household Wealth in the United States: Rising Debt and the Middle-Class Squeeze, an Update to 2007*; March 2010. www.levyinstitute.org

Wealth distribution
G. William Domhoff, Power in America – Wealth, Income, and Power; Sept 2005 (updated Sept 2010). sociology.ucsc.edu
Edward N. Wolff, Recent Trends in Household Wealth in the United States. Op cit.

Multimillionaire households
Edward N. Wolff, Recent Trends in Household Wealth in the United States. Op cit.

56–57 Immigration and Insecurity
30 states have laws…
Language Policy, Language Legislation in the USA. www.languagepolicy.net [accessed Dec 29, 2010]
Foreign-born workers
Eric Newburger and Thomas Gryn, *The Foreign-Born Labor Force in the United States: 2007*. American Community Survey Reports; Dec 2009. www.census.gov.
US population
Origins
Elizabeth M. Grieco and Edward N. Trevelyan, *Place of Birth of the Foreign-Born Population: 2009*. American Community Survey Briefs; Oct 2010. www.census.gov
Closing the gate
Jeffrey S. Passel and D'Vera Cohn, US Unauthorized Immigration Flows are down sharply. Pew Hispanic Center; Sept 1, 2010. pewresearch.org
Department of Homeland Security, Office of Immigration Statistics, Estimates of the Unauthorized Immigrant Population Residing in the United States: Jan 2009. www.dhs.gov
GAO, GAO-09-542R: CBP Could Improve Its Estimation of Funding Needed for New Border Patrol Agents; June 15, 2009. www.gao.gov
Predator Drones
Dana Priest and William Arkin, Border Control, Top Secret America series; *Washington Post*. projects.washingtonpost.com
A barrier to immigration
Building the fence along the US-Mexico frontier. www.azcentral.com
Alan Gomez, Agents' death a reminder of US-Mexican border violence. *USA Today*; Dec 21, 2010. www.usatoday.com
Dennis Wagner, US laws blamed for migrant deaths. *Arizona Republic*; May 7, 2010. www.azcentral.com
Stuart Anderson, *Death at the Border*. National Foundation for American Policy; May 2010, www.nfap.com

58–59 Khaki Country
Navy/Marine ROTC Programs. www.collegeprofiles.com
Defense Manpower Data Center, US Department of Defense. www.dmdc.osd.mil
Mark Arsenault, Senate Vote Ends 'Don't Ask, Don't Tell'. *Boston Globe*; Dec 19, 2010. www.boston.com
The Army Reserve Officers' Training Corps (ROTC). www.goarmy.com
US Air Force ROTC. www.afrotc.com
US Office of Personnel Management, Federal Employment Statistics, Employment and Trends; Table 2. www.opm.gov
Whom do Americans trust?
The Harris Poll; Feb 16–21, 2010. www.pollingreport.com
How we compare
NATO Committee on Gender Perspectives. www.nato.int
Women's Research and Education Institute. wrei.org
Anita Schjolset, *Nato and the Women: Exploring the Gender Gap in the Armed Forces*. Peace Research Institute Oslo (PRIO); July 2010.
Active-duty military
Non-White active-duty military
Defense Manpower Data Center, *Population Representation in the Military Services, Fiscal Year 2009 Report*. US Department of Defense; 2010. www.dmdc.osd.mil
Women in active-duty military
Lory Manning, *Women in the Military*, 7th edition. Women's Research and Education Institute; 2010. Table 8. www.wrei.org
Looking into the future
Frank Newport, Americans see US Military as Number 1 Now, but Not in 20 Years. Gallup Poll; Feb 26, 2010. www.gallup.com

Answering the call
Recruits from South and West
Shanea J. Watkins and James Sherk, *Who Serves in the US Military? Demographic Characteristics of Enlisted Troops and Officers*, Center for Data Analysis, The Heritage Foundation; Aug 2008. www.heritage.org.
Defense Manpower Data Center, *Population Representation in the Military Services*. Op cit.
Veterans in state population…
A Snapshot of the New Veteran. National Public Radio; May 10, 2010. www.npr.org

60–61 Shock and Awe
National Commission on Terrorist Attacks Upon the United States, *9/11 Commission Report*; 2004. www.9-11commission.gov
Jane Mayer, *The Dark Side*. New York: Doubleday; 2008
Douglas L. Kriner and Francis X. Shen, *The Casualty Gap: The Causes and Consequences of American Wartime Inequalities*. New York: Oxford University Press; 2010.
The Iraqi toll
Iraq Body Count. www.iraqbodycount.org [accessed Dec 15, 2010]
United Nations High Commissioner for Refugees. www.unhcr.org
US military deaths in Iraq War
Military deaths
Icasualties.org (Iraq Casualty Count). icasualties.org
The Afghan toll
Civilian Casualties of the War in Afghanistan (2001–present). en.wikipedia.org
United Nations High Commissioner for Refugees. www.unhcr.org
Coalitions of the "willing"
Icasualties.org. Op cit.
International Security Assistance Force. en.wikipedia.org
Amnesty International, United States Secret Detention Facilities; Feb 19, 2010. blog.amnestyusa.org
War-within-a-war
Nancy Gibbs, Sexual Assaults on Female Soldiers: Don't Ask, Don't Tell. *Time Magazine*; March 8, 2010. www.time.com
US had spent $1.15 trillion
Elizabeth Bumiller, The War: A Trillion Can Be Cheap. *New York Times*; July 25, 2010. www.nytimes.coms

64–65 Marriage and Divorce
American attitudes towards divorce
Lydia Saad, Cultural tolerance for divorce grows to 70% Gallup Poll; May 19, 2008. www.gallup.com
…Towards same sex marriage
Jeffrey M. Jones, Americans' opposition to gay marriage eases slightly. Gallup Poll; May 24, 2010. www.gallup.com
Same-sex marriage
National Conference of State Legislators. www.ncsl.prg
Marriage and divorce
US Census Bureau. www.census.gov
Marriage status
US Census Bureau, America's Families and Living Arrangements, 2009. www.census.gov
Increase in interracial marriage
Marrying Out
Making interracial marriage legal
Anti-miscegenation laws. www.search.com

66–67 Sickness and Health
How we die
Single leading cause of death
US Department of Health & Human Services. www.hhs.gov
Diabetes
Center for Disease Control, National Diabetes Fact Sheet; 2007. www.cdc.gov
Dental clinic visits

Smokers
Low birthweight
Doctors
Kaiser Family Foundation, Kaiser State Health Facts. www.statehealthfacts.org
Breast cancer
National Cancer Institute, Surveillance Epidemiology and End Results (SEER). seer.cancer.gov
AIDS
Kaiser Family Foundation, HIV/AIDS Policy Fact Sheet: Black Americans & HIV/AIDS; Sept 2009. www.kff.org

68–69 Healthcare Politics
Infant mortality
Life expectancy
Magnetic Resonance
Health expenditure
Public healthcare plans
OECD Health Care Quality Indicators, Health at a Glance; 2009. www.oecd.org
People who said they had a medical problem…
Cathy Schoen, Robin Osborn, David Squires, et al., How Health Insurance Design Affects Access to Care and Costs, by Income, in Eleven Countries. The Commonwealth Fund; Nov 2010. www.commonwealthfund.org
No health insurance
Kaiser Family Foundation, Kaiser State Health Facts. www.statehealthfacts.org
AARP, Divided We Fail: Key Findings in the Virgin Islands; 2008. assets.aarp.org
AARP, Divided we Fail: Key Findings in Puerto Rico; 2008. assets.aarp.org
Robert Wood Johnson Foundation, State Coverage Initiative. www.statecoverage.org
American attitudes to healthcare
Gallup Poll, Healthcare System; Nov 2010. www.gallup.com
Can't afford healthcare
Elizabeth Mendes, In US, Health Disparities Across Incomes Are Wide-Ranging. Gallup Poll; Oct 18, 2010. www.gallup.com
Racial/ethnic difference
Kaiser Family Foundation, Kaiser State Health Facts. www.statehealthfacts.org
Big business, big profits
Fortune 500, Ranking of America's Largest Corporations, 2010. money.cnn.com
Health Care for America, Health Insurance Industry Profits and Greed Surge Again; May 13, 2010. healthcareforamericanow.org
Matt Kapp, The Sick Business of Health-Care Profiteering. *Vanity Fair*; Sept 24, 2009. www.vanityfair.com
Abortion
NARAL Pro-Choice America. www.naral.org
National Abortion Federation. www.prochoice.org
Alan Guttmacher Institute. www.guttmacherinstitute.org

70–71 Gun Nation
FORTUNE Releases Annual Survey of Most Powerful Lobbying Organizations; Nov 15, 1999. www.timewarner.com
National Rifle Association Institute for Legislative Action. www.nraila.org
How we compare: civilian firearms
There are around 285m…
UN Office on Drugs and Crimes (UNODC), Transnational Organized Crime Threat Assessment; 2010. www.unodc.org [accessed June 24, 2010]
Gun nation
About 43% of American households have guns
Catherine A. Okoro, David E. Nelson, James A. Mercy, et al. Prevalence of Household Firearms and Firearm Storage Practices in the 50 States and the District of

Columbia: Findings from the Behavioral Risk Factor Surveillance System, 2002. *Pediatrics* Vol. 116; Sept 3, 2005.

Deaths by gun
Center for Disease Control, Injury Prevention and Control, WISQARS data. www.cdc.gov
International Action Network on Small Arms (IANSA). www.iansa.org
Of 72 school shootings…
IANSA. www.iansa.org
Homicide rates in the US…
Suicide by gun
Homicide by gun
Center for Disease Control, Injury Prevention and Control. Op cit.
US public opinion on gun control
PEW Research Center, Public Takes Conservative Turn on Gun Control, Abortion; April 30, 2009. pewresearch.org
Gun laws should be more strict
Jeffrey M. Jones, In US, Record-Low Support for Stricter Gun Laws. Gallup Poll; Oct 9, 2010. www.gallup.com

72–73 Violence Against Women
Center for Disease Control, Adverse Health Conditions and Health Risk Behaviors Associated with Intimate Partner Violence – United States – 2005; Feb 2008. www.cdc.gov
Men murdering women
1,865 women…
91% of women…
9% of females…
8% of women…
Violence Policy Center, *When Men Murder Women: An Analysis of 2007 Homicide Data;* Appendix One. Washington DC; Sept, 2009. www.vpc.org
Making violence against women an American public issue
Administration for Children and Families. www.childwelfare.gov
Caroline Johnston Polisis, Spousal Rape Laws Continue to Evolve. *Women's eNews;* July 1, 2009. www.womensenews.org
Firuzeh Shokooh Valle, Puerto Rican Women Face Rising Tide of Violence. *Women's eNews;* Aug 24, 2010. www.womensenews.org
HR 4594: International Violence Against Women Act of 2010. www.govtrack.us
National Center on Domestic and Sexual Violence. hwww.ncdsv.org
National Center for PTSD, Department of Veterans Affairs, Military Sexual Trauma. *PTSD Research Quarterly;* Spring 2009.
National Network to End Domestic Violence. www.nnedv.org
Take Back the Night. takebackthenight.org
Womens' Initiatives for Gender Justice. www.iccwomen.org
Child rape
Center for Disease Control and Prevention, Sexual Violence; Spring 2008. www.cdc.gov
18% of American women…
Joni Seager, *The Penguin Atlas of Women in the World.* NY: Penguin Books; 2009. p. 58.
2,923 reports…
John J. Kruzel, DOD Officials Release Sexual Assault Statistics. US Air Force; March 18, 2009. www.af.mil
1 in 5 women veterans…
Women Veterans Healthcare: Facts and Statistics. US Department of Veterans Affairs. www.publichealth.va.gov

74–75 Behind Bars
2.3m American adults…
Prison population
12% of federal prisoners…
Bureau of Justice Statistics, Prison Inmates at Midyear 2009. bjs.ojp.usdoj.gov
How do we compare: incarceration
Who is most likely to be behind bars?
The Pew Center on the States, 1 in 100: Behind Bars in America 2008. www.pewcenteronthestates.org
Who is behind bars?
Federal Bureau of Justice Statistics, Prison Inmate Characteristics. bjs.ojp.usdoj.gov
Prisons mean jobs
9% increase…
United States Department of Labor, Occupational Outlook Handbook 2010–11, Correctional Officers. www.bls.gov
Racial/ethnic breakdown of corrections employees
US Department of Labor and US Bureau of Labor Statistics, Labor Force Characteristics by Race and Ethnicity, 2007. Washington; Sept 2008. Table 5. www.bls.gov
51% of federal inmates…
Federal Bureau of Prisons, Quick facts about Bureau of Prisoners. www.bop.gov [accessed Sept 6, 2010]
Texas had 5 of the 13
Federal Bureau of Prisons. bjs.ojp.usdoj.gov [accessed Sept 6, 2010]
Texas has 11 of the 60…
Corrections Corporation of America. correctionscorp.com/facilities
Corrections control
Nearly 8% of people…
Pew Center on the States, One in 31: The Long Reach of American Corrections, 2010; Table A-6. www.pewcenteronthestates.org
Death penalty
The Clark County Prosecuting Attorney, The Death Penalty, US Executions Since 1976. www.clarkprosecutor.org
Death Penalty Information Center, States With and Without the Death Penalty. www.deathpenaltyinfo.org
Executions and race
Fewer than 2%…
Death Penalty Information Center. www.deathpenaltyinfo.org

76–77 Degrees and Dropouts
Sarah R. Crissey, *Educational Attainment in the United States, 2007.* US Census Bureau; Jan 2009. www.census.gov
Council for American Private Education. www.capenet.org
LG Knapp, JE Kelly-Reid, and SA Ginder, *Postsecondary Institutions and Price of Attendance in the US: Fall 2009; Degrees and Other Awards Conferred: 2008-09; 12-Month Enrollment: 2008-09.* Department of Education, National Center for Education Statistics; 2010. (NCES 2010-161). nces.ed.gov
Academic comparison
Literacy and high-school graduation: National Center for Educational Statistics, International Activities Program; Tables B.1.17, B.1.32, B.3.01, B.1.06. nces.ed.gov
University admission and graduation: OECD Highlights from Education at a Glance, 2009. oecd.org
Spending on public elementary and secondary schools
US Census Bureau, Public Elementary–Secondary Education Finance Data. www.census.gov
High school completion
US Census Bureau, Educational Attainment, CPS Historical Time Series Tables. www.census.gov
High school dropout
National Center for Educational Statistics, Digest of

Education Statistics, 2009; Table 106. nces.ed.gov
US Department of Labor and National Center for Educational Statistics, *The Condition of Education 2010 (NCES 2010-028).* nces.ed.gov
College graduates
US Census Bureau, 2009 American Community Survey. www.census.gov

80–81 The Environment
It's dangerous to live here
EPA, Final National Priorities List. www.epa.gov
EPA, Toxic Releases Inventory. www.epa.gov [accessed Dec 2010]
Waste & Recyling News. www.wasterecyclingnews.com [accessed Dec 2010]
Toxic Releases
EPA, Toxic Releases Inventory. www.epa.gov [accessed Dec 2010]
85% of Americans…
Lyman Morales, Green Behaviors Common in US, but Not Increasing. Gallup Poll; April 9, 2010. www.gallup.com
61% of Americans…
Lydia Saad, On 40th Earth Day, Image of Green Movement Still Positive. Gallup Poll; April 22, 2010. www.gallup.com
Recycling cities
Recycling rates vary widely. *New York Times;* July 29, 2008. www.nytimes.com

82–83 Big Food
5 retailers accounted for 48%…
Mary Hendrickson and William Heffernan, *Concentration of Agricultural Markets.* University of Missouri; April 2007. www.foodcircles.missouri.edu
Top US food and…
Dave Fusaro, Food processing tops 100 for 2009: Licking the recession. *Food Processing;* Aug 3, 2009. www.foodprocessing.com
Making food, making money
Hans-Wilhelm Windhorst, Recent and future dynamics in US egg production and trade. *Zootecnica,* July 1, 2008. www.zootecnicainternational.com
Mary Hendrickson and William Heffernan, *Concentration of Agricultural Markets.* Op cit.
Hog factory farms
Meat farming
USDA, National Agriculture Statistics Service, 2008 and 2009. www.nass.usda.gov
Overweight or obese adults
Fruit consumption
Kaiser Family Foundation, Kaiser State Health Facts. www.statehealthfacts.org
Centers for Disease Control and Prevention, Behavioral Risk Factor Surveillance System Survey Data; 2009. Unpublished data, information about the BRFSS is available at: www.cdc.gov
Food availability
Consumption of high-fructose corn syrup…
Hodan Farah Wells and Jean C. Buzby, *Dietary Assessment of Major Trends in US Food Consumption, 1970–2005.* Economic Research Service, US Department of Agriculture; March 2008. www.ers.usda.gov
How we compare
Beef
USDA-FAS attache reports, Livestock and Poultry: World Markets and Trade, 2006. www.fas.usda.gov
Top fat consumers
FAOSTAT. www.fao.org
Sugar and sweeteners
FAO Statistical Yearbook 2009. www.fao.org

84–85 Playing Ball

Highest paid players
Total made by LeBron James
Jonah Freedman, The 50 Highest Earning American Athletes. sportsillustrated.cnn.com
Maximum salary for experienced woman
Base salary for a rookie male...
Women's Basketball Online, WNBA Salary Scale. womensbasketballonline.com
In 2010, only six of the NFL's...
$1.6bn Value of...
Mark Yost, Major League Baseball: The Green Monster Goes It Alone. *The Wall Street Journal*; July 13, 2010. www.WSJ.com
Women's National Basketball Association. en.wikipedia.com
National Football League. en.wikipedia.org
University of Iowa news release, Study finds NFL's Rooney Rule Does Little to Help Minority Head Coach Hiring; Jan 12, 2010. news-releases.uiowa.edu
Michael Morrison and Chris Frantz, Icing the Stereotypes: Black Hockey Players in a Traditionally White Sport. www.infoplease.com
S.F. Heron, Average Salaries of NBA Players. www.helium.com
The big money
Forbes.com, NHL Team Valuations; Nov 11, 2009. www.forbes.com
Kurt Badenhausen, Michael K. Ozanian and Christina Settimi, The Business Of Hockey. Forbes; Nov 11, 2009. www.forbes.com
Sponsors and Sponsorship
Deals
Rod Palmquist, Student Campaign Takes on Nike Like Never Before. *Huffington Post*; July 12, 2010. www.huffingtonpost.com
College Athletics websites.
Gary Klein, USC's Pete Carroll Tops National Salary List. *Los Angeles Times*; Feb 23, 2009. articles.latimes.com
National Collegiate Athletic Association. www.ncaa.org
$60m Amount Adidas is paying...
Cecil Hurt, Tide Signs $30 million extension with Nike; May 14, 2010. tidesports.com
Making a stand
United Students Against Sweatshops. www.usasnet.org
The racial gap
Richard Lapchick, Keeping Score When it Counts: Graduation Rates for 2010 NCAA Men's Division I Basketball Tournament Teams. The Institute for Diversity and Ethics in Sport, University of Central Florida; 2010. www.tidesport.org
An incomplete revolution
Gwendolyn Mink, Title IX, in Wilma Mankiller, et al., editors, *The Reader's Companion to US Women's History*. Boston: Houghton Mifflin; 1998. p.593–94.
American Association of University Women, Title IX: Equity in School Athletics; April, 2010. www.aauw.org
Title IX and United States Female Sports Participation. www.faqs.org
Women's Sports Foundation. www.womenssportsfoundation.org
Increase in participants
Recipients of college/university athletic scholarships
Title IX and United States Female Sorts Participation. www.faqs.org

86–87 Auto Nation

How we compare
Number of vehicles
US Department of Energy, Vehicle Technologies Program, Fact #617; April 5, 2010. www1.eere.energy.gov
Gasoline tax

US Department of Transportation, Federal Highway Administration, Highway Statistics 2008: Motor Fuel Tax Rates for Selected Countries 1/; Dec 2009. www.fhsw.dot.gov
US share of global motor vehicle manufacturing
The International Organization of Motor Vehicle Manufacturers. www.oica.net
Employment in motor manufacturing
Stephen Cooney, *Motor Vehicle Manufacturing Employment: National and State Trends and Issues*. Congressional Research Service; Dec 27, 2007. Table 1. www.policyarchive.org
Bill Canis and Brent D. Yacobucci, *The US Motor Vehicle Industry: Confronting a New Dynamic in the Global Economy*. Congressional Research Service; March 26, 2010. www.fas.org
Anatomy of a typical auto
Consumption of resources
Economic contributions of the automobile industry to the US economy. *Manufacturing & Technology News*; Oct 17, 2003. www.manufacturingnews.com
Well-travelled
US Department of Transportation, Federal Highway Administration, Highway Statistics 2008. www.fhwa.dot.gov
Responsibility for roads
Mode of travel
US Department of Transportation, Federal Highway Administration, *Our Nation's Highways 2010*. www.fhwa.dot.gov
Fuel consumption
US Department of Transportation, Federal Highway Administration, Policy Information, Highway Statistics 2008, Motor-Fuel Use. www.fhwa.dot.gov
Vehicle ownership
Licensed to drive
US Census Bureau, American Community Survey 2010. www.census.gov
Mode of travel for getting to work
Steven E. Polzin, *The Case for Moderate Growth in Vehicle Miles of Travel: A Critical Juncture in US Travel Behavior Trends*. US Department of Transportation; April 2006. www.cutr.ust.edu
Alternative commutes
Les Christie, New Yorkers are Top Transit Users; June 29, 2007. money.cnn.com
Hybrid gas–electric vehicles were...
Hybrid Cars. www.hybridcars.com
Political identification of...
Hybrid Cars. www.hybridcars.com
Factbox: Who are hybrid car buyers in US? *Reuters*; April 8, 2008. www.reuters.com

88–89 Money Comes, Money Goes

How we compare
CIA World Factbook. www.cia.gov
Where federal government money comes from
Where federal government money goes to
US Debt Clock.org. www.usdebtclock.org
Congressional Budget Office, The Budget and Economic Outlook: Fiscal Years 2010 to 2020; Jan 2010. www.cbo.gov
Center on Budget and Policy Priorities. www.cbpp.org
The deficit trendline
US national gross debt...
Time Series Chart of US Government Spending. www.usgovernmentspending.com
Personal debt
26% of adults...
US Debt Clock.org. www.usdebtclock.org
National Foundation for Credit Counselling, *The 2009 Consumer Financial Literacy Survey*; April 2010. www.nfcc.org
Value of loans
Federal Deposit Insurance Corporation, Payday

Lending; Jan 29, 2003. www.fdic.gov
Kevin Connor & Matthew Skomarovsky, *The Predator's Creditors*. National People's Action; 2009.
Payday Loan and Cash Advance Consumer Guide. www.paydayloanscashadvance.org
Personal bankruptcy filings
There was a 14%...
American Bankruptcy Institute. www.abiworld.org
Credit Card Country
Fortune 500, Ranking America's Largest Corporations; 2010. money.cnn.com
Jose Garcia & Tamara Draut, *The Plastic Safety Net*. Demos Institute; 2009.
Credit Card.Com. www.creditcards.com
Credit Card Rates Remain High; Dec 31, 2010. www.indexcreditcards

92–93 Exporting Democracy

Number of overseas bases or installations
US Department of Defense, *Base Structure Report, Fiscal Year 2009 Baseline*; Figure 1. www.defense.gov
US military presence
US Department of Defense, *Base Structure Report, Fiscal Year 2009 Baseline*. www.defense.gov
David Vine, *Island of Shame: The Secret History of the US Military Base on Diego Garcia*. Princeton: Princeton University Press; 2009.
Catherine Lutz, editor, *The Bases of Empire*. London: Pluto Press; 2009.
US foreign aid
Congressional Research Service, State, Foreign Operations, and Related Programs: FY2009 Appropriations, Table 6. www.fas.org
Net foreign aid
Bill and Melinda Gates Foundation, 2010 Annual Letter from Bill Gates: Rich Countries' Aid Generosity. www.gatesfoundation.org
37% of Americans support foreign aid
Harris Interactive/Harris Polls, Medicare, Crime-fighting, Social Security, Defense – the Most Popular Federal Government Services; June 14, 2010. www.harrisinteractive.com
Peace Corps
Peace Corps Map Country List. www.peacecorps.gov
37% of Peace Corps
200,000 Peace Corps Volunteers
Peace Corps. peacecorps.gov

94–95 Arms Seller to the World

Top ten customers for US arms
Richard F. Grimmett, *US Arms Sales. Agreement with and Deliveries to Major Clients, 2000–2008*, Washington, DC: Congressional Research Service; Dec 2, 2009.
Top arms exporters
$31.5 billion...
Stockholm International Peace Research Institute (SIPRI), *SIPRI Yearbook, 2010*. www.sipri.org
World's top arms manufacturers
SPIRI, *SIPRI Yearbook, 2010*; Appendix 6A.1. www.sipri.org
The Big Players
Boeing. www.boeing.com
Lockheed Martin. wwwlockheedmartin.com

96–97 Nuclear State

Government Accountability Office, letter to the US Senate Judiciary Committee, Radiation Exposure Compensation Act: Program Status; Sept 7, 2007.
Stockpiles of nuclear warheads
Stockholm International Peace Research Institute (SIPRI), *SIPRI Yearbook, 2010*. www.sipri.org
American attitudes to nuclear weapons
AP-GfK Poll, conducted by GfK Roper Public Affairs & Media; Nov 3–8, 2010. www.ap-gfkpoll.com
CNN/Opinion Research Corporation Poll, Foreign

Affairs and Defense issues; April 9–11, 2010. www.pollingreport.com

Nuclear landscape
Atomic Archive. www.atomicarchive.com [accessed Dec 5, 2010]
Brookings, 50 Facts About US Nuclear Weapons. www.brookings.edu
Joni Seager, *Earth Follies*. NY: Routledge; 1993.
Arjun Makhijani, Howard Hu, and Katherine Yih (editors) *Nuclear Wastelands: A Global Guide to Nuclear Weapons Production and its Health and Environmental Effects*. Cambridge: MIT Press; 2000.
Global Security.org. www.globalsecurity.org [accessed Dec 4, 2010]
Natural Resources Defense Council, *Nuclear Weapons Databook*; 1987. www.nrdc.org

98–99 Climate Change
Political differences
Yale Project on Climate Change Communication. environment.yale.edu [accessed Dec 5, 2010]
A. Leiserowitz, E. Maibach, C. Roser-Renouf, et al., *Climate change in the American Mind: Public support for climate & energy policies in June 2010*. Yale Project on Climate Change Communication; 2010. environment.yale.edu
Pew Research Center for the People and the Press, Fewer Americans See Solid Evidence of Global Warming; Oct 22, 2009. people-press.org

Gender differences
Aaron McCright, The Effects of Gender on Climate Change Knowledge. *Population & Environment* 32(1); 2010.

Key climate change impacts in the USA
US Global Change Research Program, *Global Climate Change Impacts in the US*; 2009. www.globalchange.gov

Greenhouse gases
Major sources of emissions
US EPA, Inventory of US Greenhouse Gas Emissions and Sinks: 1990–2008; April 2010. www.epa.gov [accessed Dec 5, 2010]

Carbon footprints
US Department of Energy, Energy Information Administration, International Energy Statistics. tonto.eia.doe.gov [accessed Dec 4, 2010]

Climate-change deniers
Greenpeace, ExonMobil's Continued Funding of Global Warming Denial Industry; May 2007. www.greenpeace.org [accessed Dec 4, 2010]
Greenpeace, Koch Industries Secretly Funding the Climate Change Denial Machine; March 2010. www.greenpeace.org [accessed Dec 4, 2010]
Jeff Goodall & Tom Dickinson, The Climate Killers. *Rolling Stone*; Jan 2009.
Josh Harkinson, The Dirty Dozen of Climate Change Denial. *Mother Jones*; Dec 4, 2009. motherjones.com [accessed Dec 5, 2010]
Union of Concerned Scientists, Global Warming Skeptic Organizations. www.ucsusa.org [accessed Dec 4, 2010]

100–01 Playing Well with Others
Most favored countries
Lydia Saad, Canada Remains Americans' Favored Nation. Gallup Poll; April 23, 2009. www.gallup.com

Where is that?
National Geographic and Roper Public Affairs, *Final Report: National Geographic-Roper Public Affairs 2006 Geographic Literacy Study*. Washington DC; 2006.

Major international organizations
Council on Foreign Relations, Group of Eight Industrialized Nations. www.cfr.org
Catherine Rampell, The Group of 20: A Primer. *New York Times Blog*; Nov 14, 2008. economix.blogs.nytimes.com
Group of 8. www.britannica.com

Group of 20. www.g20.org
International Monetary Fund. www.imf.org
North Atlantic Treaty Organization. www.nato.int
The World Bank. www.worldbank.org
United Nations. www.un.org

The US contributes 22%…
Better World Campaign, US Dues and Contributions to the United Nations. www.betterworldcampaign.org

International treaties
United States Senate, Treaties. www.senate.gov
UNICEF, Convention on the Rights of the Child. www.unicef.org
Amnesty USA, Convention on the Elimination of All Forms of Discrimination Against Women. www.amnestyusa.org
The Ottawa Treaty. en.wikipedia.org
List of United States Treaties. en.wikipedia.org
Feminist Majority Foundation, Fact Sheet: United States Failure To Ratify Key International Conventions, Treaties and Laws. www.iccnow.org

How others see the US
Pew Global Attitudes Project, Key Indicators Database, US Consideration of Other Countries' Interests. pewglobal.org

102–03 Culture Abroad
Top 10 movies: all US produces
The Voyage of the Dawn Treader
Box Office Mojo, All Time Box Office Worldwide Grosses. boxofficemojo.com

Starbucks
World Franchise Associates, Starbucks (US) to Double Rate of International Store Openings; Nov 22, 2010. www.worldfranchiseassociates.com

McDonald's
McDonald's, Our Company. www.aboutmcdonalds.com

The world drinks Cola
The Coca-Cola Company, Per Capita Consumption of Company Beverage Products. www.thecoca-colacompany.com

Barbies
1bn Barbies…
Paul Burns, *Corporate Entrepreneurship*. London: Palgrave, 2008.
Barbie Deemed a Threat to Saudi Morality. *USA Today*; Sept 10, 2003. www.usatoday.com
Barbie. en.wikipedia.org

Walmart
Walmart's 2.1m…
Walmart. walmartstores.com

106 State profiles
Federal money
US Census Bureau, Federal Aid to States for Fiscal Year 2009; Aug 2010. www.census.gov
US Census Bureau, Consolidated Federal Funds Report for Fiscal Year 2009. www.census.gov
Dennis Cauchon, Federal Aid is Top Revenue for States; May 4, 2009. 222.usatoday.com
Andrew D. Reamer and Rachel Blanchard Carpenter, *Counting for Dollars: The Role of the Decennial Census in the Distribution of Federal Funds*. Brookings; March 9, 2010. www.brookings.edu
The Tax Foundation, Federal Spending Received Per Dollar of Taxes Paid by State, 2005; Oct 9, 2007. www.taxfoundation.org

Land area
US Census Bureau, Census 2000 Summary. www.census.gov
Guam: www.guamchamber.com.gu
USVI: tonto.eia.doe.gov

Total GDP 2009
US Census Bureau, Federal Aid to States for Fiscal Year 2009; Aug 2010. www.census.gov

Guam *2005 est*, Puerto Rico *2010 est*, USVI *2004 est*. www.cia.gov

Total population 2010
US Census 2010. www.2010.census.gov
Guam, USVI: CIA; July 2010 *est*. www.cia.gov

White, not Hispanic or Latino 2009
Black alone 2009
American Indian and Alaska Native alone 2009
Asian alone 2009
Native Hawaiian and other Pacific Islander alone 2009
US Census Bureau, 2009 American Community Survey 1-Year Estimates. www.census.gov
Guam, USVI: Census; 2000. www.census.gov

Hispanic or Latino origin 2008
US Census Bureau, 2008 American Community Survey.
USVI: Census; 2000. www.census.gov

Percentage of people over age 65 2009
US Census Bureau, 2009 American Community Survey 1-Year Estimate.
Guam, USVI: CIA; July 2010 *est*. www.cia.gov

Median household income 2009
Poverty rate (official) 2009
US Census Bureau, 2009 American Community Survey 1-Year Estimate.
Guam, USVI; 2000. coris.noaa.gov

Physicians (nonfederal) per 10,000 people 2009
State Health Facts, Population 2009. www.statehealthfacts.org

High school completion rate (people aged 25+) 2009
US Census Bureau, 2009 American Community Survey 1-Year Estimate.
Guam, USVI; 2000. coris.noaa.gov

People under correctional control 2007
PEW, 2007 Public Safety Performance Project, One in 31, Table A-6. www.pewcenteronthestates.org

People living in households with guns 2001
Gun ownership by state. *Washington Post*; 2004, citing BRFSS Survey Results; 2001

Women as representatives in state legislature 2009
NCSL, 2009. www.ncsl.org

Walmart Supercenters 2010
Walmart Corporate, 2010. www.walmartstores.com

Starbucks (company-operated and licensed) 2010
Starbucks – Investor Relations, 2010. www.investor.starbucks.com

Farmland 2008
USDA, 2008. www.usda.mannlib.cornell.edu
Guam, USVI; 2007. www.agcensus.usda.gov

Hogs 2008
National Agriculture Statistics Service, 2008. www.nass.usda.gov
Guam, USVI; 2007. www.agcensus.usda.gov

Index

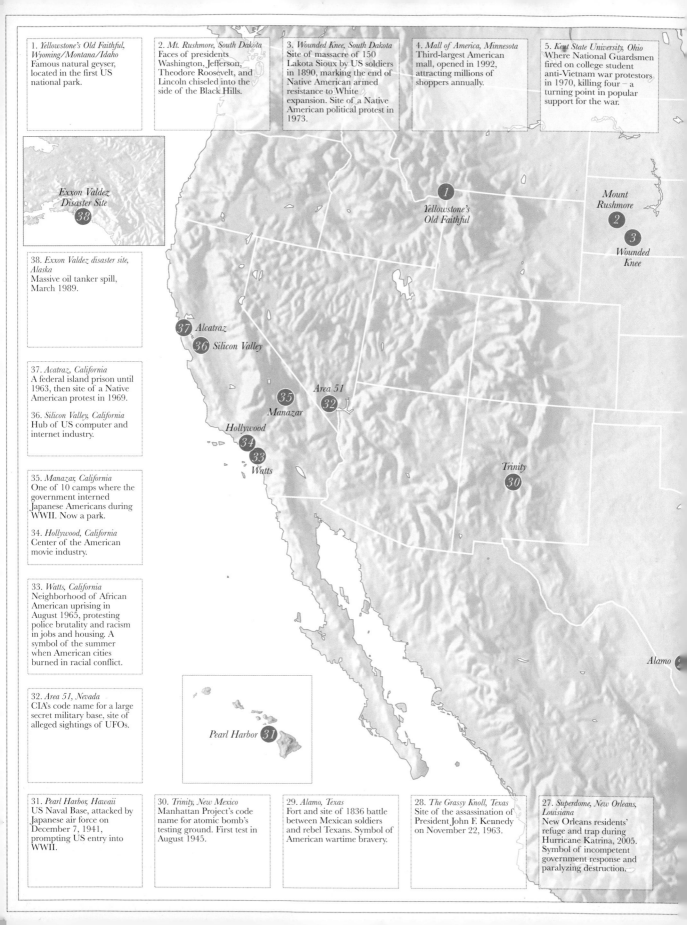

1. *Yellowstone's Old Faithful, Wyoming/Montana/Idaho* Famous natural geyser, located in the first US national park.

2. *Mt. Rushmore, South Dakota* Faces of presidents Washington, Jefferson, Theodore Roosevelt, and Lincoln chiseled into the side of the Black Hills.

3. *Wounded Knee, South Dakota* Site of massacre of 150 Lakota Sioux by US soldiers in 1890, marking the end of Native American armed resistance to White expansion. Site of a Native American political protest in 1973.

4. *Mall of America, Minnesota* Third-largest American mall, opened in 1992, attracting millions of shoppers annually.

5. *Kent State University, Ohio* Where National Guardsmen fired on college student anti-Vietnam war protestors in 1970, killing four – a turning point in popular support for the war.

38. *Exxon Valdez disaster site, Alaska* Massive oil tanker spill, March 1989.

37. *Acatraz, California* A federal island prison until 1963, then site of a Native American protest in 1969.

36. *Silicon Valley, California* Hub of US computer and internet industry.

35. *Manazar, California* One of 10 camps where the government interned Japanese Americans during WWII. Now a park.

34. *Hollywood, California* Center of the American movie industry.

33. *Watts, California* Neighborhood of African American uprising in August 1965, protesting police brutality and racism in jobs and housing. A symbol of the summer when American cities burned in racial conflict.

32. *Area 51, Nevada* CIA's code name for a large secret military base, site of alleged sightings of UFOs.

31. *Pearl Harbor, Hawaii* US Naval Base, attacked by Japanese air force on December 7, 1941, prompting US entry into WWII.

30. *Trinity, New Mexico* Manhattan Project's code name for atomic bomb's testing ground. First test in August 1945.

29. *Alamo, Texas* Fort and site of 1836 battle between Mexican soldiers and rebel Texans. Symbol of American wartime bravery.

28. *The Grassy Knoll, Texas* Site of the assassination of President John F. Kennedy on November 22, 1963.

27. *Superdome, New Orleans, Louisiana* New Orleans residents' refuge and trap during Hurricane Katrina, 2005. Symbol of incompetent government response and paralyzing destruction.

Exxon Valdez Disaster Site 38

Yellowstone's Old Faithful 1

Mount Rushmore 2

3 *Wounded Knee*

37 *Alcatraz*

36 *Silicon Valley*

Area 51 32

35 *Manazar*

Hollywood 34

33 *Watts*

Trinity 30

Pearl Harbor 31

Alamo